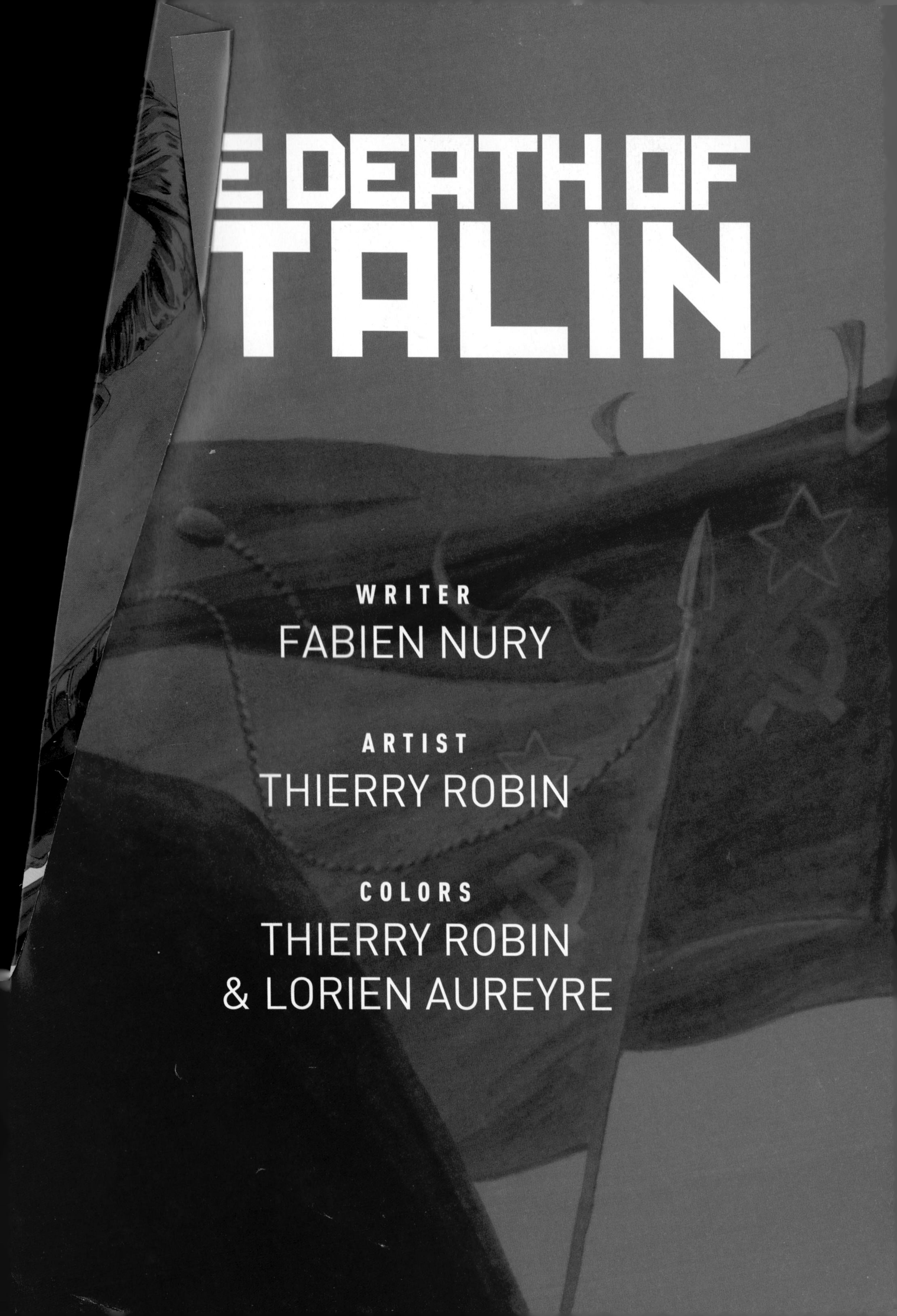

E DEATH OF TALIN

WRITER

FABIEN NURY

ARTIST

THIERRY ROBIN

COLORS

THIERRY ROBIN
& LORIEN AUREYRE

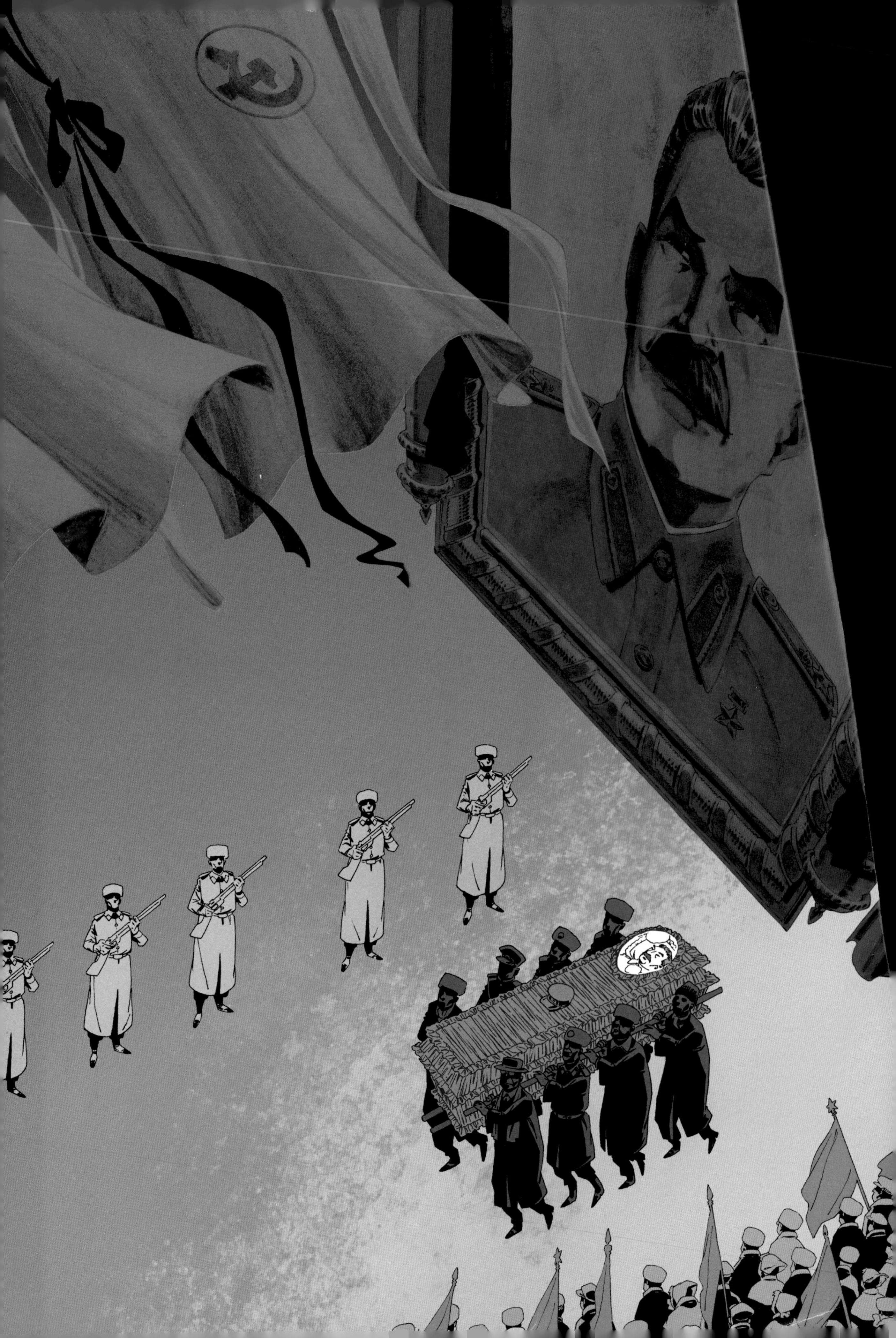

DISCLAIMER

Although inspired by real events, this book is nonetheless a work of fiction: artistic license has been used to construct a story from historical evidence that was at best patchy, at times partial, and often contradictory.

Having said this, the authors would like to make clear that their imaginations were scarcely stretched in the creation of this story, since it would have been impossible for them to come up with anything half as insane as the real events surrounding the death of Stalin.

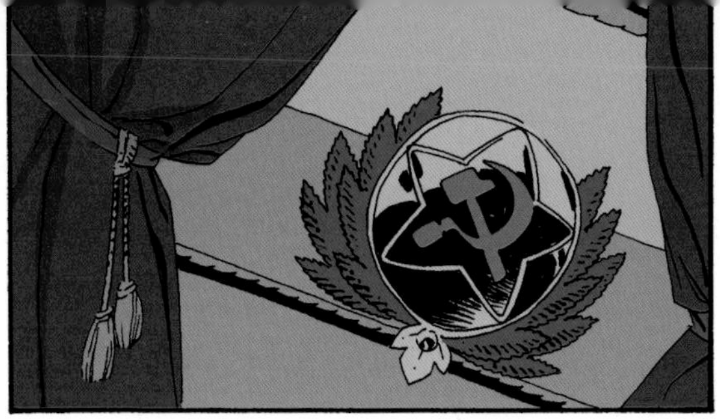

February 28, 1953.

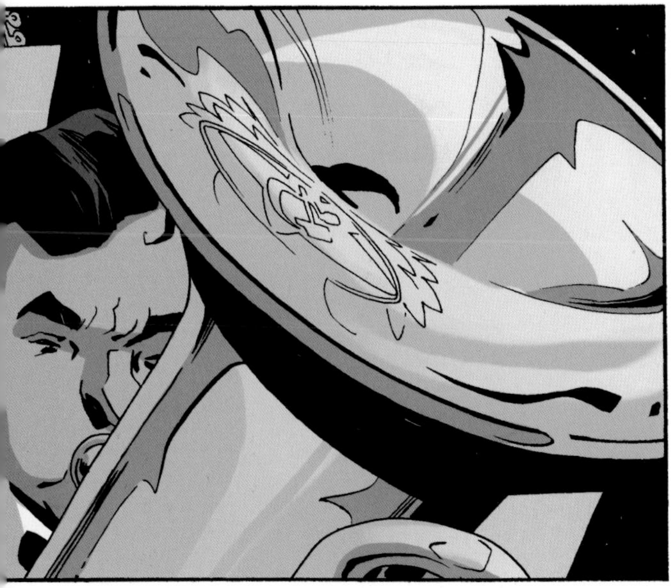

Radio Moscow.

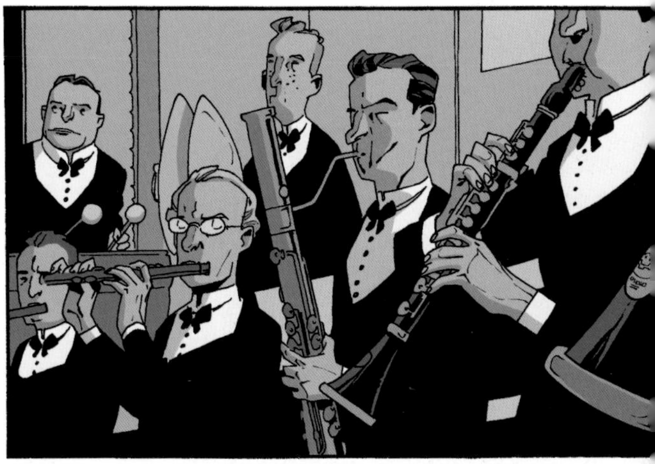

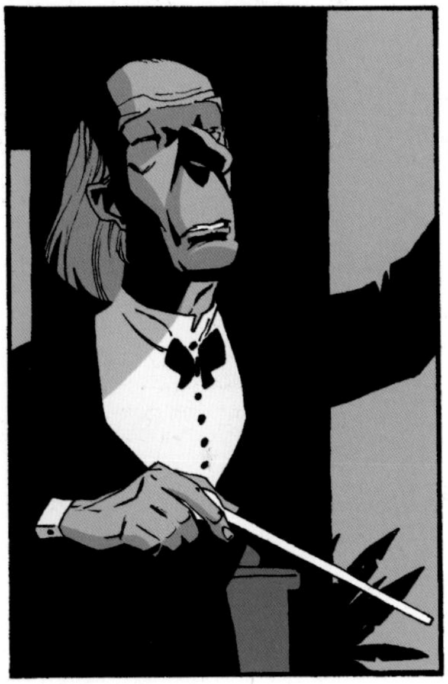

Program:
Wolfgang Amadeus Mozart's
PIANO CONCERTO No. 23.

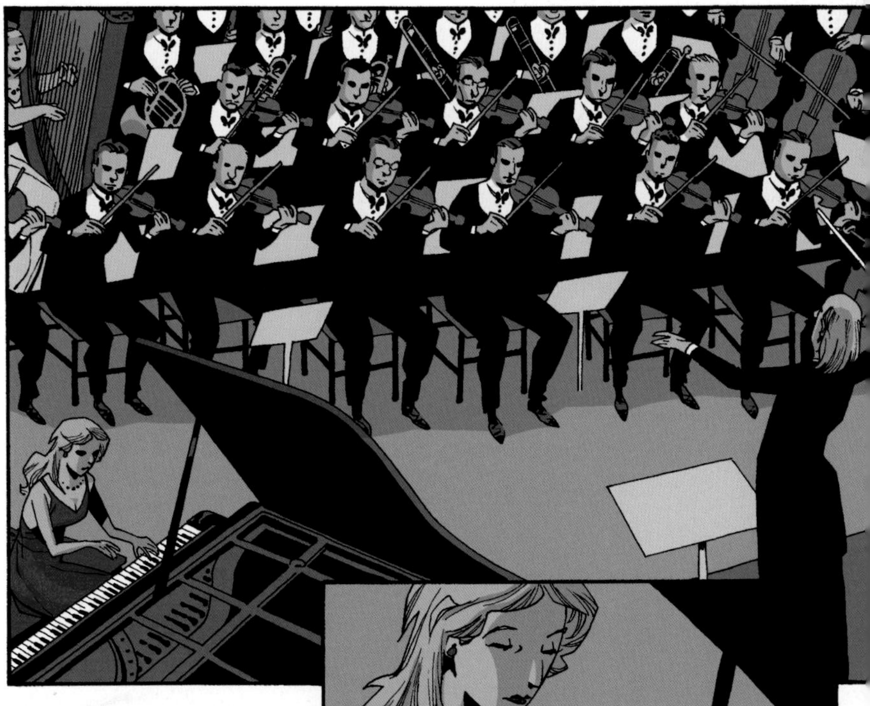

Soloist:
Maria Yudina.

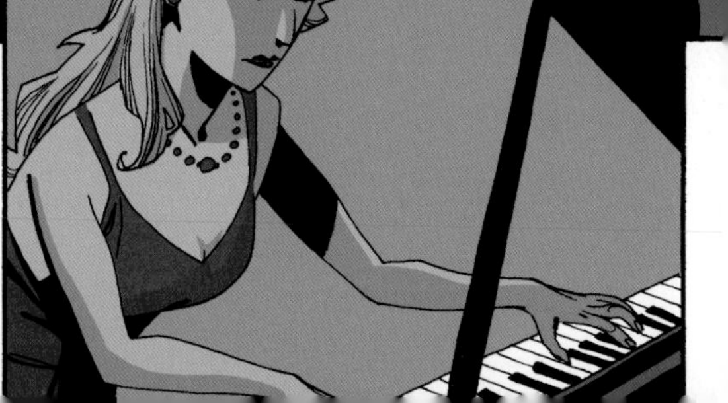

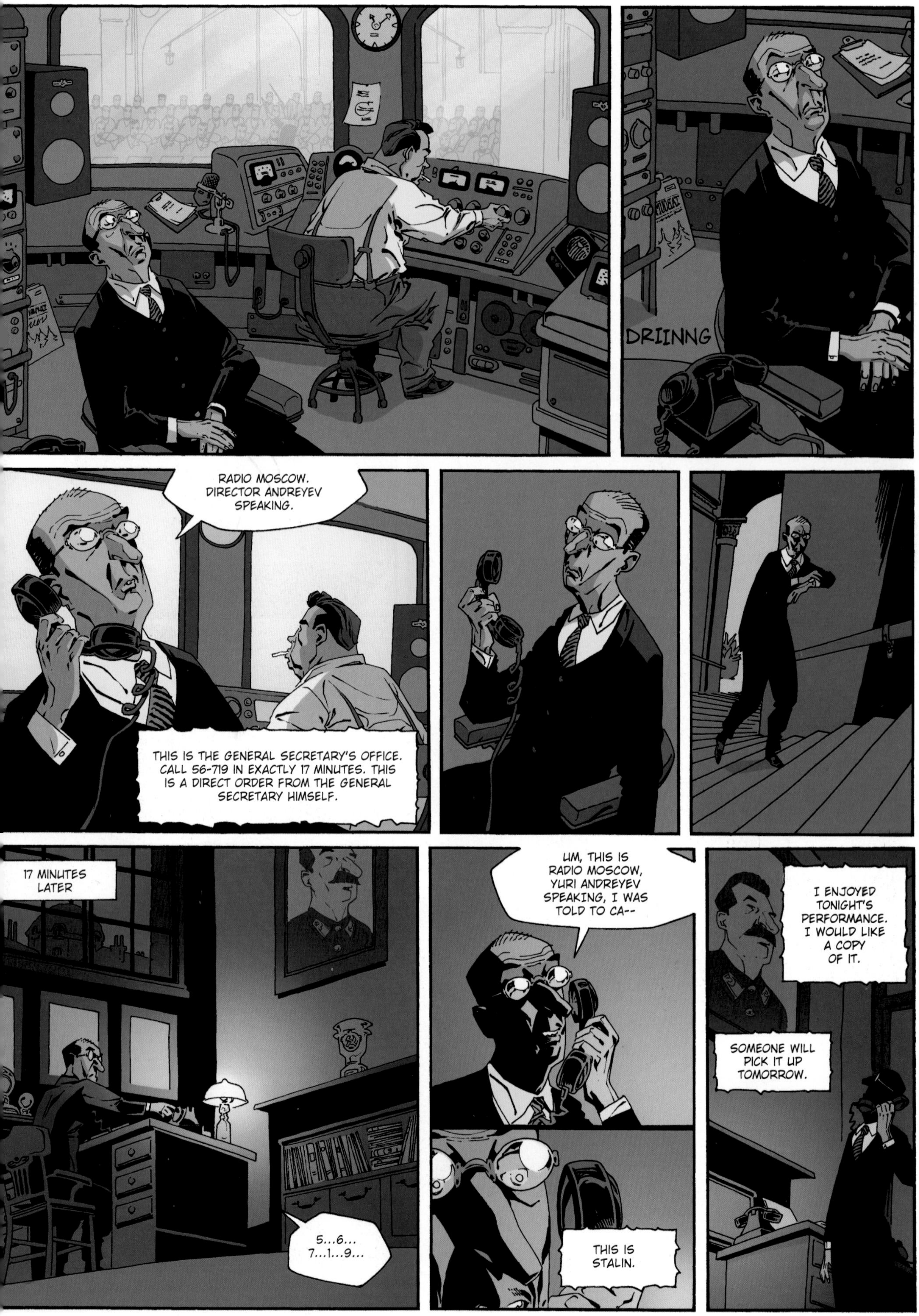
DRIINNG
RADIO MOSCOW. DIRECTOR ANDREYEV SPEAKING.
THIS IS THE GENERAL SECRETARY'S OFFICE. CALL 56-719 IN EXACTLY 17 MINUTES. THIS IS A DIRECT ORDER FROM THE GENERAL SECRETARY HIMSELF.
17 MINUTES LATER
5...6... 7...1...9...
UM, THIS IS RADIO MOSCOW, YURI ANDREYEV SPEAKING, I WAS TOLD TO CA--
THIS IS STALIN.
I ENJOYED TONIGHT'S PERFORMANCE. I WOULD LIKE A COPY OF IT.
SOMEONE WILL PICK IT UP TOMORROW.

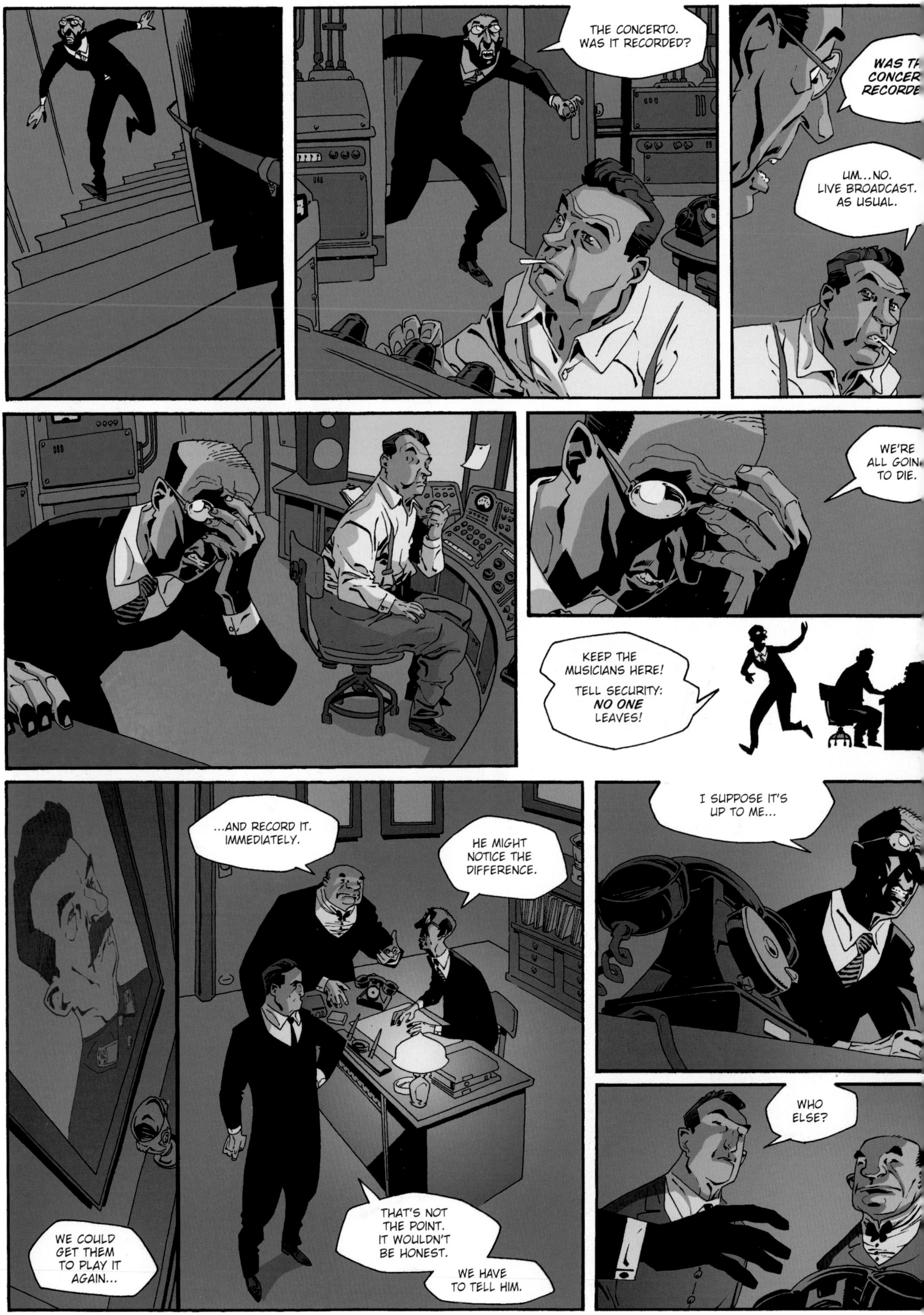
THE CONCERTO. WAS IT RECORDED?
WAS T CONCER RECORDE
UM...NO. LIVE BROADCAST. AS USUAL.
WE'RE ALL GOIN TO DIE.
KEEP THE MUSICIANS HERE! TELL SECURITY: ***NO ONE*** LEAVES!
WE COULD GET THEM TO PLAY IT AGAIN...
...AND RECORD IT. IMMEDIATELY.
HE MIGHT NOTICE THE DIFFERENCE.
THAT'S NOT THE POINT. IT WOULDN'T BE HONEST.
WE HAVE TO TELL HIM.
I SUPPOSE IT'S UP TO ME...
WHO ELSE?

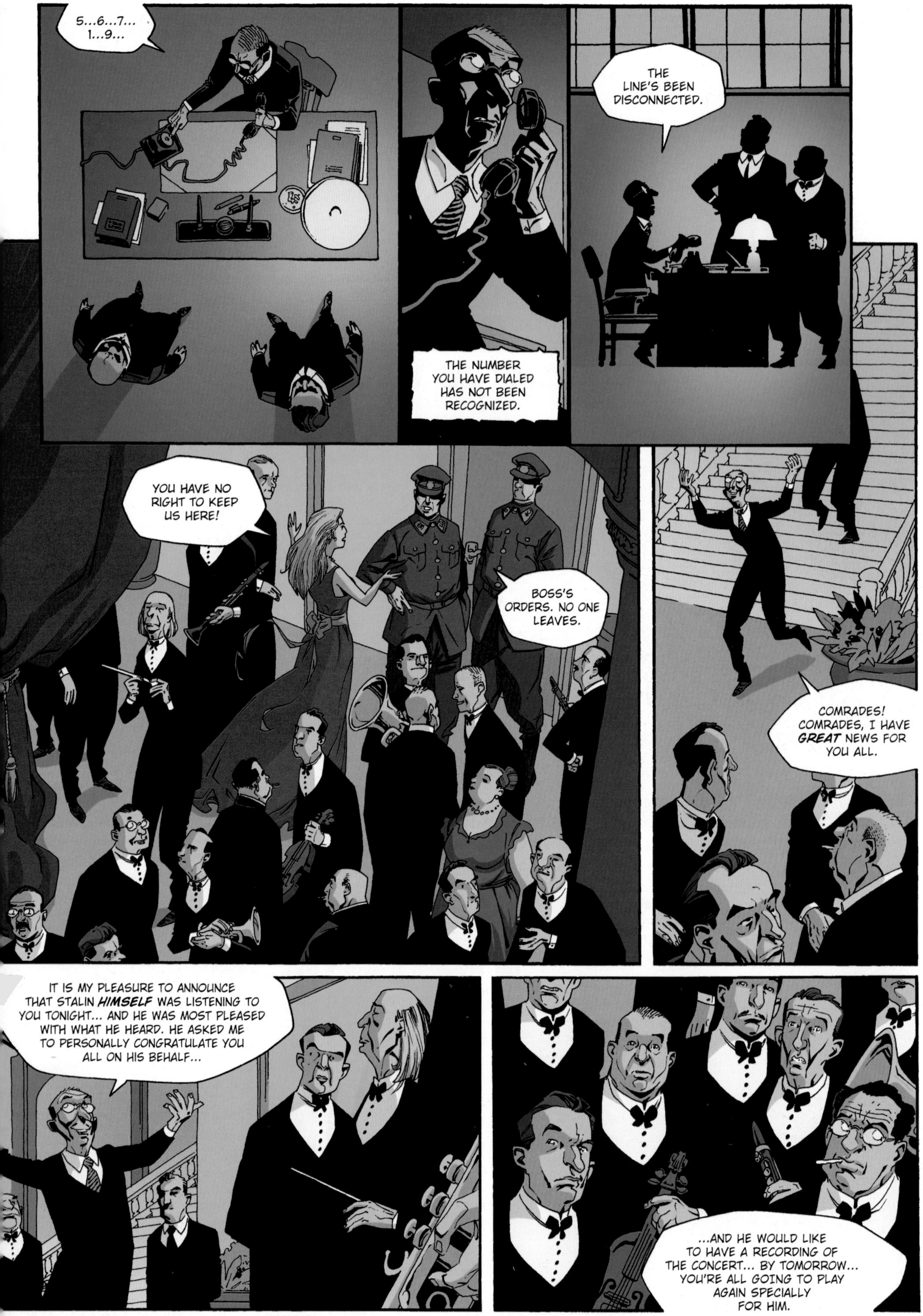
5...6...7...
1...9...
THE NUMBER YOU HAVE DIALED HAS NOT BEEN RECOGNIZED.
THE LINE'S BEEN DISCONNECTED.
YOU HAVE NO RIGHT TO KEEP US HERE!
BOSS'S ORDERS. NO ONE LEAVES.
COMRADES! COMRADES, I HAVE ***GREAT*** NEWS FOR YOU ALL.
IT IS MY PLEASURE TO ANNOUNCE THAT STALIN ***HIMSELF*** WAS LISTENING TO YOU TONIGHT... AND HE WAS MOST PLEASED WITH WHAT HE HEARD. HE ASKED ME TO PERSONALLY CONGRATULATE YOU ALL ON HIS BEHALF...
...AND HE WOULD LIKE TO HAVE A RECORDING OF THE CONCERT... BY TOMORROW... YOU'RE ALL GOING TO PLAY AGAIN SPECIALLY FOR HIM.

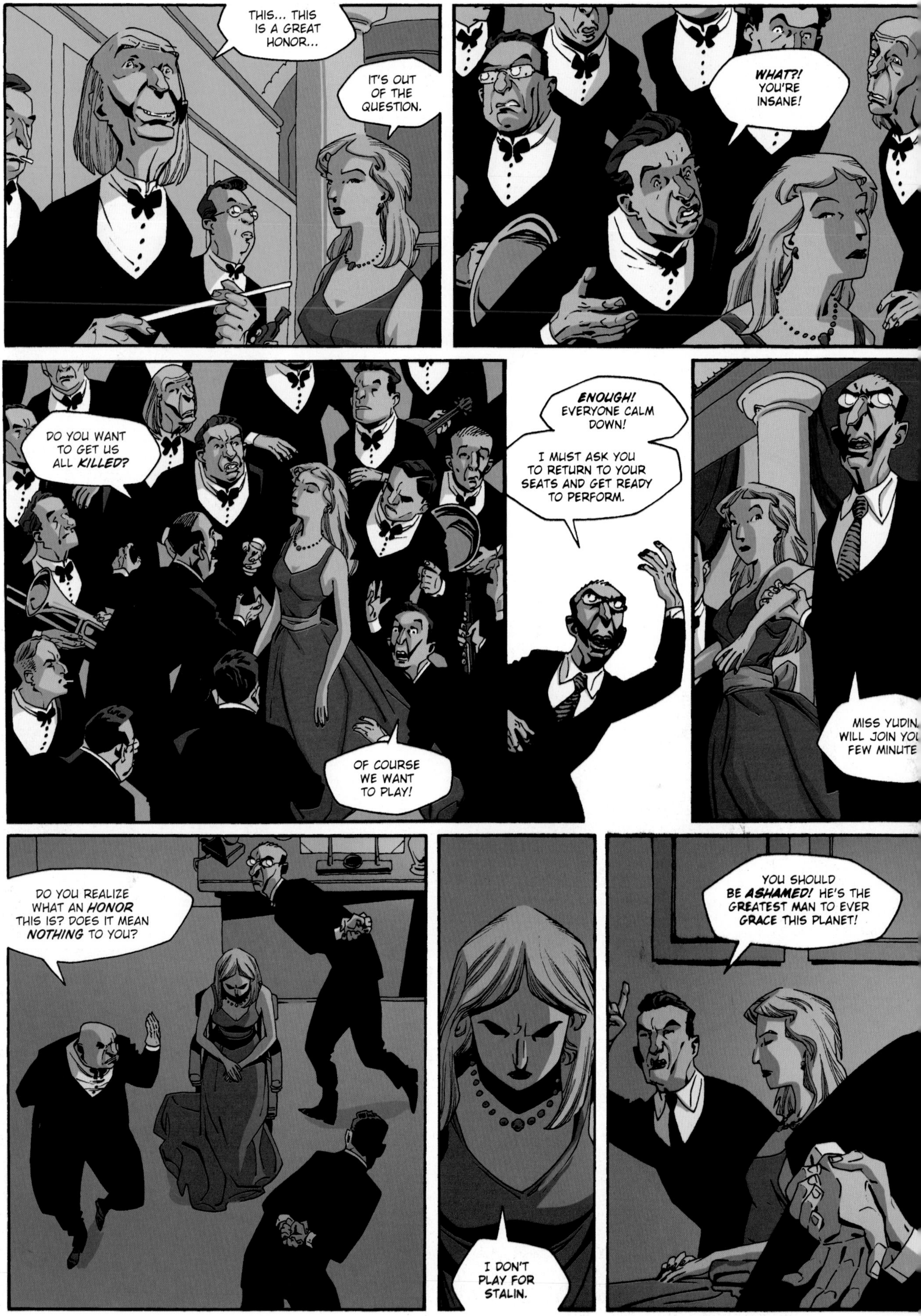
THIS... THIS IS A GREAT HONOR...
IT'S OUT OF THE QUESTION.
WHAT?! YOU'RE INSANE!
DO YOU WANT TO GET US ALL KILLED?
OF COURSE WE WANT TO PLAY!
ENOUGH! EVERYONE CALM DOWN!
I MUST ASK YOU TO RETURN TO YOUR SEATS AND GET READY TO PERFORM.
MISS YUDIN WILL JOIN YO FEW MINUTE
DO YOU REALIZE WHAT AN HONOR THIS IS? DOES IT MEAN NOTHING TO YOU?
I DON'T PLAY FOR STALIN.
YOU SHOULD BE ASHAMED! HE'S THE GREATEST MAN TO EVER GRACE THIS PLANET!

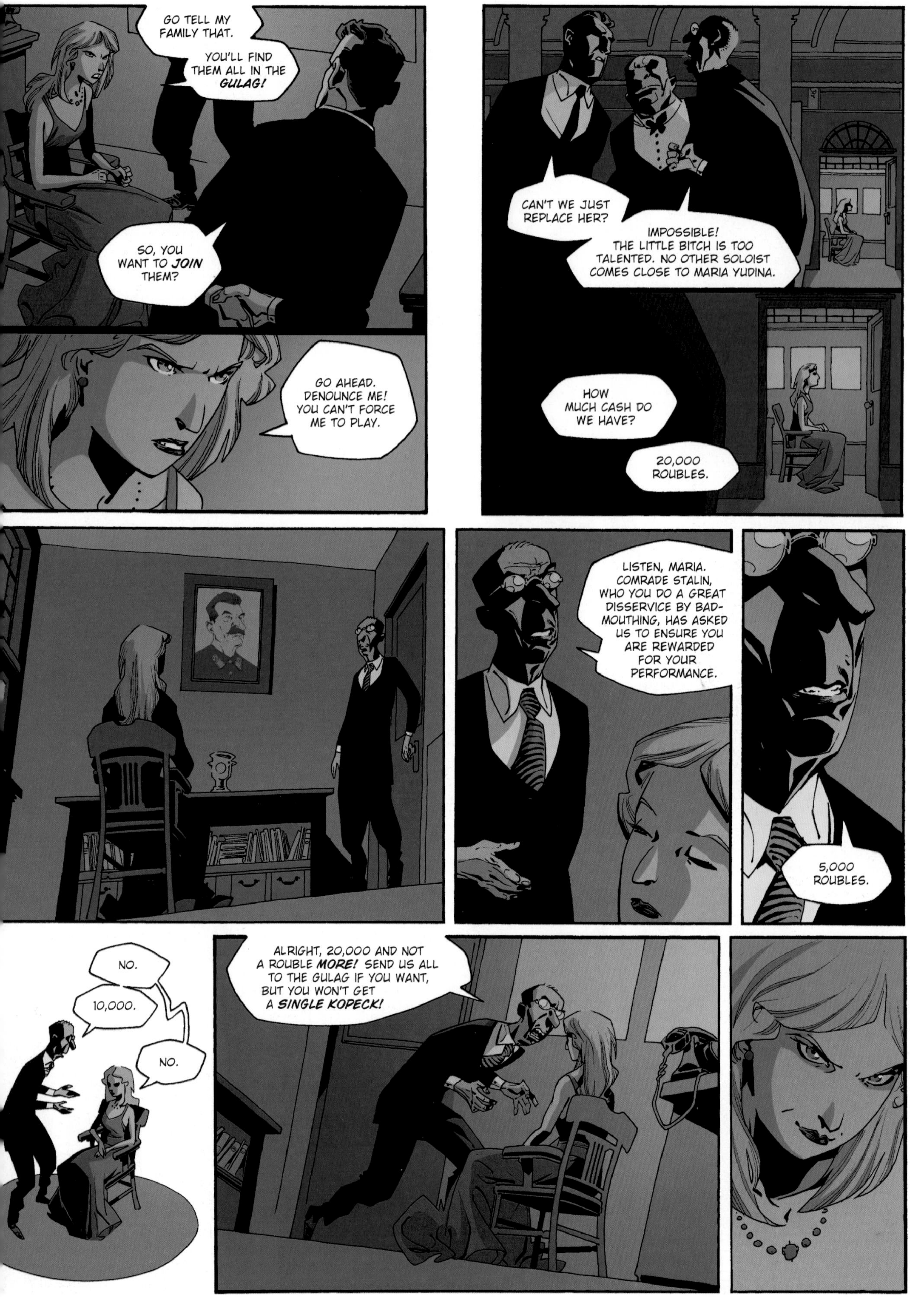
GO TELL MY FAMILY THAT.
YOU'LL FIND THEM ALL IN THE ***GULAG!***
SO, YOU WANT TO ***JOIN*** THEM?
GO AHEAD. DENOUNCE ME! YOU CAN'T FORCE ME TO PLAY.
CAN'T WE JUST REPLACE HER?
IMPOSSIBLE! THE LITTLE BITCH IS TOO TALENTED. NO OTHER SOLOIST COMES CLOSE TO MARIA YUDINA.
HOW MUCH CASH DO WE HAVE?
20,000 ROUBLES.
LISTEN, MARIA. COMRADE STALIN, WHO YOU DO A GREAT DISSERVICE BY BAD-MOUTHING, HAS ASKED US TO ENSURE YOU ARE REWARDED FOR YOUR PERFORMANCE.
5,000 ROUBLES.
NO.
10,000.
NO.
ALRIGHT, 20,000 AND NOT A ROUBLE ***MORE!*** SEND US ALL TO THE GULAG IF YOU WANT, BUT YOU WON'T GET A ***SINGLE KOPECK!***

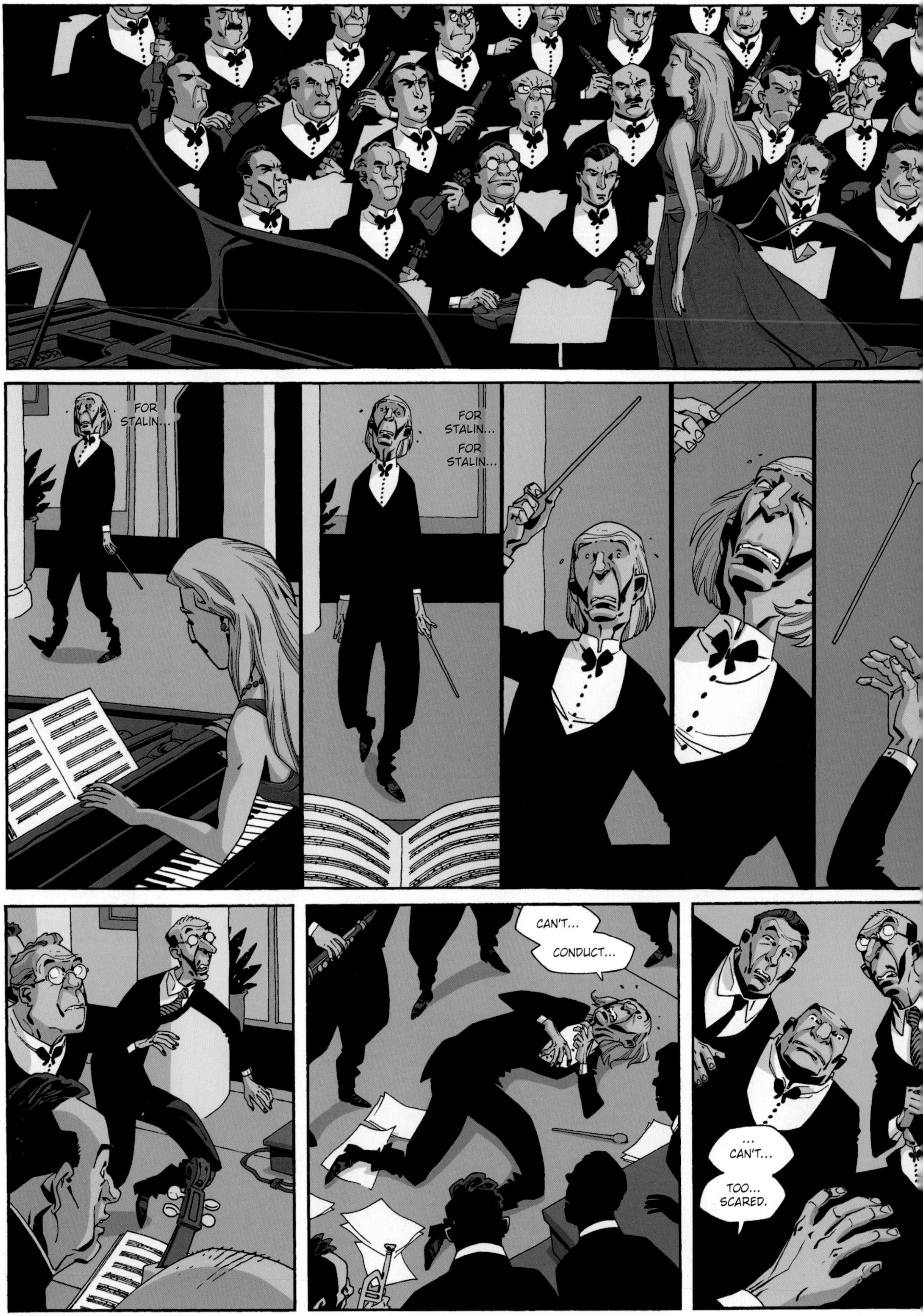
FOR STALIN...
FOR STALIN...
FOR STALIN...
CAN'T...
CONDUCT...
... CAN'T...
TOO... SCARED.

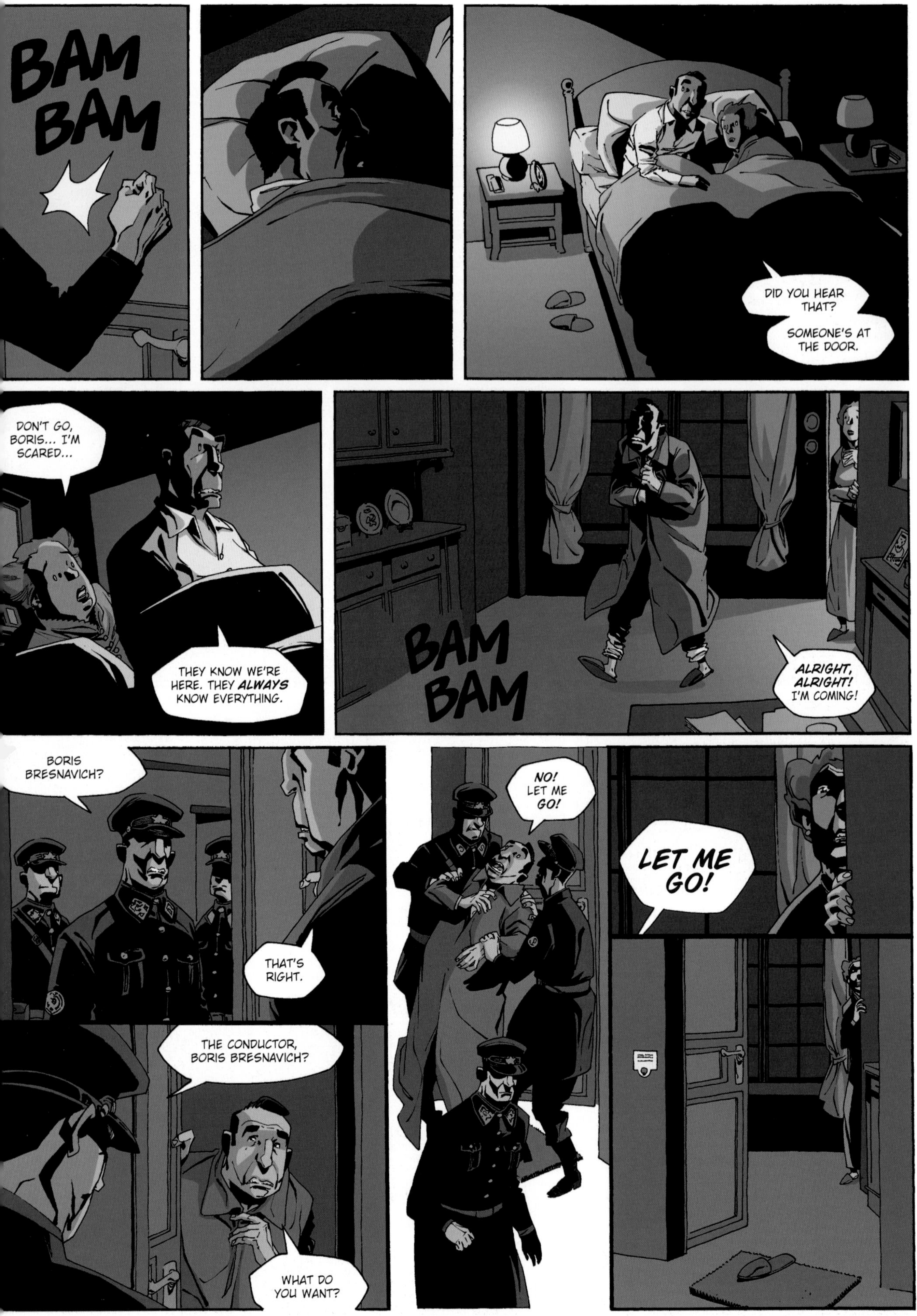
BAM
BAM
DID YOU HEAR THAT?
SOMEONE'S AT THE DOOR.
DON'T GO, BORIS... I'M SCARED...
THEY KNOW WE'RE HERE. THEY ALWAYS KNOW EVERYTHING.
BAM
BAM
ALRIGHT, ALRIGHT! I'M COMING!
BORIS BRESNAVICH?
THAT'S RIGHT.
THE CONDUCTOR, BORIS BRESNAVICH?
WHAT DO YOU WANT?
NO! LET ME GO!
LET ME GO!

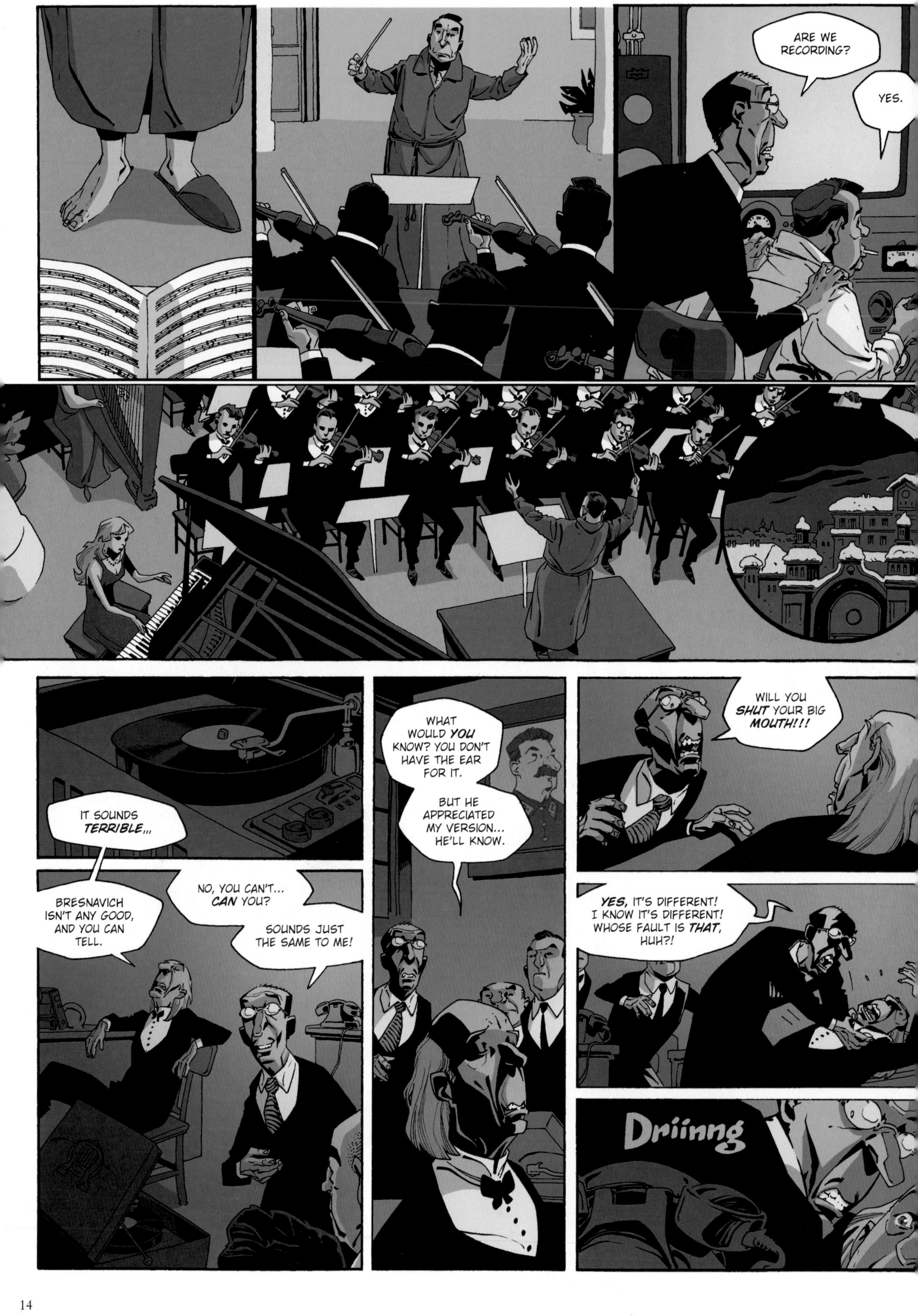
ARE WE RECORDING?
YES.
IT SOUNDS TERRIBLE...
BRESNAVICH ISN'T ANY GOOD, AND YOU CAN TELL.
NO, YOU CAN'T... CAN YOU?
SOUNDS JUST THE SAME TO ME!
WHAT WOULD YOU KNOW? YOU DON'T HAVE THE EAR FOR IT.
BUT HE APPRECIATED MY VERSION... HE'LL KNOW.
WILL YOU SHUT YOUR BIG MOUTH!!!
YES, IT'S DIFFERENT! I KNOW IT'S DIFFERENT! WHOSE FAULT IS THAT, HUH?!
Driinng

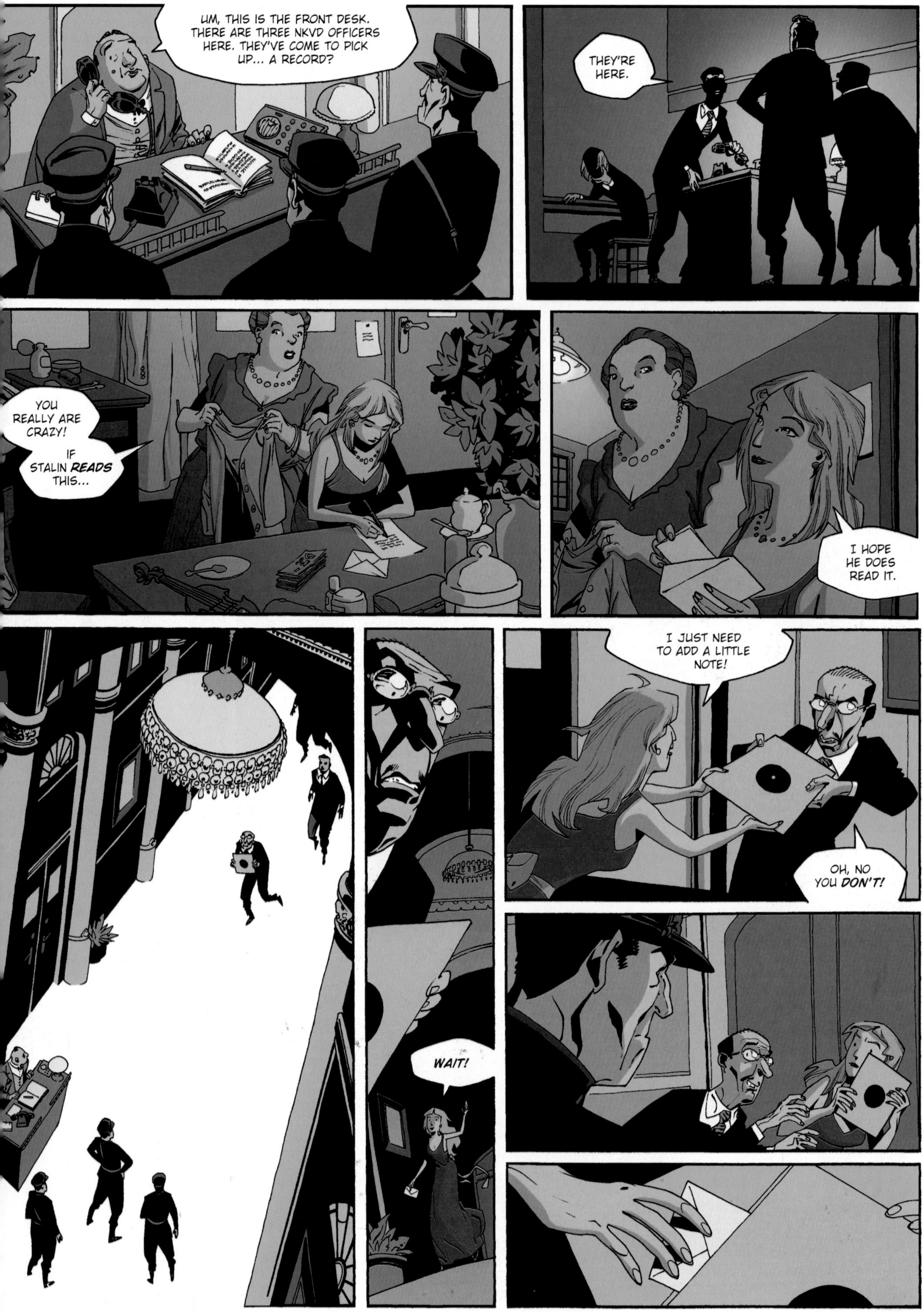
UM, THIS IS THE FRONT DESK. THERE ARE THREE NKVD OFFICERS HERE. THEY'VE COME TO PICK UP... A RECORD?
THEY'RE HERE.
YOU REALLY ARE CRAZY!
IF STALIN **READS** THIS...
I HOPE HE DOES READ IT.
WAIT!
I JUST NEED TO ADD A LITTLE NOTE!
OH, NO YOU **DON'T!**

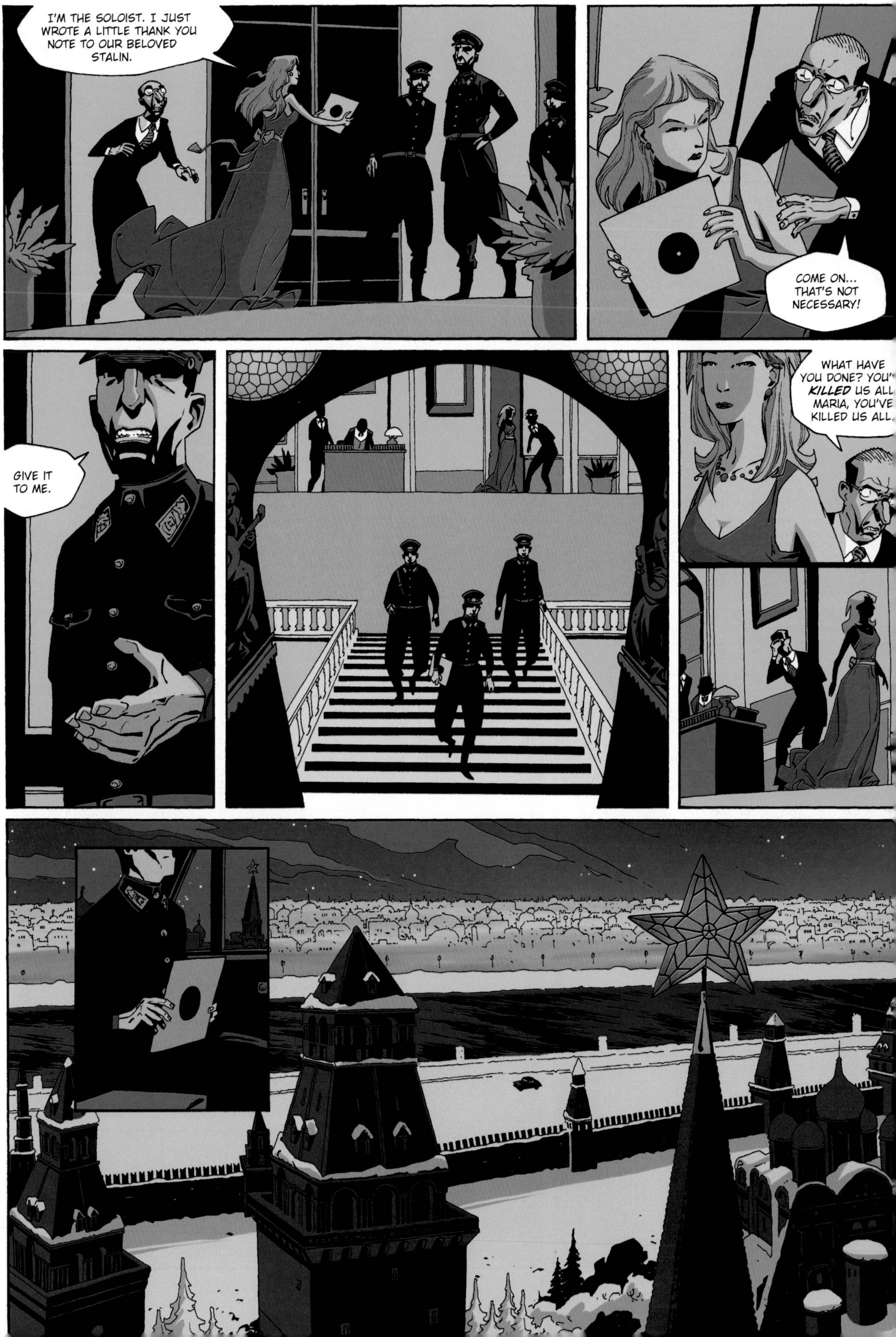
I'M THE SOLOIST. I JUST WROTE A LITTLE THANK YOU NOTE TO OUR BELOVED STALIN.
COME ON... THAT'S NOT NECESSARY!
GIVE IT TO ME.
WHAT HAVE YOU DONE? YOU'VE KILLED US ALL. MARIA, YOU'VE KILLED US ALL.

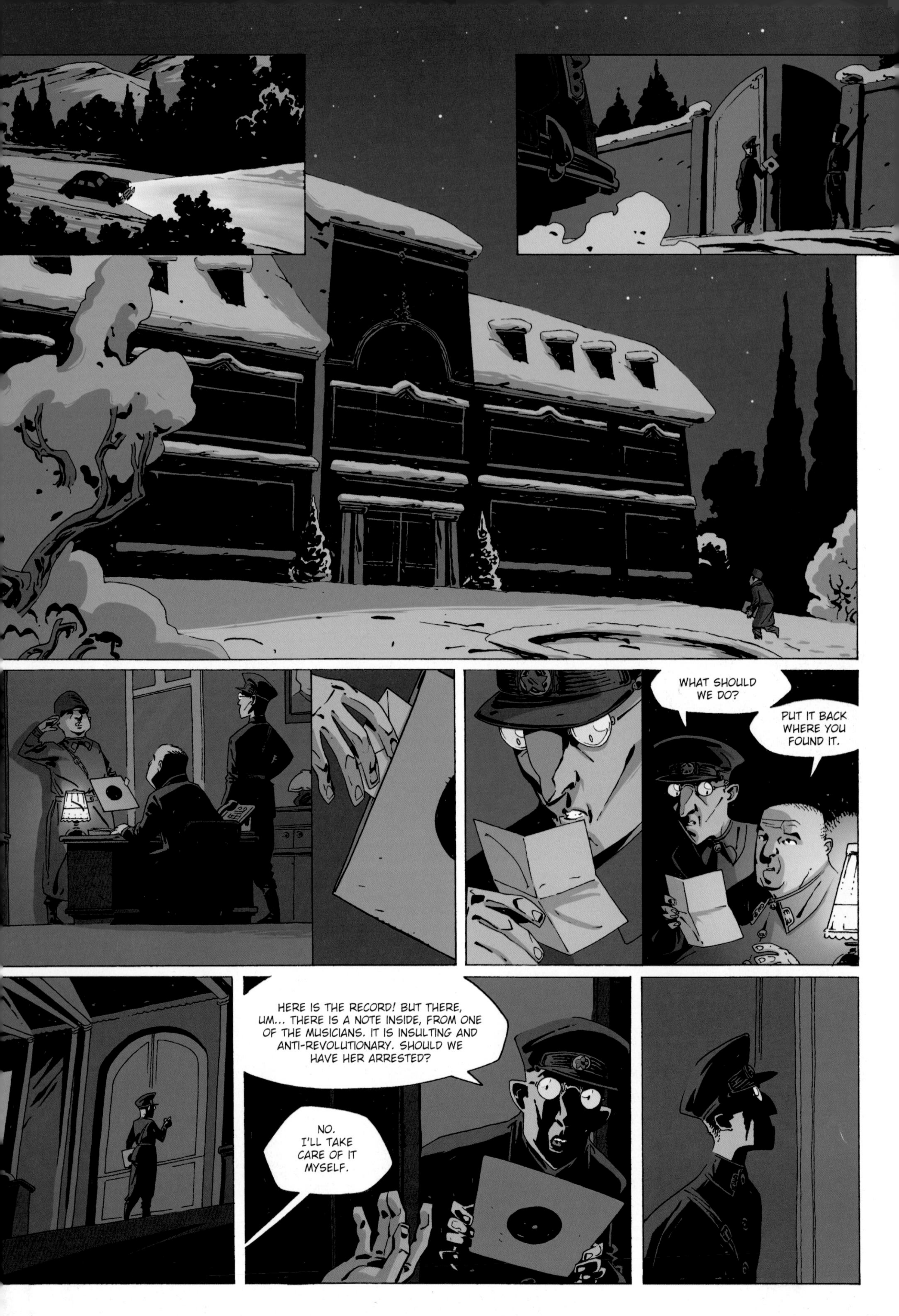
WHAT SHOULD WE DO?
PUT IT BACK WHERE YOU FOUND IT.
HERE IS THE RECORD! BUT THERE, UM... THERE IS A NOTE INSIDE, FROM ONE OF THE MUSICIANS. IT IS INSULTING AND ANTI-REVOLUTIONARY. SHOULD WE HAVE HER ARRESTED?
NO. I'LL TAKE CARE OF IT MYSELF.

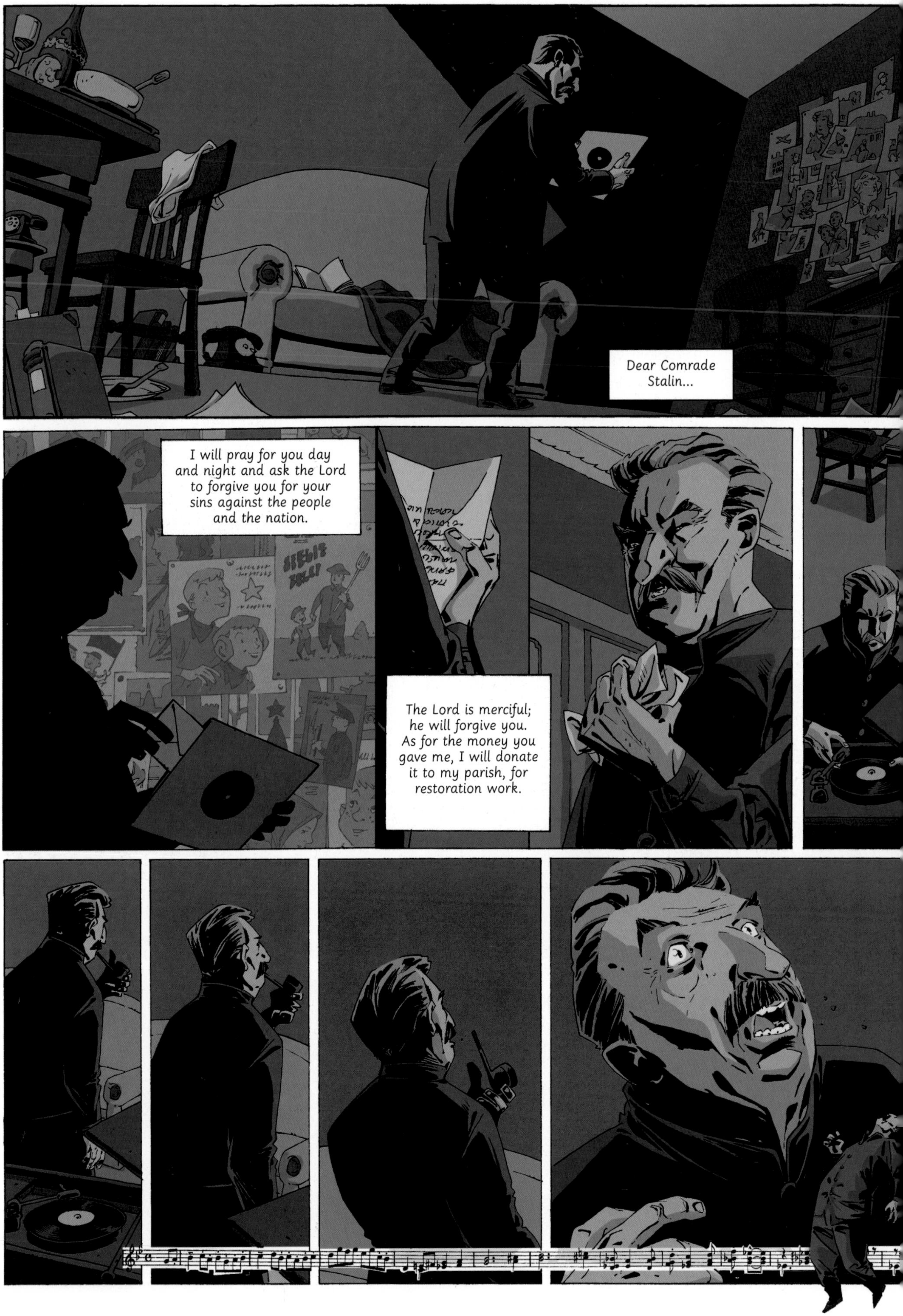
Dear Comrade Stalin...
I will pray for you day and night and ask the Lord to forgive you for your sins against the people and the nation.
The Lord is merciful; he will forgive you. As for the money you gave me, I will donate it to my parish, for restoration work.

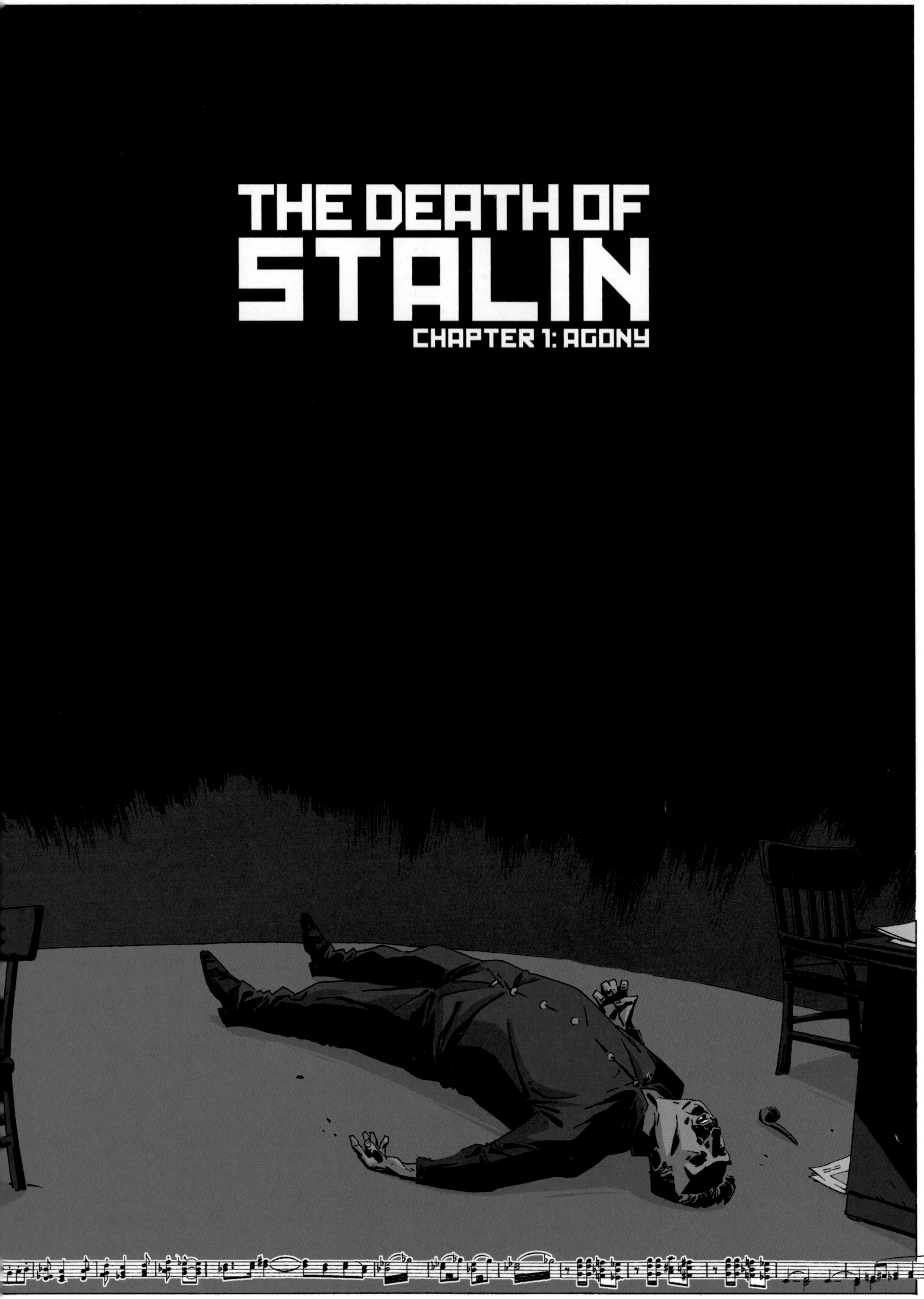
THE DEATH OF STALIN
CHAPTER 1: AGONY

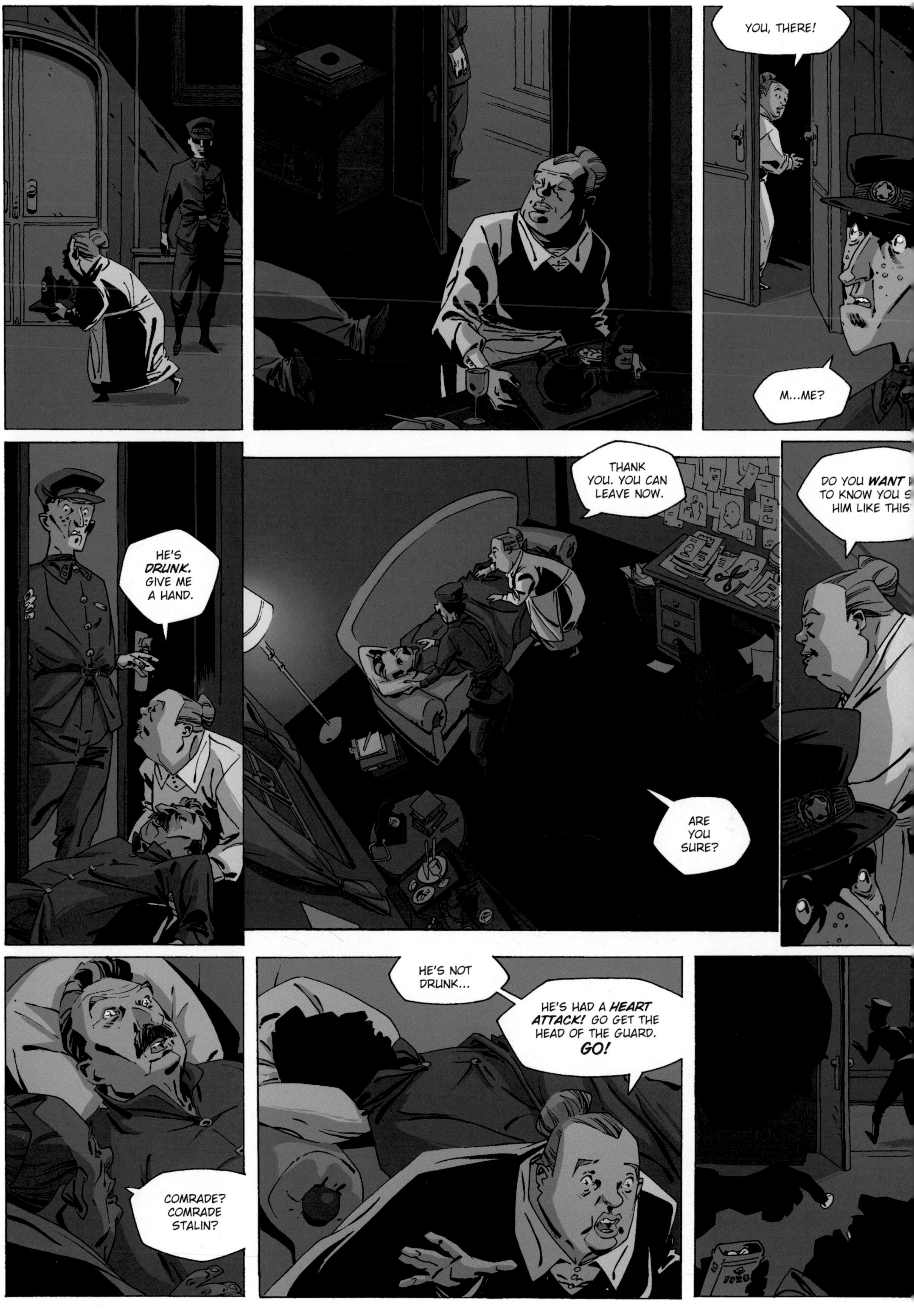
YOU, THERE!
M...ME?
HE'S **DRUNK.** GIVE ME A HAND.
THANK YOU. YOU CAN LEAVE NOW.
ARE YOU SURE?
DO YOU **WANT**
TO KNOW YOU
HIM LIKE THIS
COMRADE? COMRADE STALIN?
HE'S NOT DRUNK...
HE'S HAD A **HEART ATTACK!** GO GET THE HEAD OF THE GUARD. **GO!**

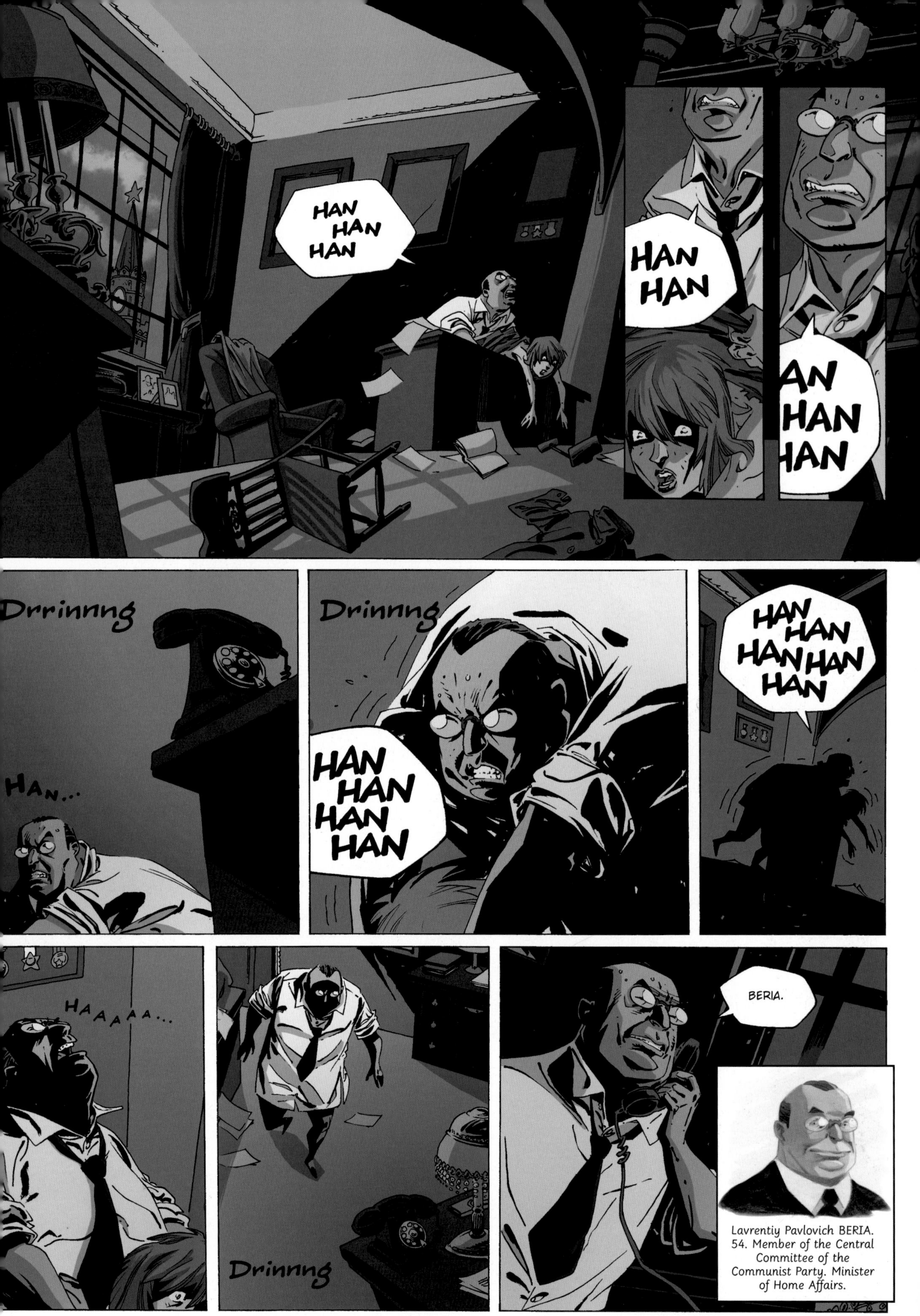
HAN HAN HAN
HAN HAN
HAN HAN HAN
Drrinnng
HAN...
Drinnng
HAN HAN HAN HAN
HAN HAN HAN HAN HAN
HAAAAA...
Drinnng
BERIA.
Lavrentiy Pavlovich BERIA. 54. Member of the Central Committee of the Communist Party. Minister of Home Affairs.

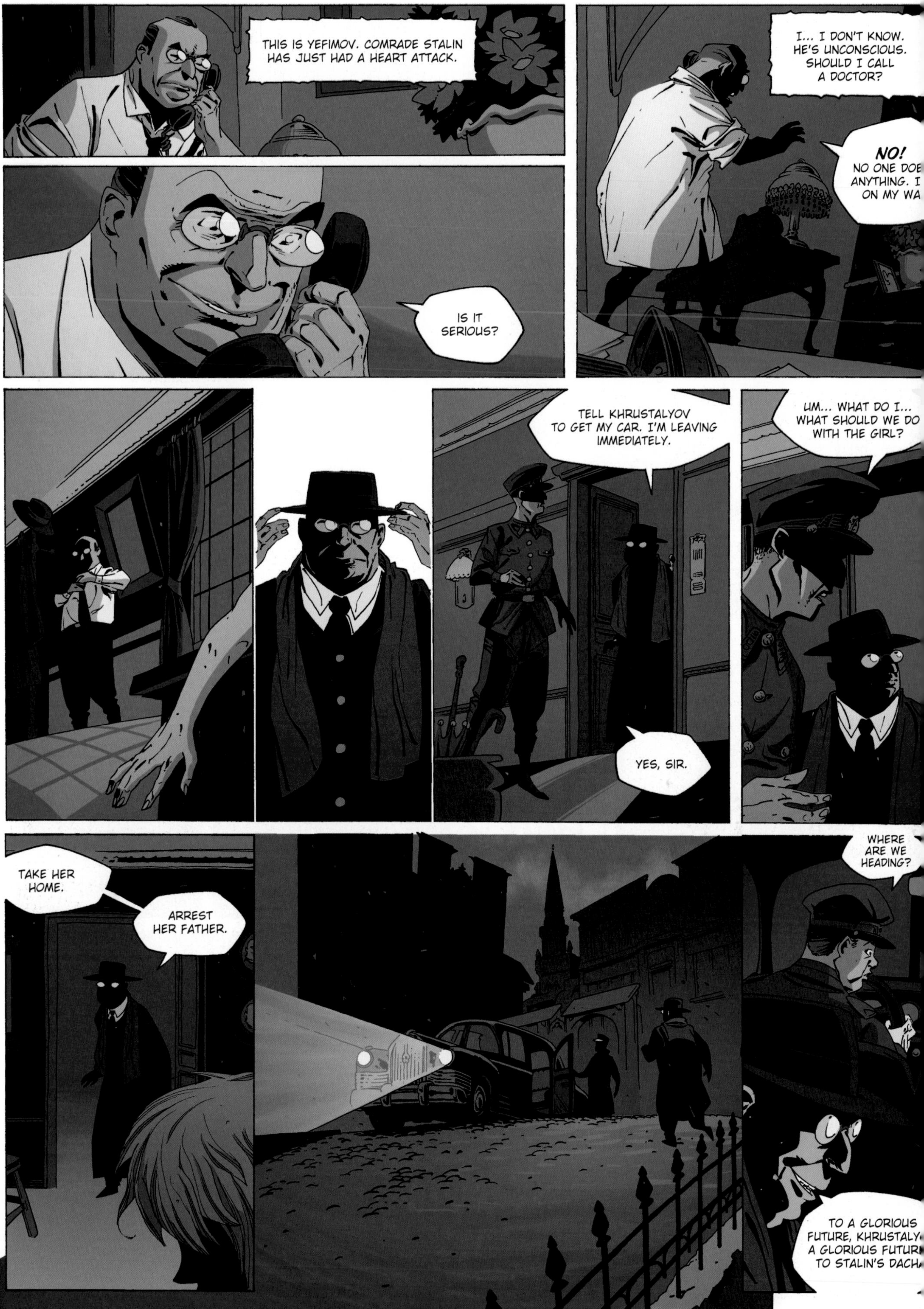
THIS IS YEFIMOV. COMRADE STALIN HAS JUST HAD A HEART ATTACK.
IS IT SERIOUS?
I... I DON'T KNOW. HE'S UNCONSCIOUS. SHOULD I CALL A DOCTOR?
NO! NO ONE DOE ANYTHING. I ON MY WA
TELL KHRUSTALYOV TO GET MY CAR. I'M LEAVING IMMEDIATELY.
YES, SIR.
UM... WHAT DO I... WHAT SHOULD WE DO WITH THE GIRL?
TAKE HER HOME.
ARREST HER FATHER.
WHERE ARE WE HEADING?
TO A GLORIOUS FUTURE, KHRUSTALY A GLORIOUS FUTUR TO STALIN'S DACH

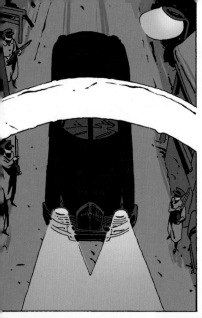
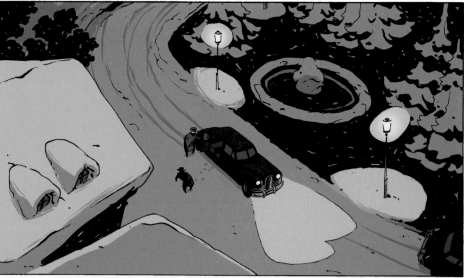

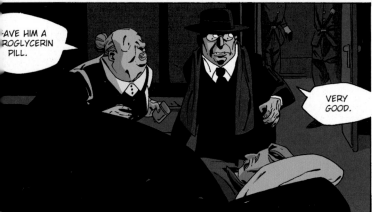

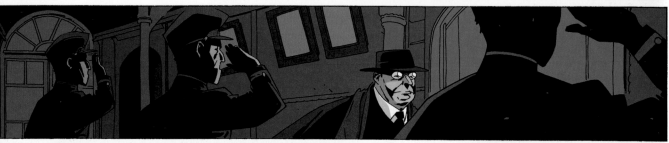

AVE HIM A
ROGLYCERIN
PILL.

VERY
GOOD.

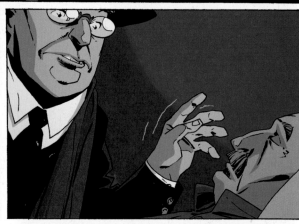

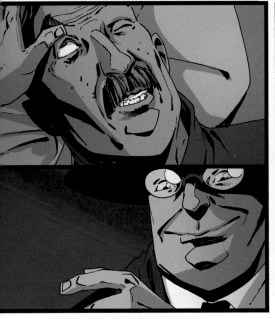

AND THE DOCTOR?
IS HE COMING?

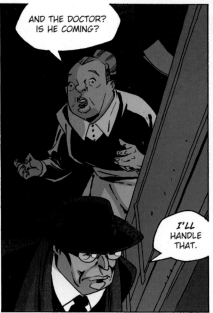

I'LL
HANDLE
THAT.

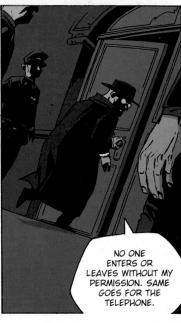

NO ONE
ENTERS OR
LEAVES WITHOUT MY
PERMISSION. SAME
GOES FOR THE
TELEPHONE.

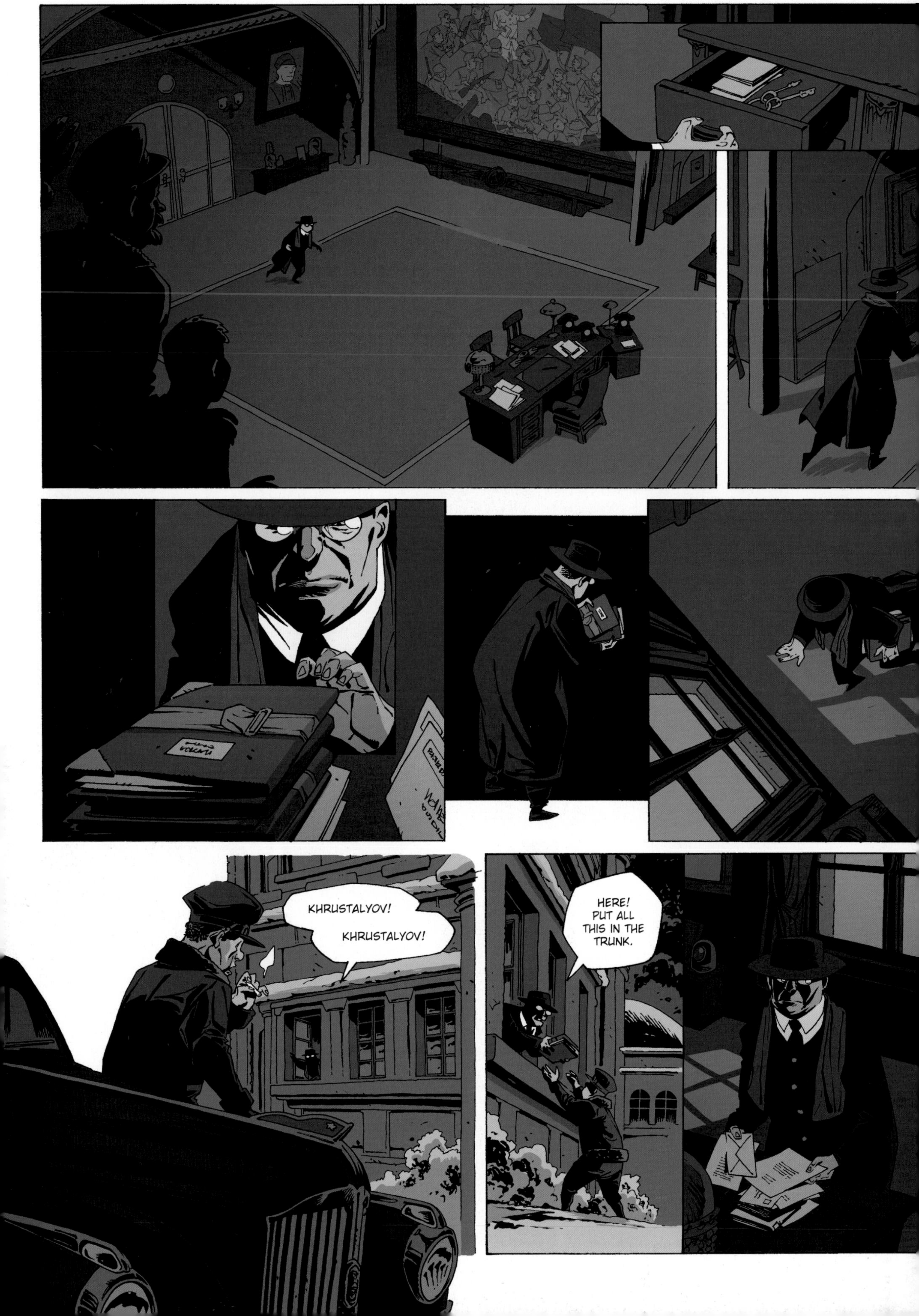
KHRUSTALYOV!
KHRUSTALYOV!
HERE! PUT ALL THIS IN THE TRUNK.

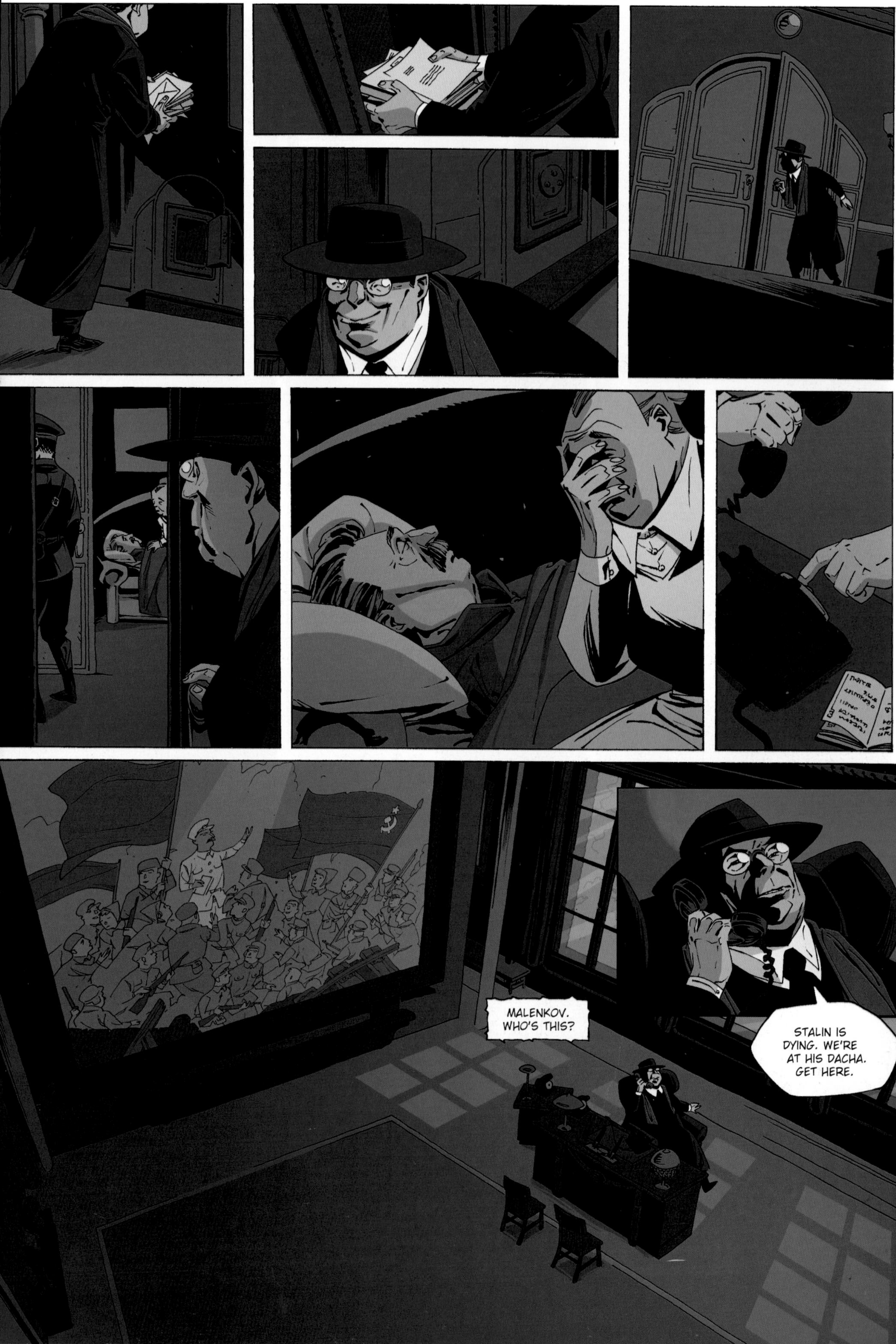
MALENKOV. WHO'S THIS?
STALIN IS DYING. WE'RE AT HIS DACHA. GET HERE.

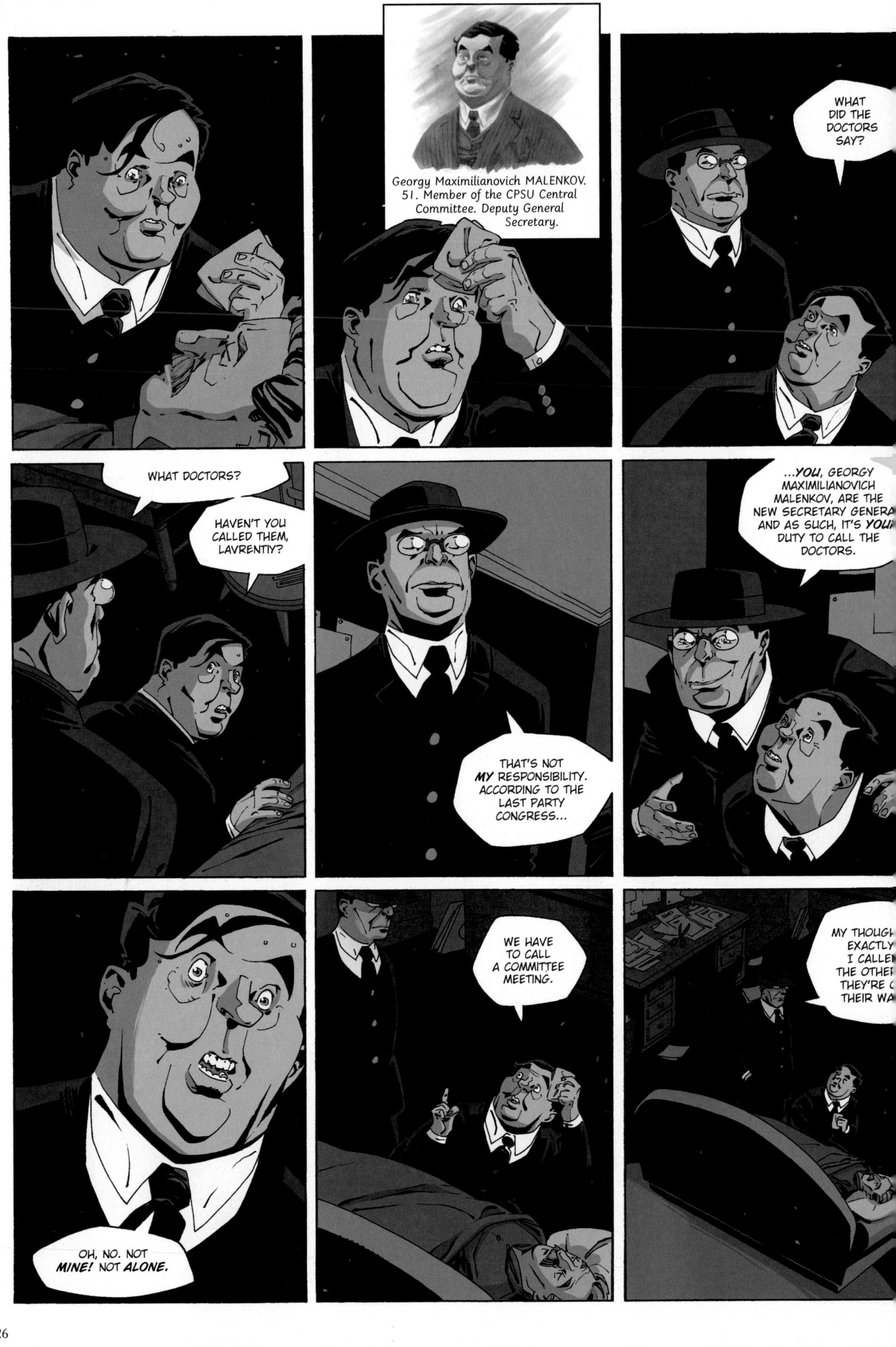
Georgy Maximilianovich MALENKOV. 51. Member of the CPSU Central Committee. Deputy General Secretary.
WHAT DID THE DOCTORS SAY?
WHAT DOCTORS?
HAVEN'T YOU CALLED THEM, LAVRENTIY?
THAT'S NOT *MY* RESPONSIBILITY. ACCORDING TO THE LAST PARTY CONGRESS...
...*YOU*, GEORGY MAXIMILIANOVICH MALENKOV, ARE THE NEW SECRETARY GENERA AND AS SUCH, IT'S *YOU* DUTY TO CALL THE DOCTORS.
OH, NO. NOT *MINE!* NOT *ALONE.*
WE HAVE TO CALL A COMMITTEE MEETING.
MY THOUG EXACTLY I CALLE THE OTHE THEY'RE THEIR WA

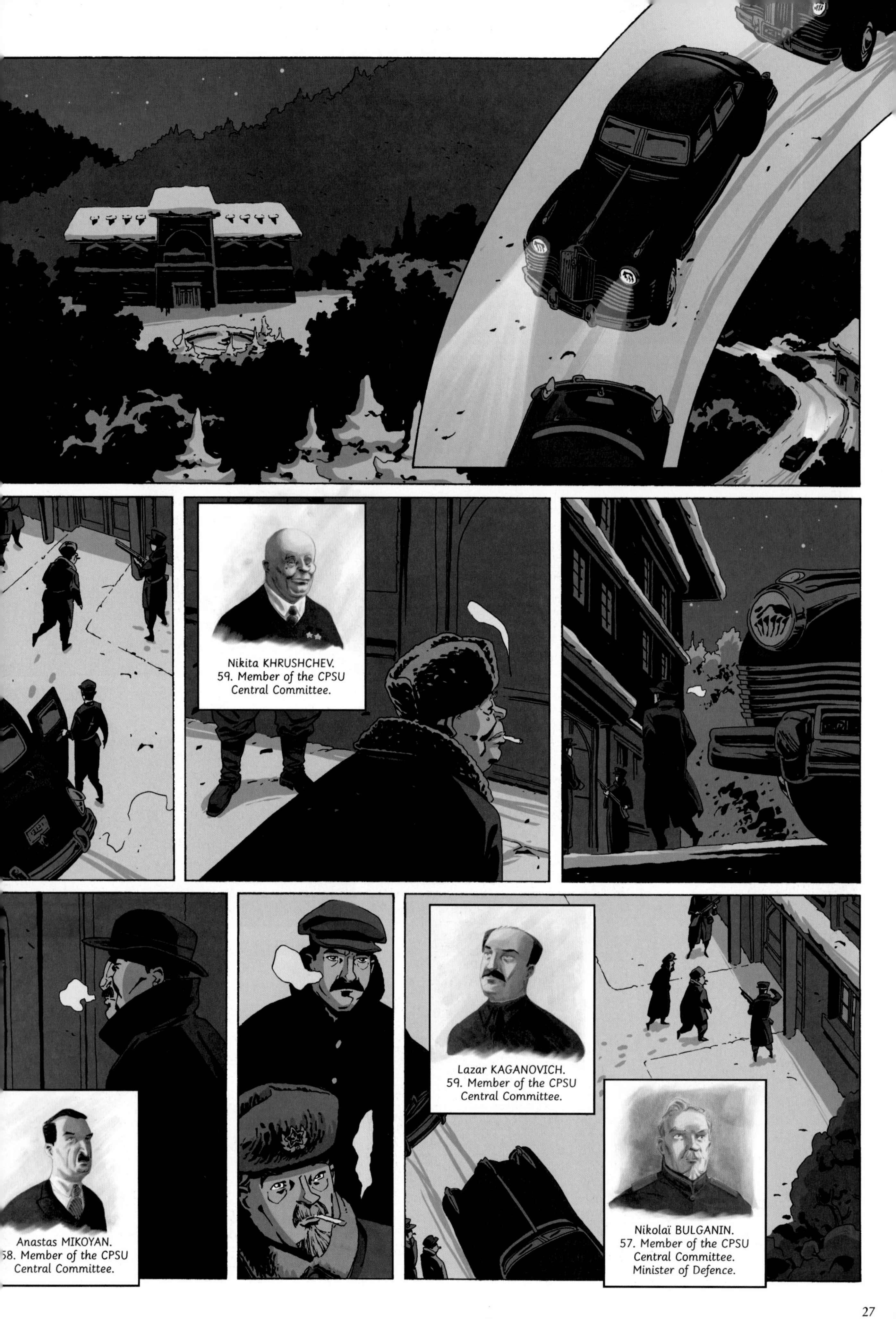
Nikita KHRUSHCHEV.
59. Member of the CPSU Central Committee.
Anastas MIKOYAN.
58. Member of the CPSU Central Committee.
Lazar KAGANOVICH.
59. Member of the CPSU Central Committee.
Nikolaï BULGANIN.
57. Member of the CPSU Central Committee.
Minister of Defence.

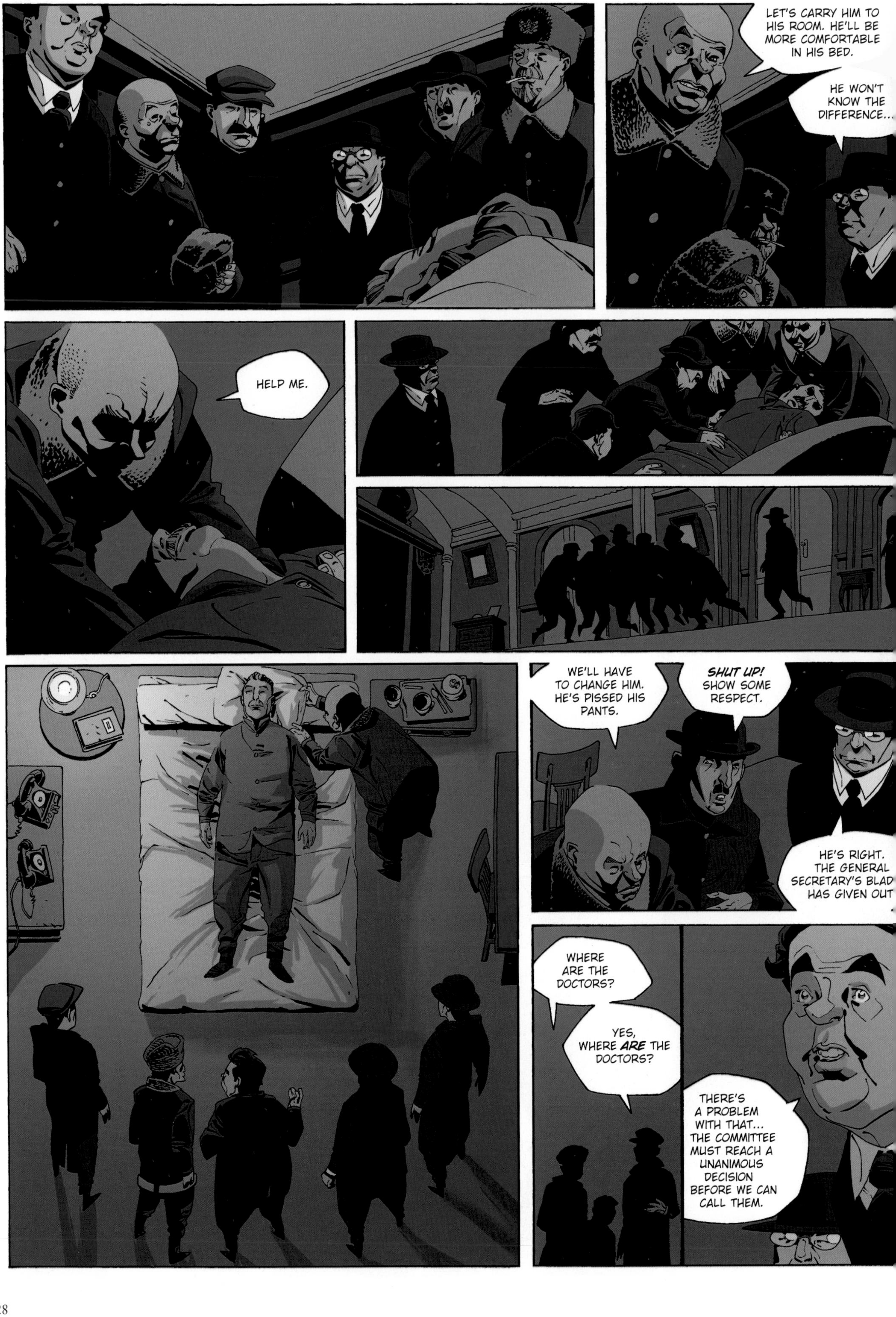
LET'S CARRY HIM TO HIS ROOM. HE'LL BE MORE COMFORTABLE IN HIS BED.
HE WON'T KNOW THE DIFFERENCE...
HELP ME.
WE'LL HAVE TO CHANGE HIM. HE'S PISSED HIS PANTS.
SHUT UP! SHOW SOME RESPECT.
HE'S RIGHT. THE GENERAL SECRETARY'S BLAD HAS GIVEN OUT
WHERE ARE THE DOCTORS?
YES, WHERE ARE THE DOCTORS?
THERE'S A PROBLEM WITH THAT... THE COMMITTEE MUST REACH A UNANIMOUS DECISION BEFORE WE CAN CALL THEM.

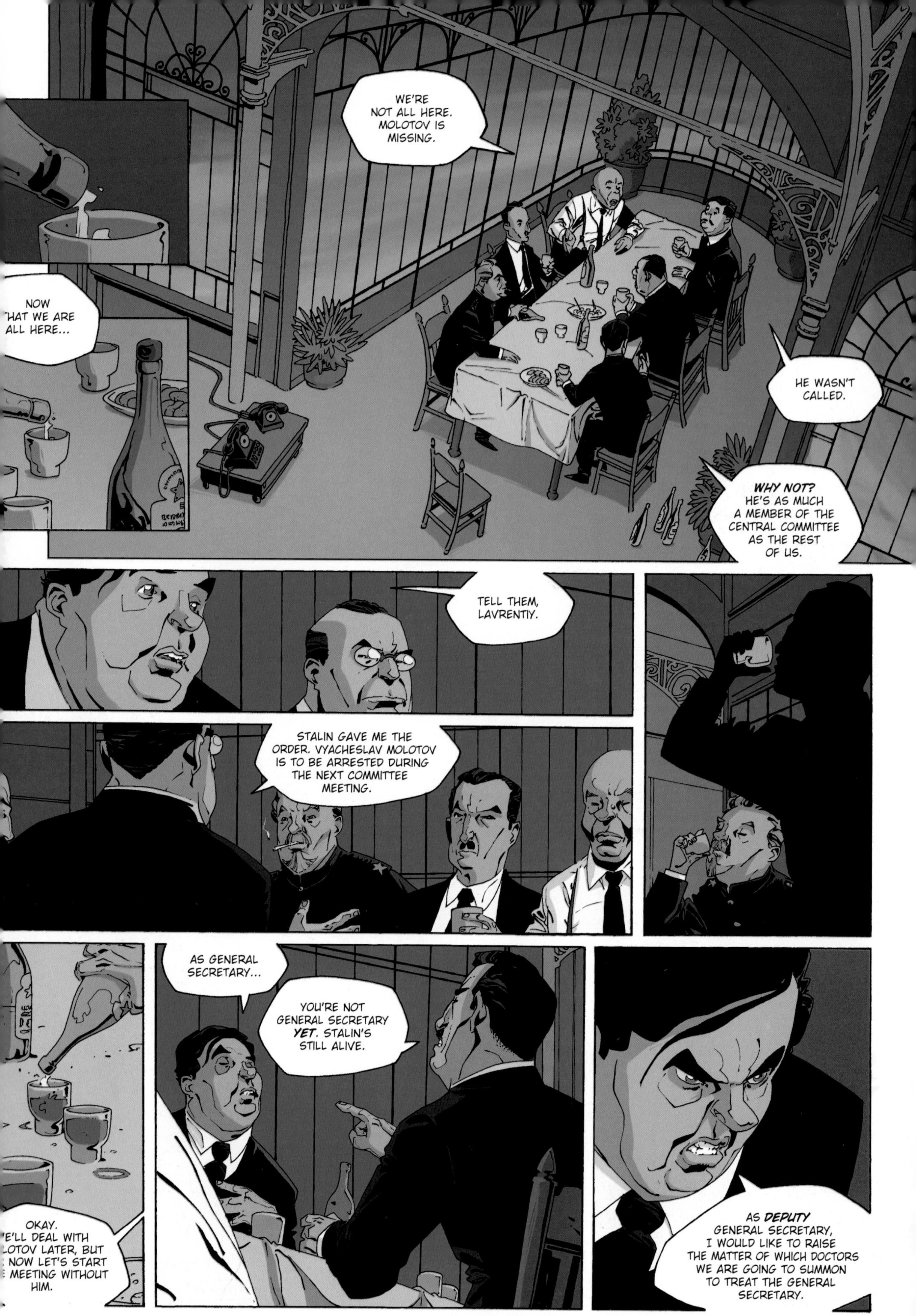
NOW 'HAT WE ARE ALL HERE...
WE'RE NOT ALL HERE. MOLOTOV IS MISSING.
HE WASN'T CALLED.
WHY NOT? HE'S AS MUCH A MEMBER OF THE CENTRAL COMMITTEE AS THE REST OF US.
TELL THEM, LAVRENTIY.
STALIN GAVE ME THE ORDER. VYACHESLAV MOLOTOV IS TO BE ARRESTED DURING THE NEXT COMMITTEE MEETING.
OKAY. 'E'LL DEAL WITH LOTOV LATER, BUT NOW LET'S START E MEETING WITHOUT HIM.
AS GENERAL SECRETARY...
YOU'RE NOT GENERAL SECRETARY *YET*. STALIN'S STILL ALIVE.
AS *DEPUTY* GENERAL SECRETARY, I WOULD LIKE TO RAISE THE MATTER OF WHICH DOCTORS WE ARE GOING TO SUMMON TO TREAT THE GENERAL SECRETARY.

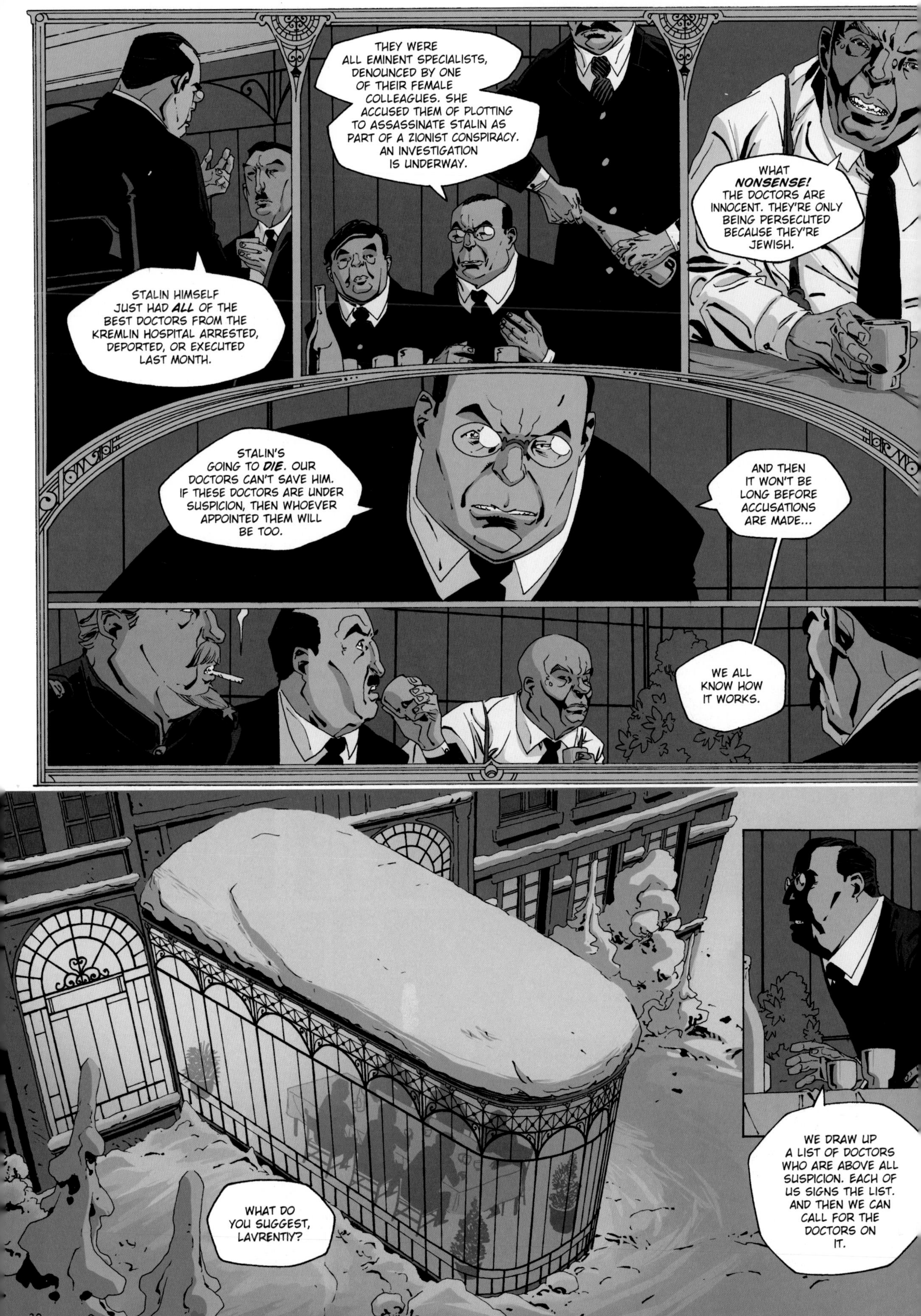
STALIN HIMSELF JUST HAD ALL OF THE BEST DOCTORS FROM THE KREMLIN HOSPITAL ARRESTED, DEPORTED, OR EXECUTED LAST MONTH.
THEY WERE ALL EMINENT SPECIALISTS, DENOUNCED BY ONE OF THEIR FEMALE COLLEAGUES. SHE ACCUSED THEM OF PLOTTING TO ASSASSINATE STALIN AS PART OF A ZIONIST CONSPIRACY. AN INVESTIGATION IS UNDERWAY.
WHAT NONSENSE! THE DOCTORS ARE INNOCENT. THEY'RE ONLY BEING PERSECUTED BECAUSE THEY'RE JEWISH.
STALIN'S GOING TO DIE. OUR DOCTORS CAN'T SAVE HIM. IF THESE DOCTORS ARE UNDER SUSPICION, THEN WHOEVER APPOINTED THEM WILL BE TOO.
AND THEN IT WON'T BE LONG BEFORE ACCUSATIONS ARE MADE...
WE ALL KNOW HOW IT WORKS.
WHAT DO YOU SUGGEST, LAVRENTIY?
WE DRAW UP A LIST OF DOCTORS WHO ARE ABOVE ALL SUSPICION. EACH OF US SIGNS THE LIST. AND THEN WE CAN CALL FOR THE DOCTORS ON IT.

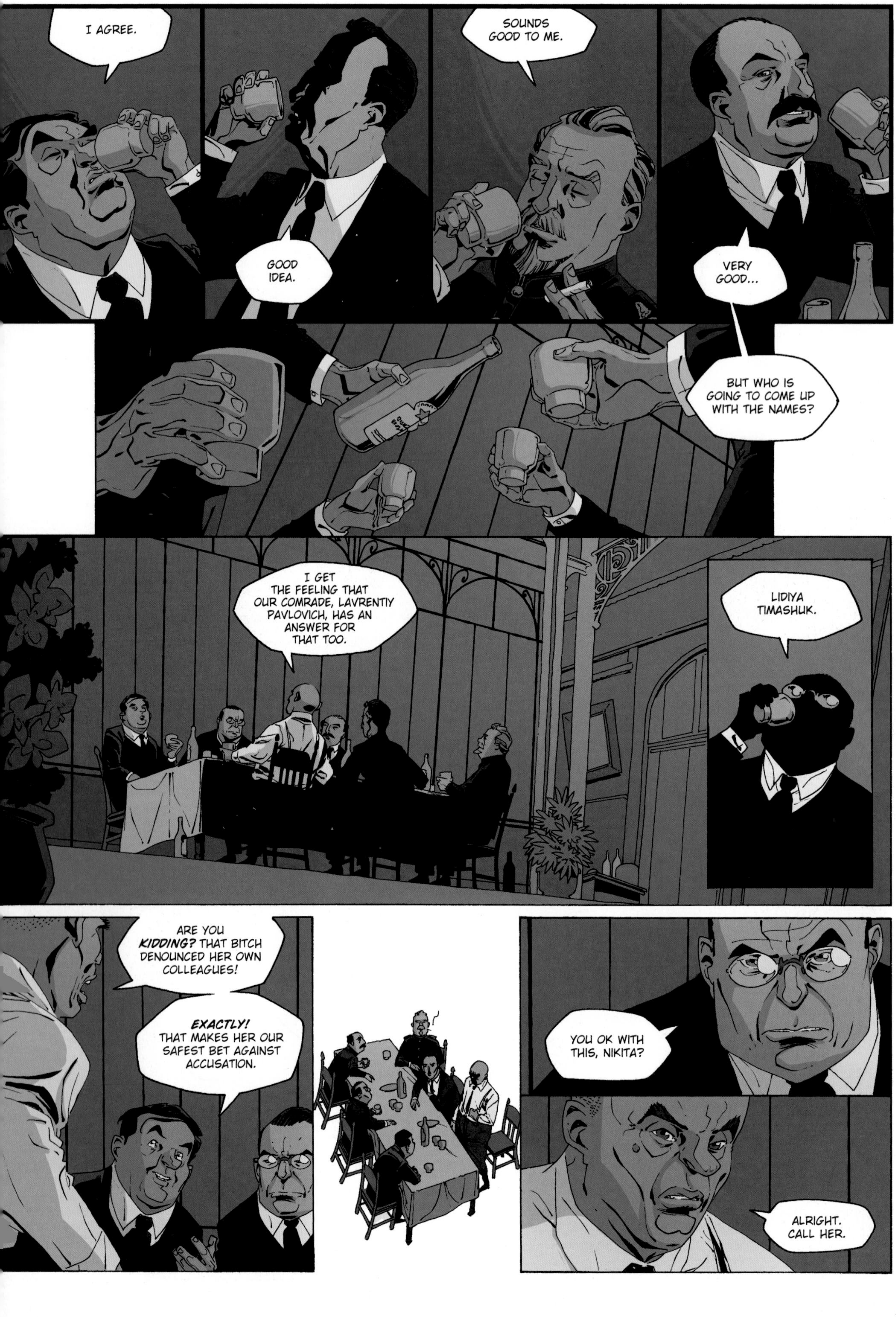
I AGREE.
GOOD IDEA.
SOUNDS GOOD TO ME.
VERY GOOD...
BUT WHO IS GOING TO COME UP WITH THE NAMES?
I GET THE FEELING THAT OUR COMRADE, LAVRENTIY PAVLOVICH, HAS AN ANSWER FOR THAT TOO.
LIDIYA TIMASHUK.
ARE YOU *KIDDING?* THAT BITCH DENOUNCED HER OWN COLLEAGUES!
EXACTLY! THAT MAKES HER OUR SAFEST BET AGAINST ACCUSATION.
YOU OK WITH THIS, NIKITA?
ALRIGHT. CALL HER.

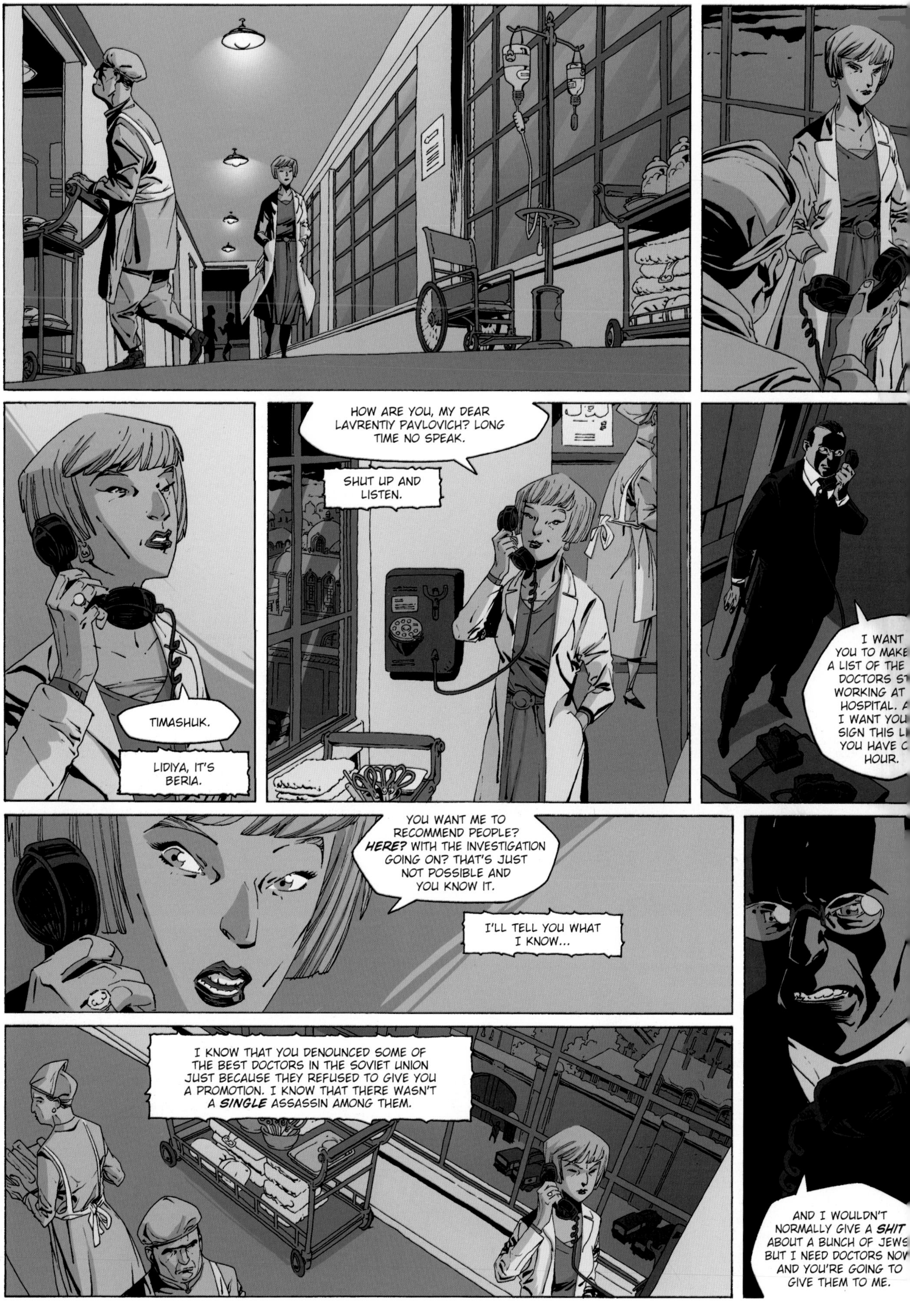
TIMASHUK.
LIDIYA, IT'S BERIA.
HOW ARE YOU, MY DEAR LAVRENTIY PAVLOVICH? LONG TIME NO SPEAK.
SHUT UP AND LISTEN.
I WANT YOU TO MAKE A LIST OF THE DOCTORS ST WORKING AT HOSPITAL. A I WANT YOU SIGN THIS L YOU HAVE O HOUR.
YOU WANT ME TO RECOMMEND PEOPLE? ***HERE?*** WITH THE INVESTIGATION GOING ON? THAT'S JUST NOT POSSIBLE AND YOU KNOW IT.
I'LL TELL YOU WHAT I KNOW...
I KNOW THAT YOU DENOUNCED SOME OF THE BEST DOCTORS IN THE SOVIET UNION JUST BECAUSE THEY REFUSED TO GIVE YOU A PROMOTION. I KNOW THAT THERE WASN'T A ***SINGLE*** ASSASSIN AMONG THEM.
AND I WOULDN'T NORMALLY GIVE A ***SHIT*** ABOUT A BUNCH OF JEWS BUT I NEED DOCTORS NOW AND YOU'RE GOING TO GIVE THEM TO ME.

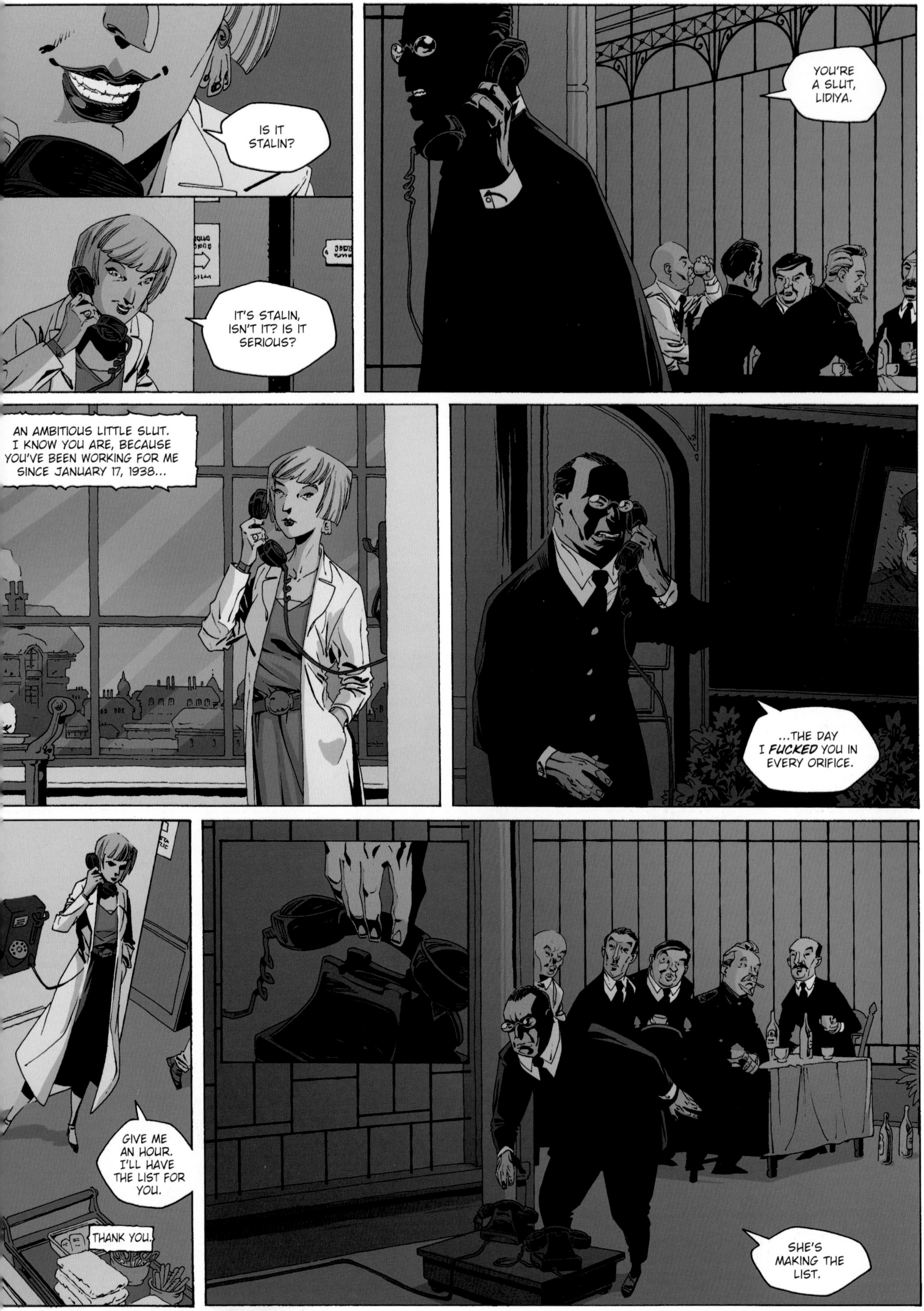
IS IT STALIN?
IT'S STALIN, ISN'T IT? IS IT SERIOUS?
YOU'RE A SLUT, LIDIYA.
AN AMBITIOUS LITTLE SLUT. I KNOW YOU ARE, BECAUSE YOU'VE BEEN WORKING FOR ME SINCE JANUARY 17, 1938...
...THE DAY I ***FUCKED*** YOU IN EVERY ORIFICE.
GIVE ME AN HOUR. I'LL HAVE THE LIST FOR YOU.
THANK YOU.
SHE'S MAKING THE LIST.

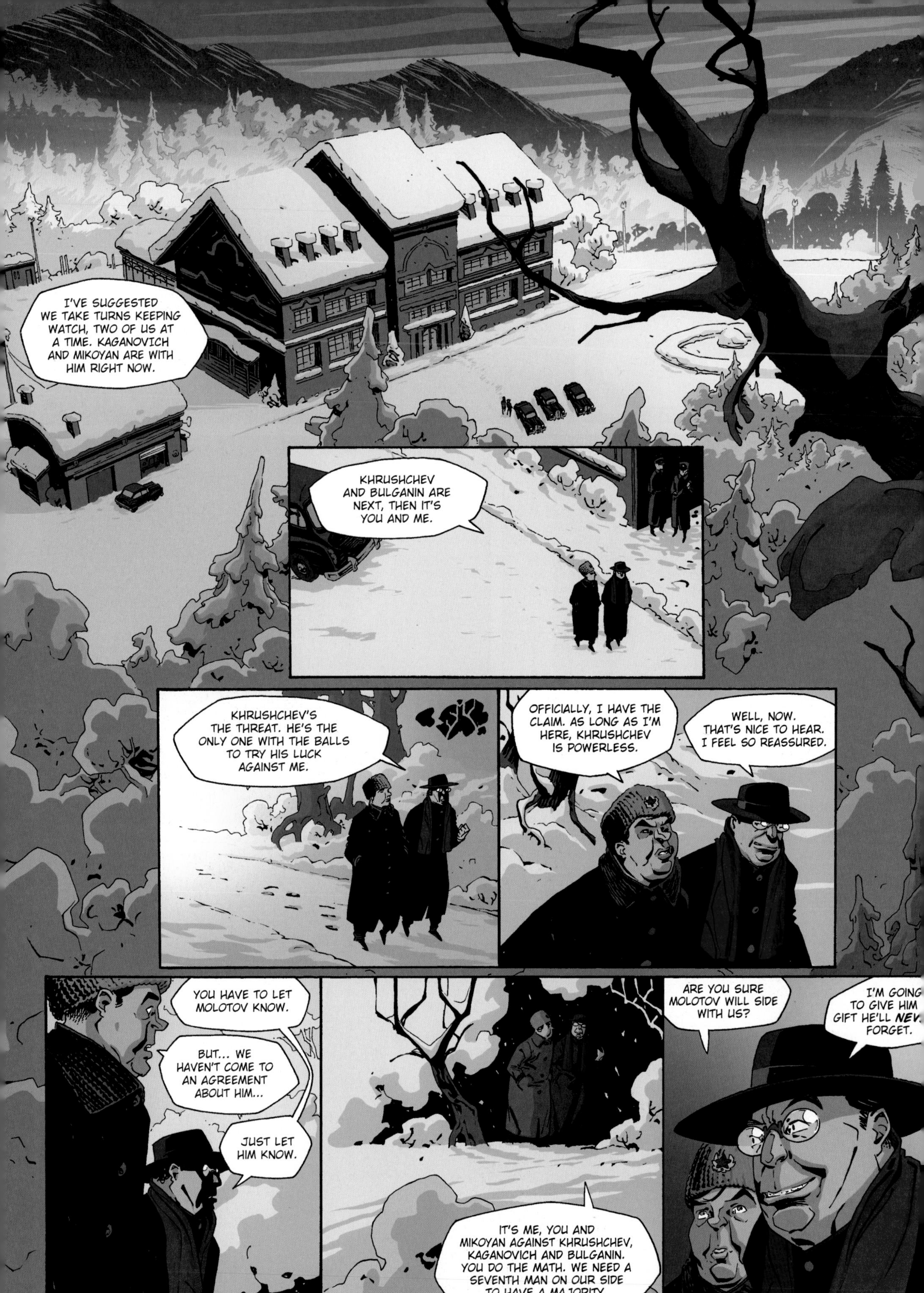
I'VE SUGGESTED WE TAKE TURNS KEEPING WATCH, TWO OF US AT A TIME. KAGANOVICH AND MIKOYAN ARE WITH HIM RIGHT NOW.
KHRUSHCHEV AND BULGANIN ARE NEXT, THEN IT'S YOU AND ME.
KHRUSHCHEV'S THE THREAT. HE'S THE ONLY ONE WITH THE BALLS TO TRY HIS LUCK AGAINST ME.
OFFICIALLY, I HAVE THE CLAIM. AS LONG AS I'M HERE, KHRUSHCHEV IS POWERLESS.
WELL, NOW. THAT'S NICE TO HEAR. I FEEL SO REASSURED.
YOU HAVE TO LET MOLOTOV KNOW.
BUT... WE HAVEN'T COME TO AN AGREEMENT ABOUT HIM...
JUST LET HIM KNOW.
IT'S ME, YOU AND MIKOYAN AGAINST KHRUSHCHEV, KAGANOVICH AND BULGANIN. YOU DO THE MATH. WE NEED A SEVENTH MAN ON OUR SIDE TO HAVE A MAJORITY.
ARE YOU SURE MOLOTOV WILL SIDE WITH US?
I'M GOING TO GIVE HIM GIFT HE'LL *NEV* FORGET.

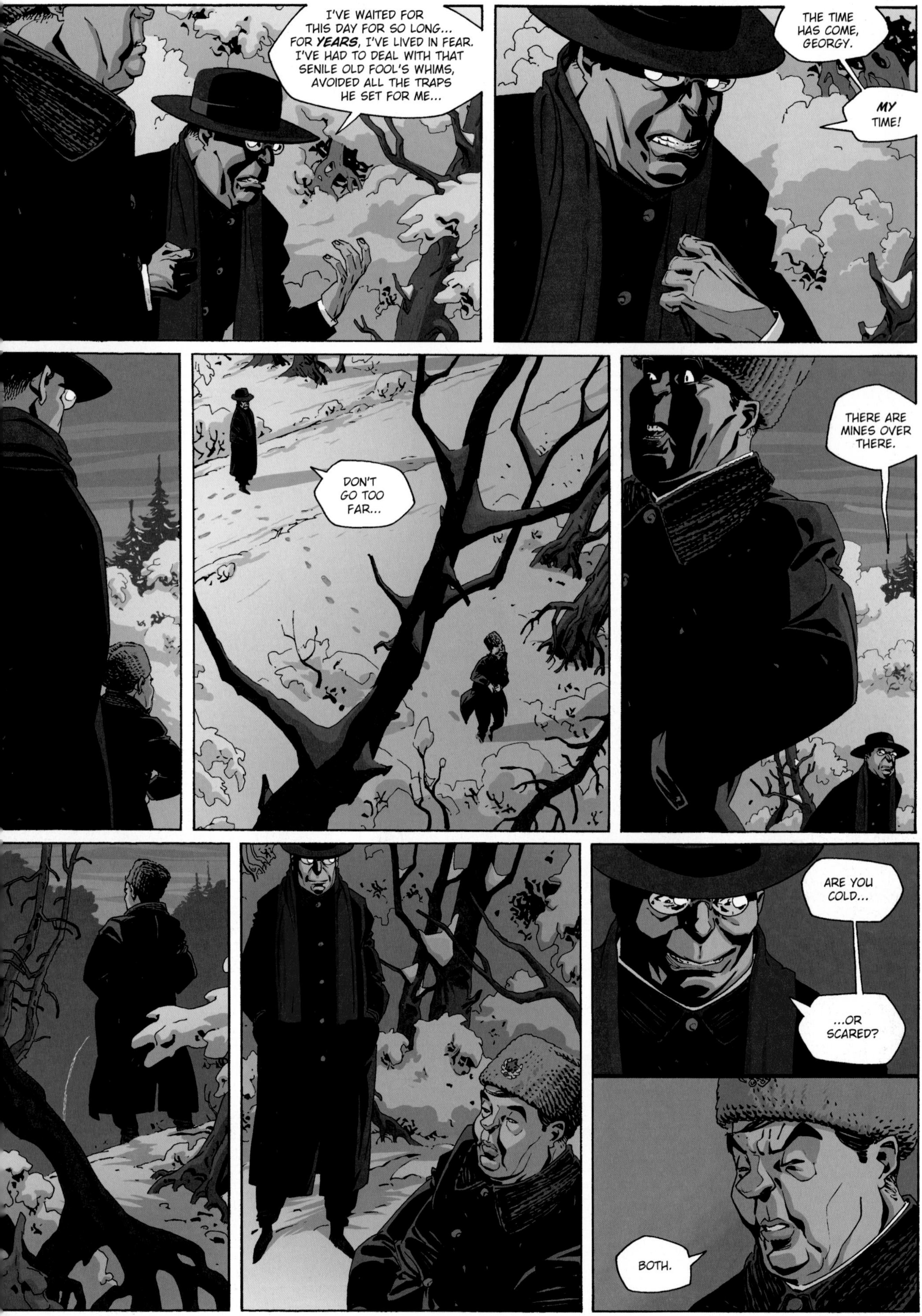
I'VE WAITED FOR THIS DAY FOR SO LONG... FOR YEARS, I'VE LIVED IN FEAR. I'VE HAD TO DEAL WITH THAT SENILE OLD FOOL'S WHIMS, AVOIDED ALL THE TRAPS HE SET FOR ME...
THE TIME HAS COME, GEORGY.
MY TIME!
DON'T GO TOO FAR...
THERE ARE MINES OVER THERE.
ARE YOU COLD...
...OR SCARED?
BOTH.

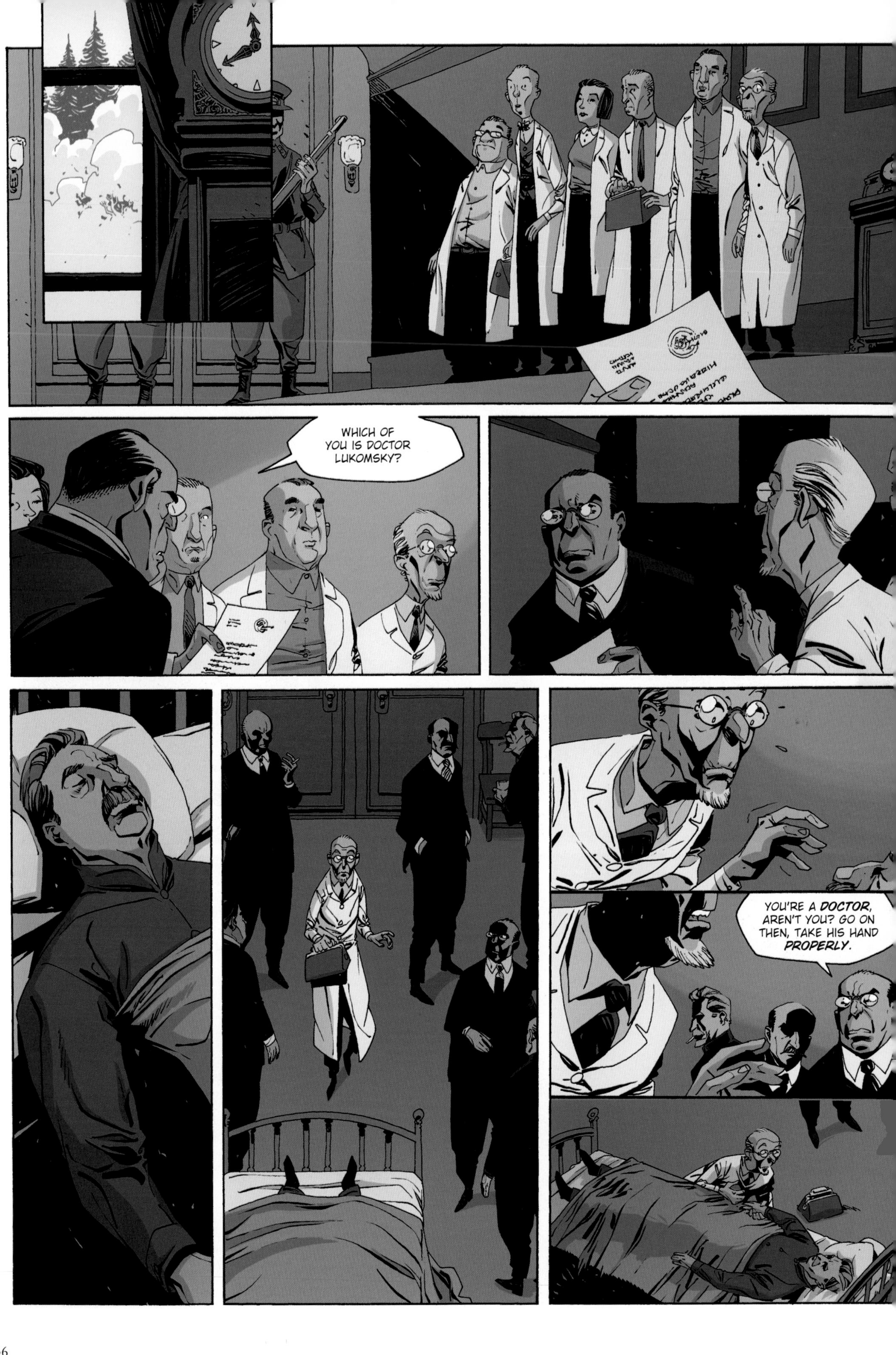
WHICH OF YOU IS DOCTOR LUKOMSKY?
YOU'RE A **DOCTOR**, AREN'T YOU? GO ON THEN, TAKE HIS HAND **PROPERLY**.

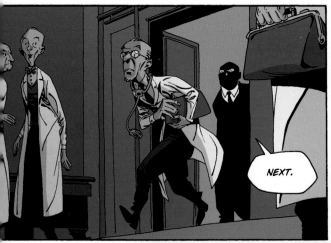

NEXT.

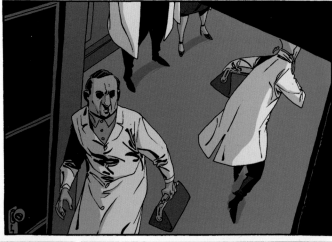

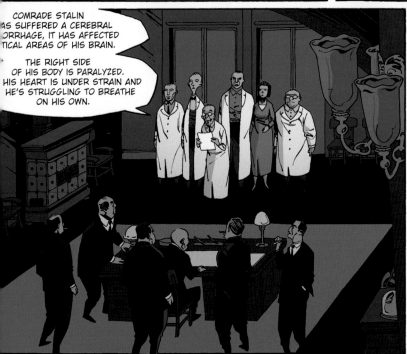

COMRADE STALIN HAS SUFFERED A CEREBRAL HEMORRHAGE, IT HAS AFFECTED CRITICAL AREAS OF HIS BRAIN.

THE RIGHT SIDE OF HIS BODY IS PARALYZED. HIS HEART IS UNDER STRAIN AND HE'S STRUGGLING TO BREATHE ON HIS OWN.

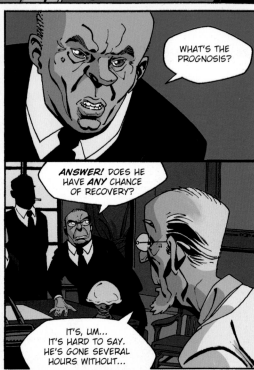

WHAT'S THE PROGNOSIS?

ANSWER! DOES HE HAVE ANY CHANCE OF RECOVERY?

IT'S, UM... IT'S HARD TO SAY. HE'S GONE SEVERAL HOURS WITHOUT...

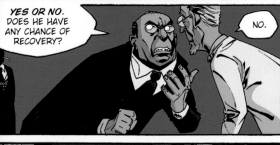

YES OR NO. DOES HE HAVE ANY CHANCE OF RECOVERY?

NO.

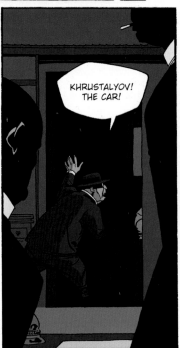

KHRUSTALYOV! THE CAR!

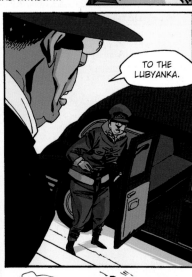

TO THE LUBYANKA.

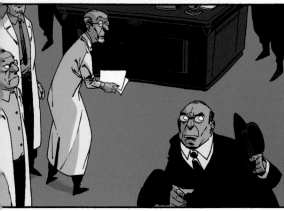

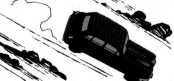

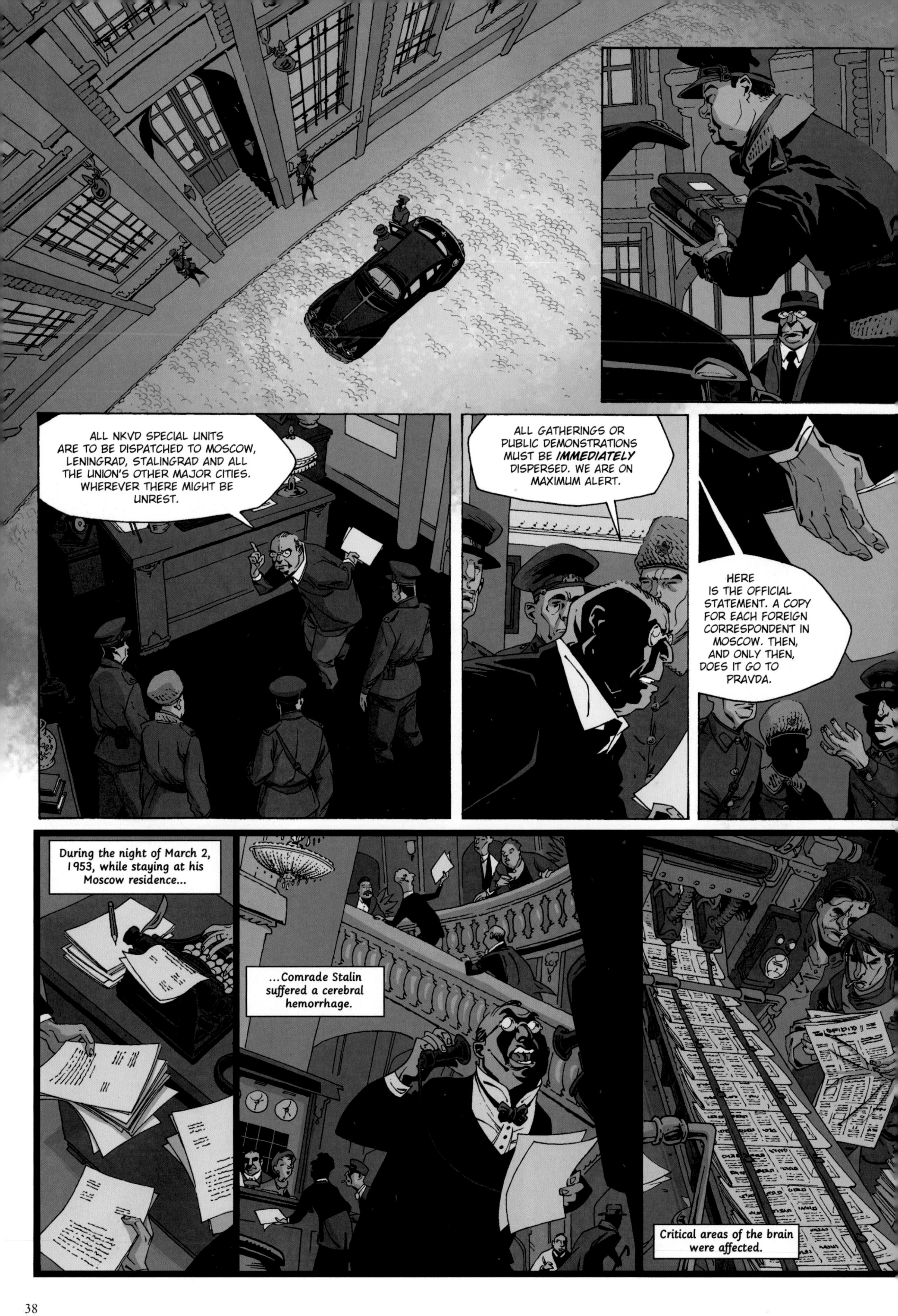
ALL NKVD SPECIAL UNITS ARE TO BE DISPATCHED TO MOSCOW, LENINGRAD, STALINGRAD AND ALL THE UNION'S OTHER MAJOR CITIES. WHEREVER THERE MIGHT BE UNREST.
ALL GATHERINGS OR PUBLIC DEMONSTRATIONS MUST BE *IMMEDIATELY* DISPERSED. WE ARE ON MAXIMUM ALERT.
HERE IS THE OFFICIAL STATEMENT. A COPY FOR EACH FOREIGN CORRESPONDENT IN MOSCOW. THEN, AND ONLY THEN, DOES IT GO TO PRAVDA.
During the night of March 2, 1953, while staying at his Moscow residence...
...Comrade Stalin suffered a cerebral hemorrhage.
Critical areas of the brain were affected.

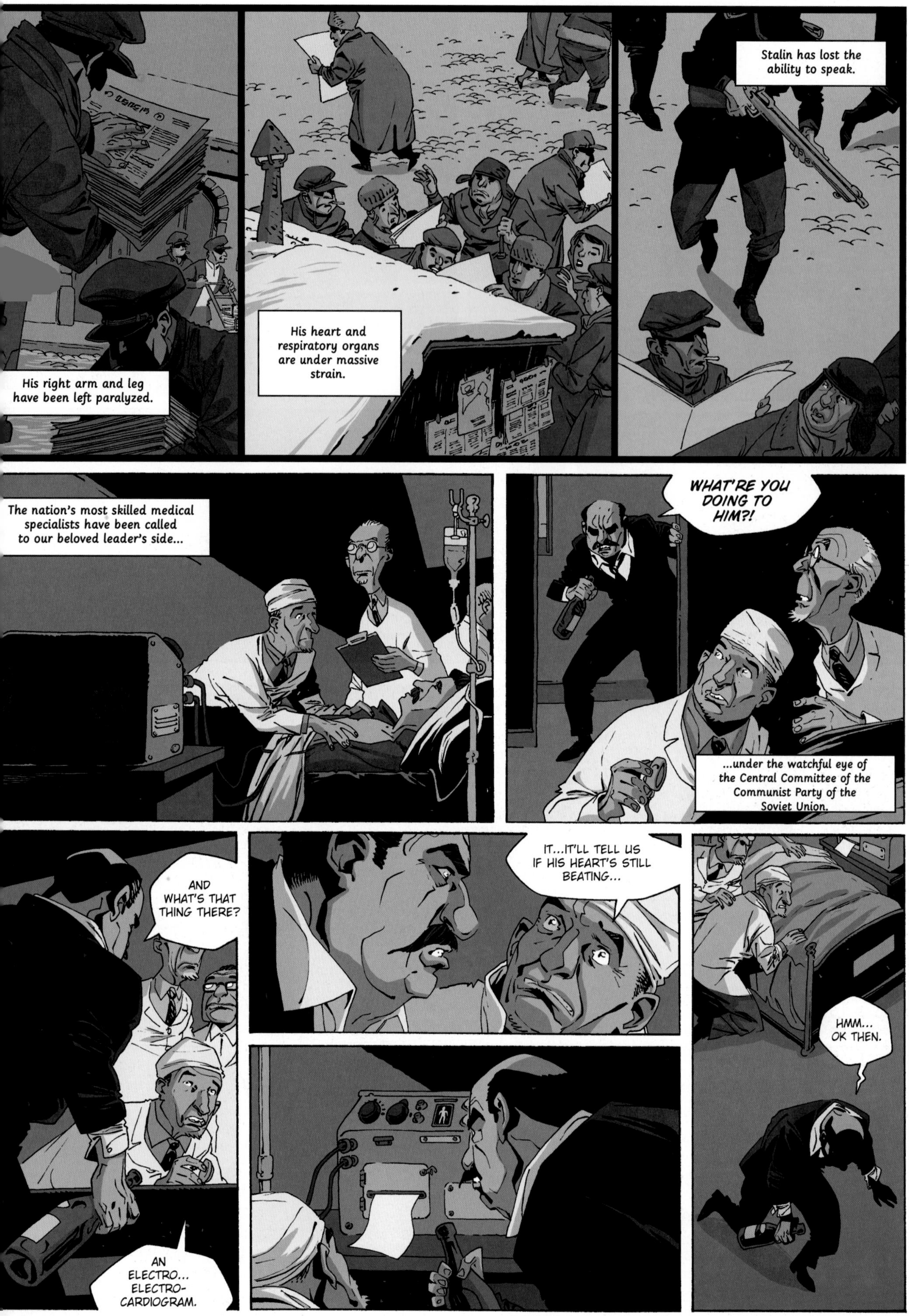

His right arm and leg have been left paralyzed.
His heart and respiratory organs are under massive strain.
Stalin has lost the ability to speak.
The nation's most skilled medical specialists have been called to our beloved leader's side...
WHAT'RE YOU DOING TO HIM?!
...under the watchful eye of the Central Committee of the Communist Party of the Soviet Union.
AND WHAT'S THAT THING THERE?
AN ELECTRO... ELECTRO-CARDIOGRAM.
IT...IT'LL TELL US IF HIS HEART'S STILL BEATING...
HMM... OK THEN.

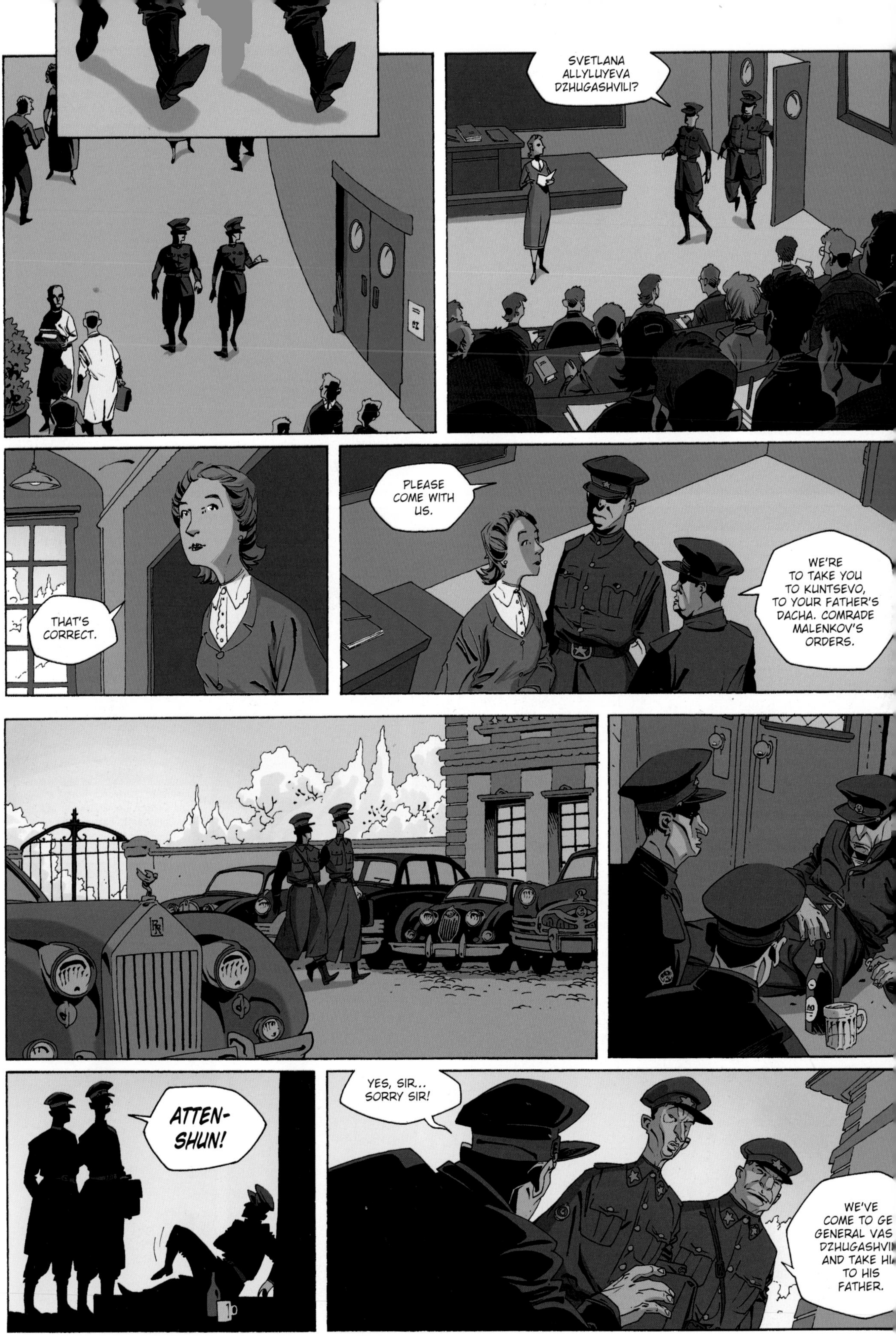
SVETLANA ALLYLUYEVA DZHUGASHVILI?
THAT'S CORRECT.
PLEASE COME WITH US.
WE'RE TO TAKE YOU TO KUNTSEVO, TO YOUR FATHER'S DACHA. COMRADE MALENKOV'S ORDERS.
ATTEN-SHUN!
YES, SIR... SORRY SIR!
WE'VE COME TO GE
GENERAL VAS
DZHUGASHVI
AND TAKE HI
TO HIS
FATHER.

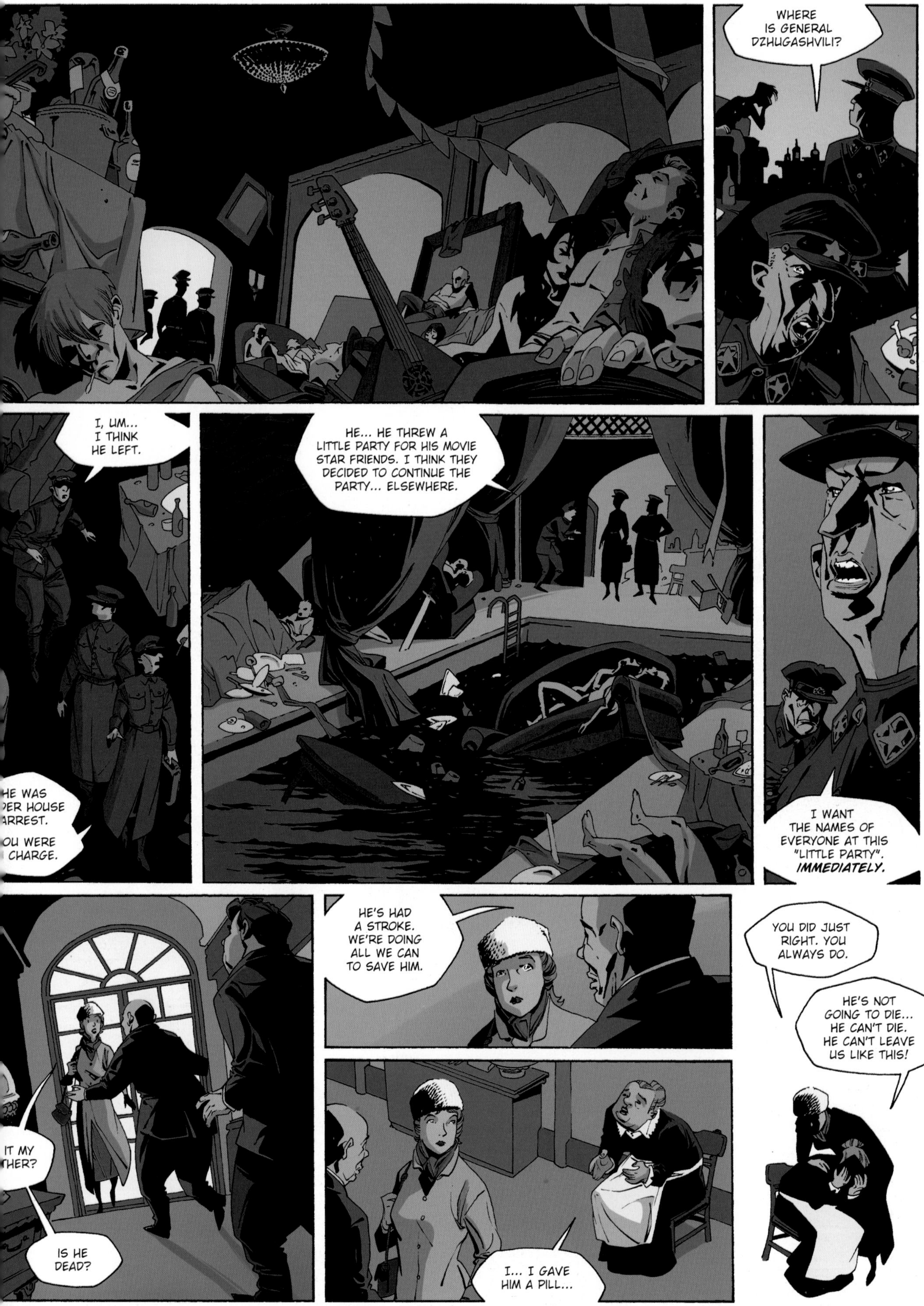
WHERE IS GENERAL DZHUGASHVILI?
I, UM... I THINK HE LEFT.
HE WAS DER HOUSE ARREST.
OU WERE CHARGE.
HE... HE THREW A LITTLE PARTY FOR HIS MOVIE STAR FRIENDS. I THINK THEY DECIDED TO CONTINUE THE PARTY... ELSEWHERE.
I WANT THE NAMES OF EVERYONE AT THIS "LITTLE PARTY". ***IMMEDIATELY.***
IT MY THER?
IS HE DEAD?
HE'S HAD A STROKE. WE'RE DOING ALL WE CAN TO SAVE HIM.
I... I GAVE HIM A PILL...
YOU DID JUST RIGHT. YOU ALWAYS DO.
HE'S NOT GOING TO DIE... HE CAN'T DIE. HE CAN'T LEAVE US LIKE THIS!

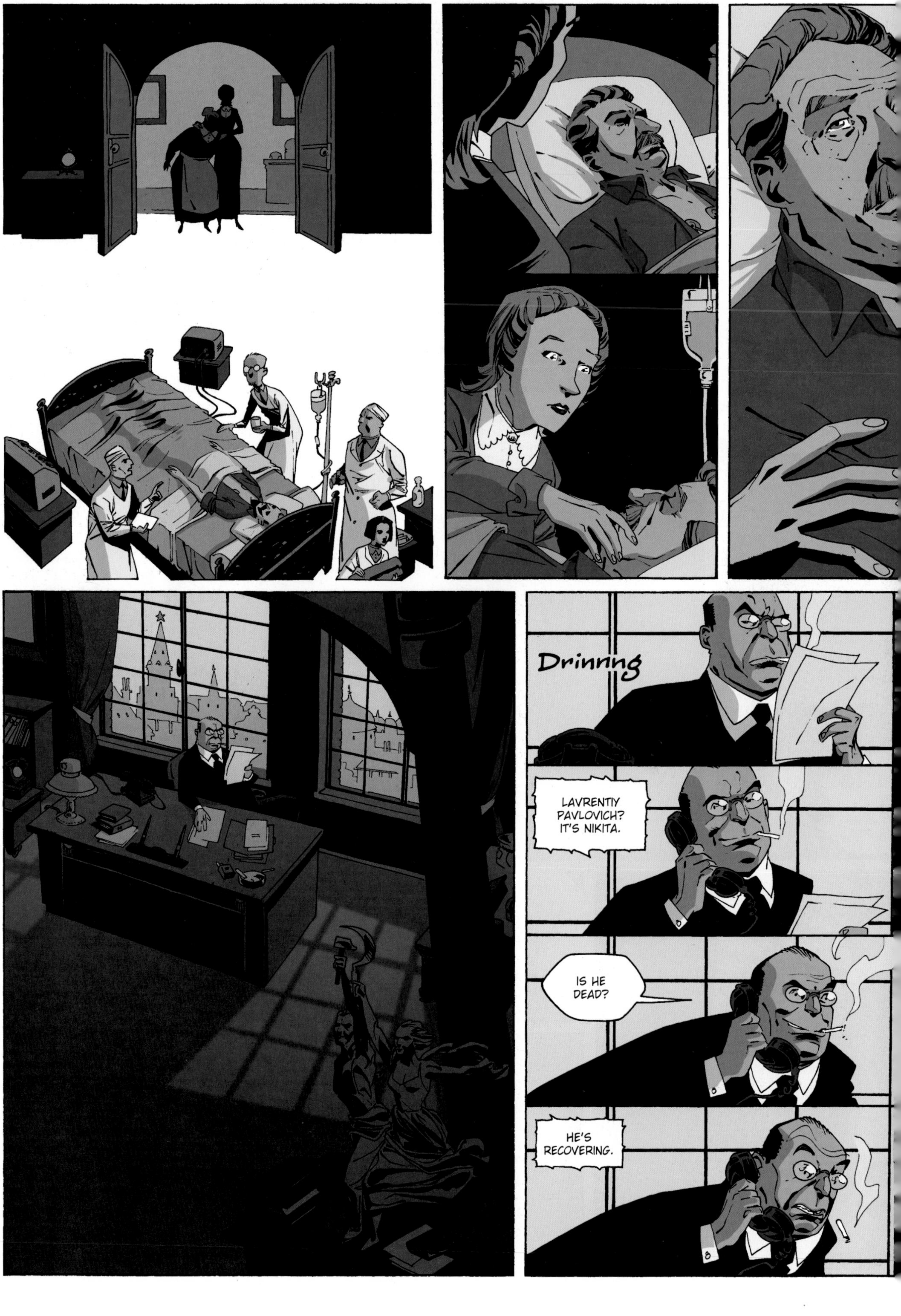

Drinnng
LAVRENTIY PAVLOVICH? IT'S NIKITA.
IS HE DEAD?
HE'S RECOVERING.

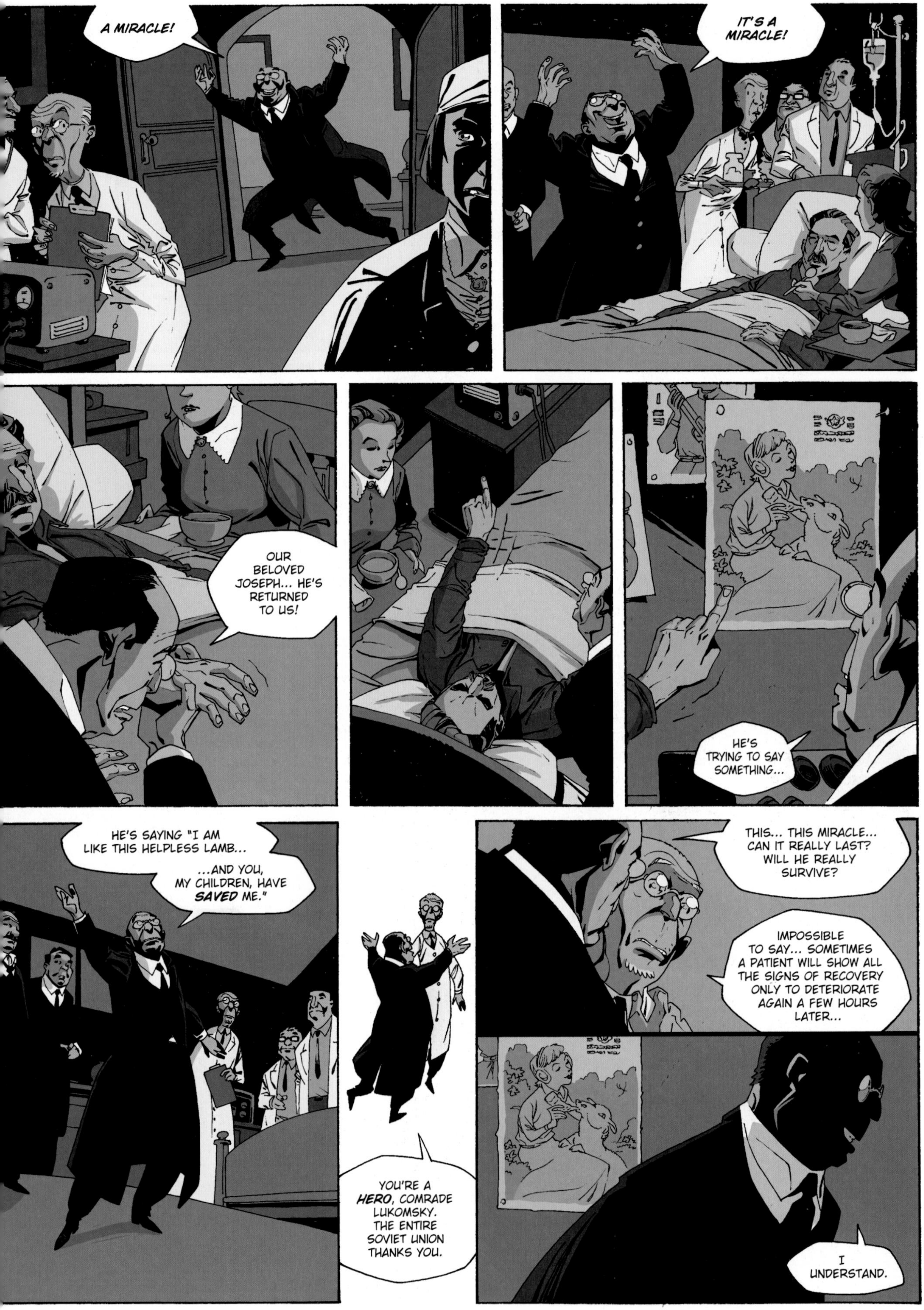
A MIRACLE!
IT'S A MIRACLE!
OUR BELOVED JOSEPH... HE'S RETURNED TO US!
HE'S TRYING TO SAY SOMETHING...
HE'S SAYING "I AM LIKE THIS HELPLESS LAMB...
...AND YOU, MY CHILDREN, HAVE **SAVED** ME."
YOU'RE A **HERO**, COMRADE LUKOMSKY. THE ENTIRE SOVIET UNION THANKS YOU.
THIS... THIS MIRACLE... CAN IT REALLY LAST? WILL HE REALLY SURVIVE?
IMPOSSIBLE TO SAY... SOMETIMES A PATIENT WILL SHOW ALL THE SIGNS OF RECOVERY ONLY TO DETERIORATE AGAIN A FEW HOURS LATER...
I UNDERSTAND.

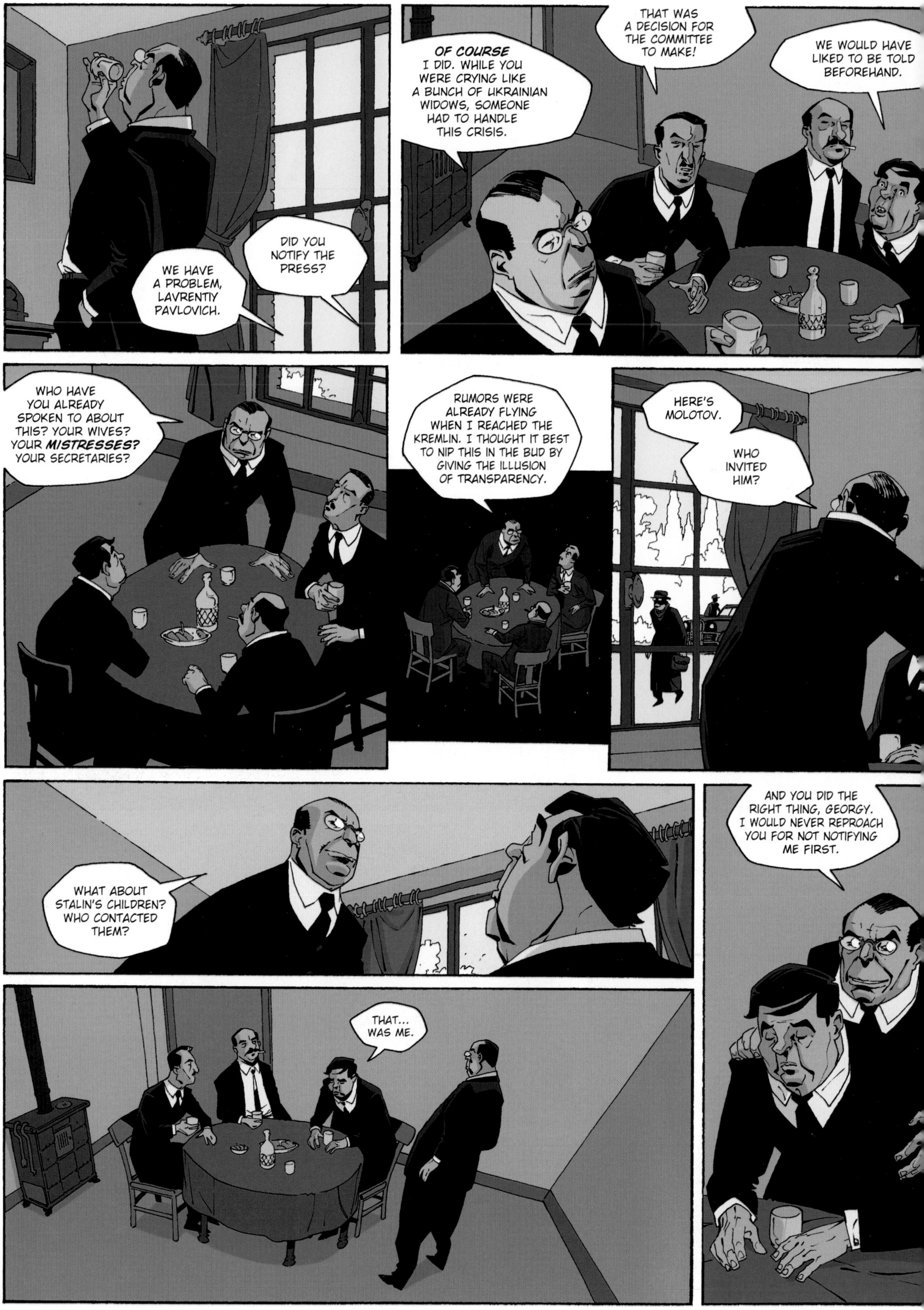

WE HAVE A PROBLEM, LAVRENTIY PAVLOVICH.
DID YOU NOTIFY THE PRESS?
OF COURSE I DID. WHILE YOU WERE CRYING LIKE A BUNCH OF UKRAINIAN WIDOWS, SOMEONE HAD TO HANDLE THIS CRISIS.
THAT WAS A DECISION FOR THE COMMITTEE TO MAKE!
WE WOULD HAVE LIKED TO BE TOLD BEFOREHAND.
WHO HAVE YOU ALREADY SPOKEN TO ABOUT THIS? YOUR WIVES? YOUR ***MISTRESSES?*** YOUR SECRETARIES?
RUMORS WERE ALREADY FLYING WHEN I REACHED THE KREMLIN. I THOUGHT IT BEST TO NIP THIS IN THE BUD BY GIVING THE ILLUSION OF TRANSPARENCY.
HERE'S MOLOTOV.
WHO INVITED HIM?
WHAT ABOUT STALIN'S CHILDREN? WHO CONTACTED THEM?
THAT... WAS ME.
AND YOU DID THE RIGHT THING, GEORGY. I WOULD NEVER REPROACH YOU FOR NOT NOTIFYING ME FIRST.

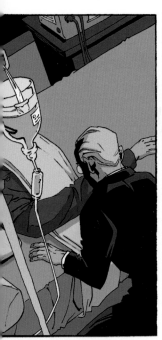

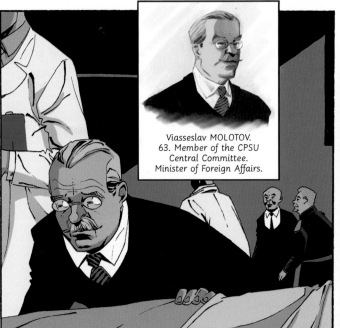

Viasseslav MOLOTOV. 63. Member of the CPSU Central Committee. Minister of Foreign Affairs.

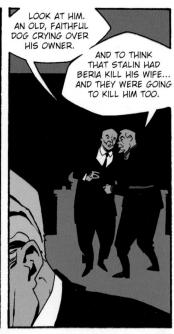

LOOK AT HIM. AN OLD, FAITHFUL DOG CRYING OVER HIS OWNER.

AND TO THINK THAT STALIN HAD BERIA KILL HIS WIFE... AND THEY WERE GOING TO KILL HIM TOO.

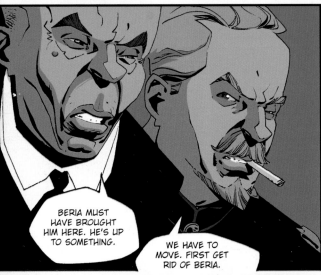

BERIA MUST HAVE BROUGHT HIM HERE. HE'S UP TO SOMETHING.

WE HAVE TO MOVE. FIRST GET RID OF BERIA.

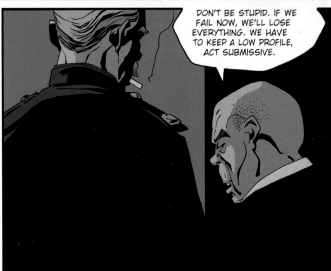

DON'T BE STUPID. IF WE FAIL NOW, WE'LL LOSE EVERYTHING. WE HAVE TO KEEP A LOW PROFILE, ACT SUBMISSIVE.

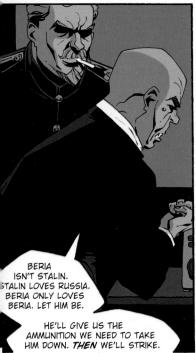

BERIA ISN'T STALIN. STALIN LOVES RUSSIA. BERIA ONLY LOVES BERIA. LET HIM BE.

HE'LL GIVE US THE AMMUNITION WE NEED TO TAKE HIM DOWN. *THEN* WE'LL STRIKE.

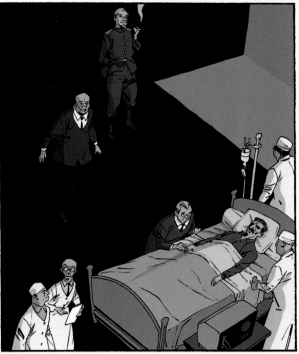

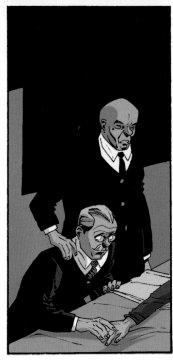

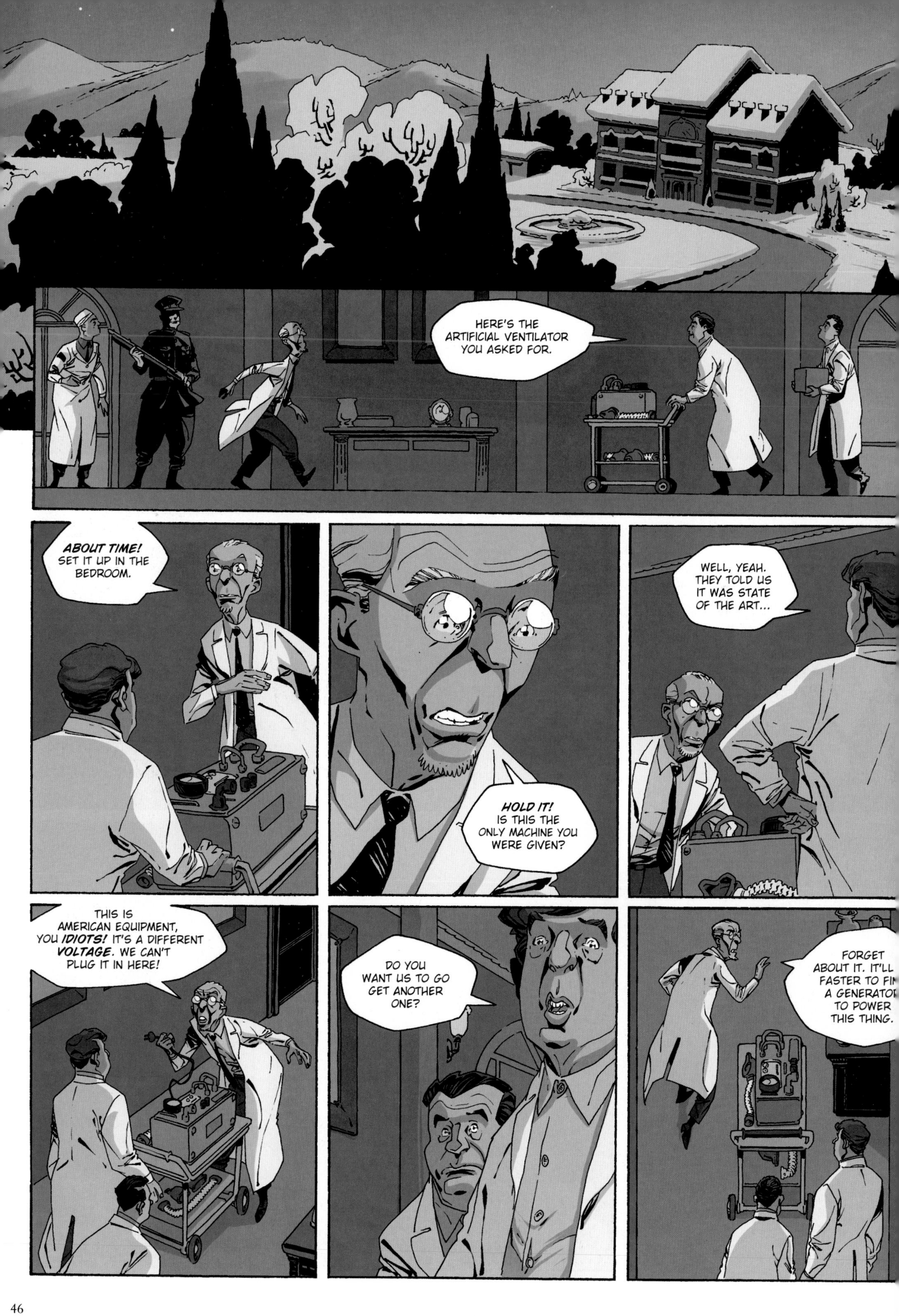
HERE'S THE ARTIFICIAL VENTILATOR YOU ASKED FOR.
ABOUT TIME! SET IT UP IN THE BEDROOM.
HOLD IT! IS THIS THE ONLY MACHINE YOU WERE GIVEN?
WELL, YEAH. THEY TOLD US IT WAS STATE OF THE ART...
THIS IS AMERICAN EQUIPMENT, YOU IDIOTS! IT'S A DIFFERENT VOLTAGE. WE CAN'T PLUG IT IN HERE!
DO YOU WANT US TO GO GET ANOTHER ONE?
FORGET ABOUT IT. IT'LL FASTER TO FI A GENERATO TO POWER THIS THING.

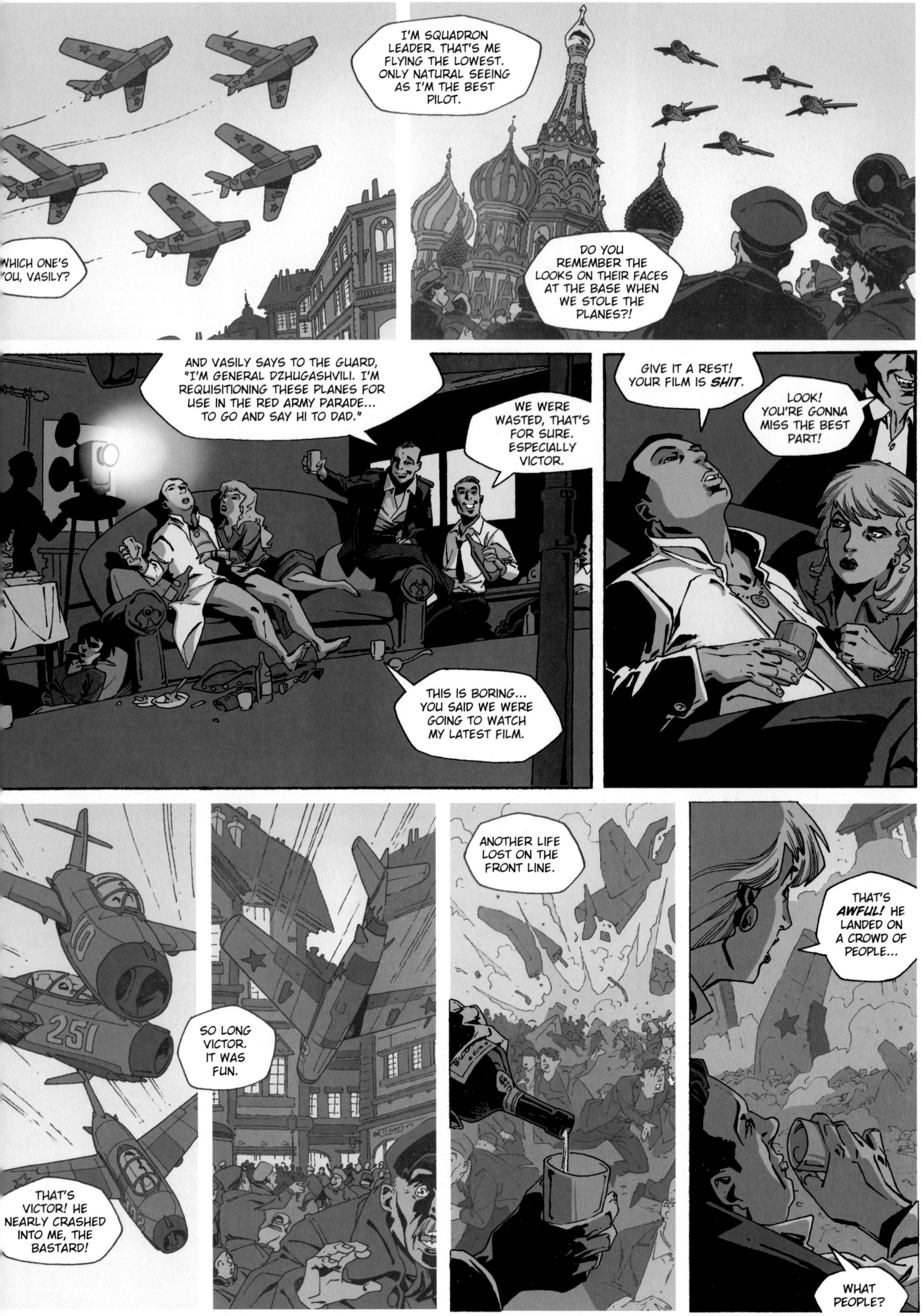
WHICH ONE'S YOU, VASILY?
I'M SQUADRON LEADER. THAT'S ME FLYING THE LOWEST. ONLY NATURAL SEEING AS I'M THE BEST PILOT.
DO YOU REMEMBER THE LOOKS ON THEIR FACES AT THE BASE WHEN WE STOLE THE PLANES?!
AND VASILY SAYS TO THE GUARD, "I'M GENERAL DZHUGASHVILI. I'M REQUISITIONING THESE PLANES FOR USE IN THE RED ARMY PARADE... TO GO AND SAY HI TO DAD."
WE WERE WASTED, THAT'S FOR SURE. ESPECIALLY VICTOR.
THIS IS BORING... YOU SAID WE WERE GOING TO WATCH MY LATEST FILM.
GIVE IT A REST! YOUR FILM IS ***SHIT***.
LOOK! YOU'RE GONNA MISS THE BEST PART!
THAT'S VICTOR! HE NEARLY CRASHED INTO ME, THE BASTARD!
SO LONG VICTOR. IT WAS FUN.
ANOTHER LIFE LOST ON THE FRONT LINE.
THAT'S ***AWFUL!*** HE LANDED ON A CROWD OF PEOPLE...
WHAT PEOPLE?

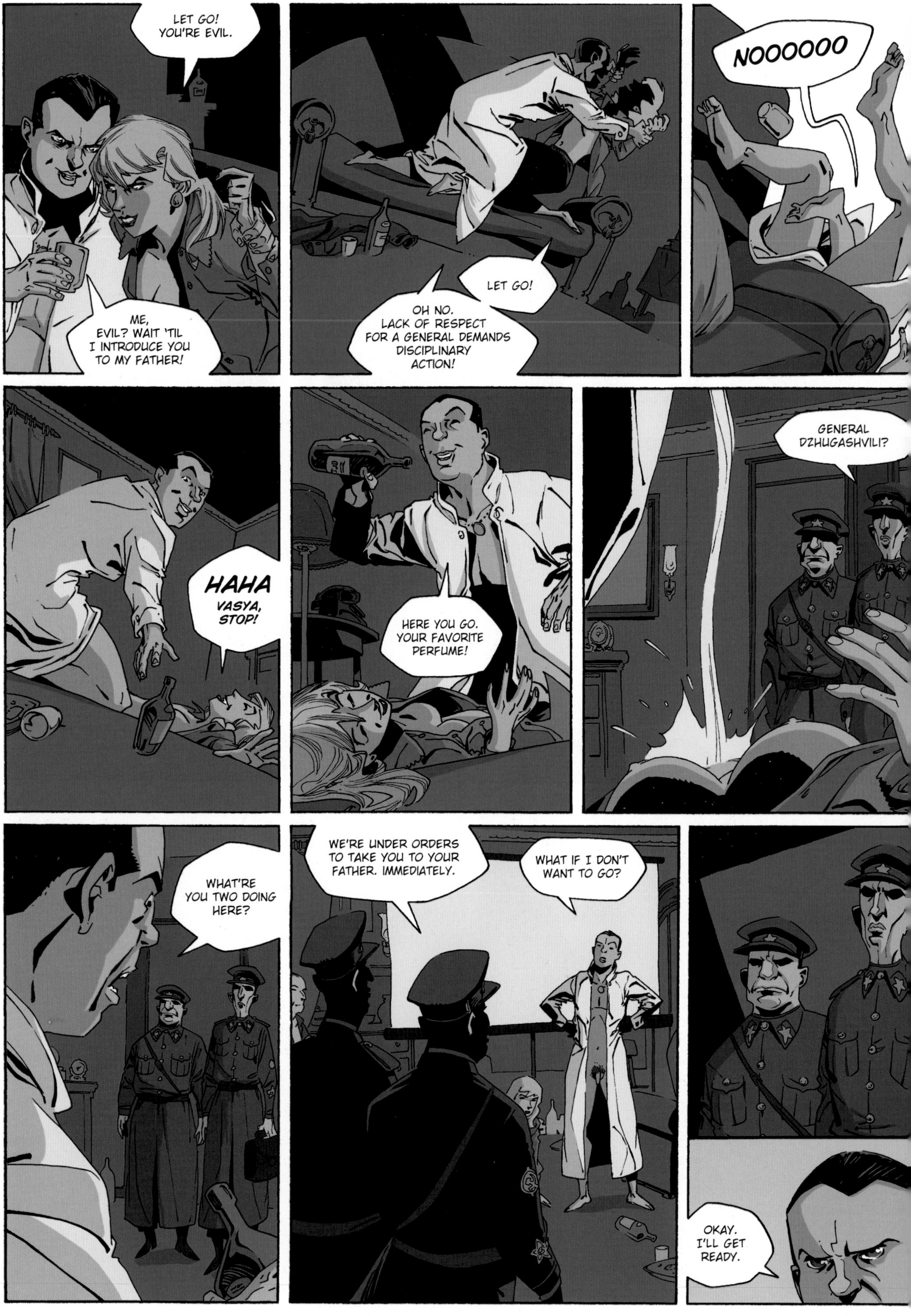
LET GO! YOU'RE EVIL.
ME, EVIL? WAIT 'TIL I INTRODUCE YOU TO MY FATHER!
LET GO!
OH NO. LACK OF RESPECT FOR A GENERAL DEMANDS DISCIPLINARY ACTION!
NOOOOOO
HAHA
VASYA, STOP!
HERE YOU GO. YOUR FAVORITE PERFUME!
GENERAL DZHUGASHVILI?
WHAT'RE YOU TWO DOING HERE?
WE'RE UNDER ORDERS TO TAKE YOU TO YOUR FATHER. IMMEDIATELY.
WHAT IF I DON'T WANT TO GO?
OKAY. I'LL GET READY.

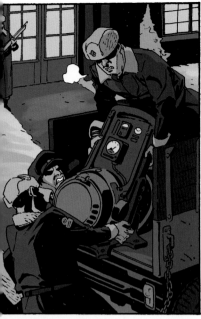

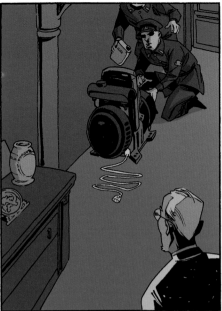

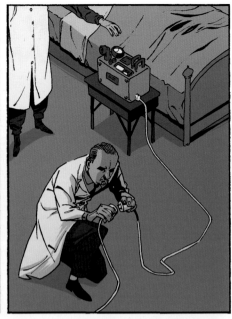

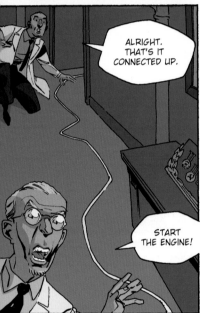

ALRIGHT. THAT'S IT CONNECTED UP.

START THE ENGINE!

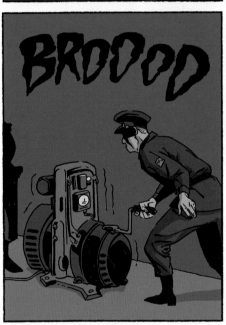

BRDOOD

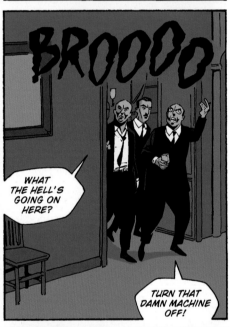

BROOOO

WHAT THE HELL'S GOING ON HERE?

TURN THAT DAMN MACHINE OFF!

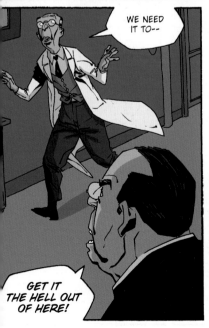

WE NEED IT TO--

GET IT THE HELL OUT OF HERE!

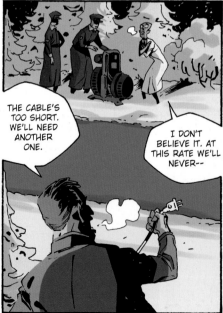

THE CABLE'S TOO SHORT. WE'LL NEED ANOTHER ONE.

I DON'T BELIEVE IT. AT THIS RATE WE'LL NEVER--

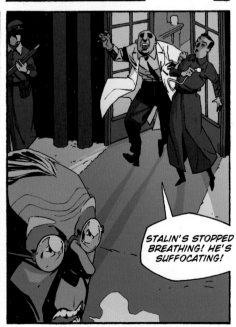

STALIN'S STOPPED BREATHING! HE'S SUFFOCATING!

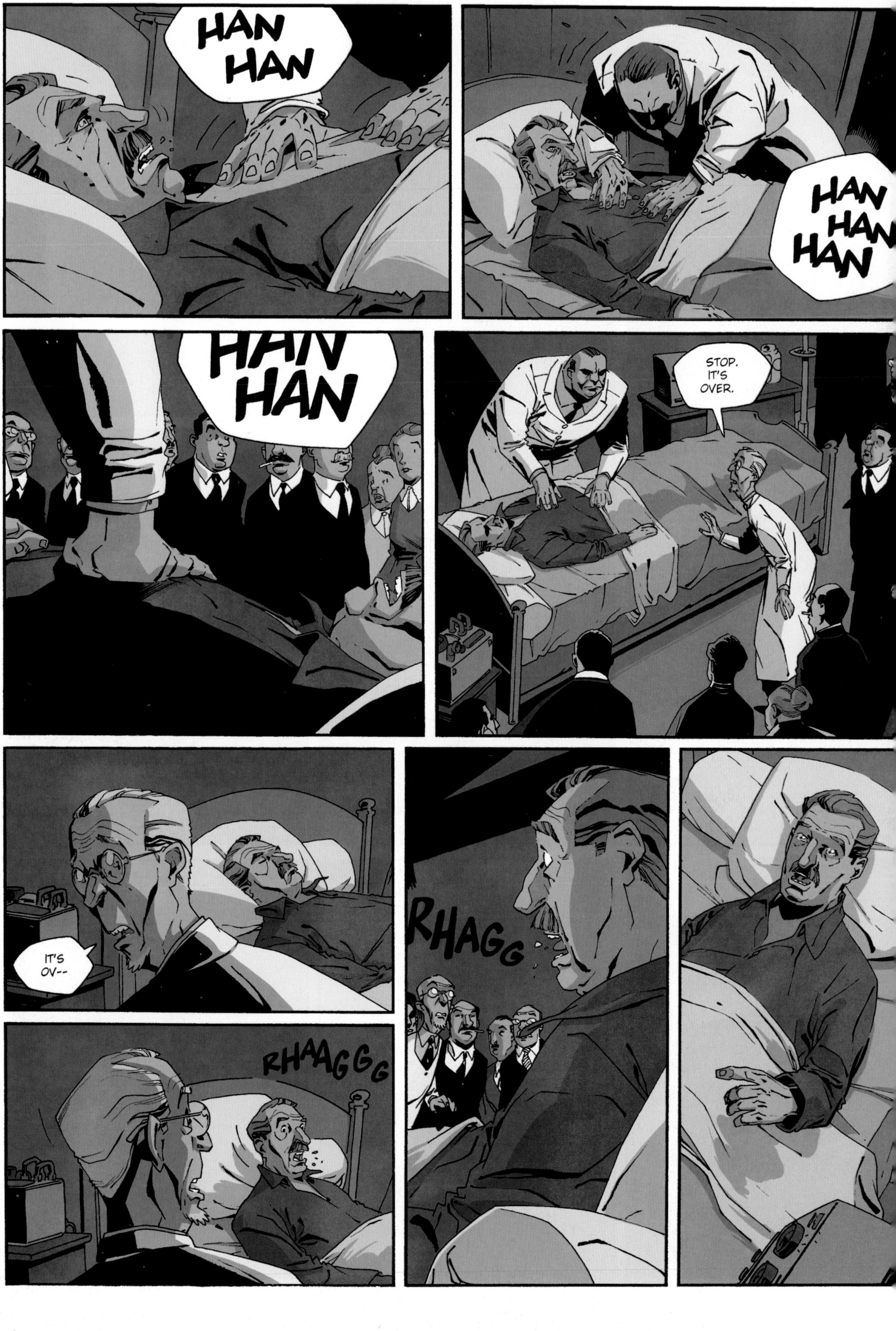
HAN HAN
HAN HAN HAN
HAN HAN
STOP. IT'S OVER.
IT'S OV--
RHAAGGG
RHAGG

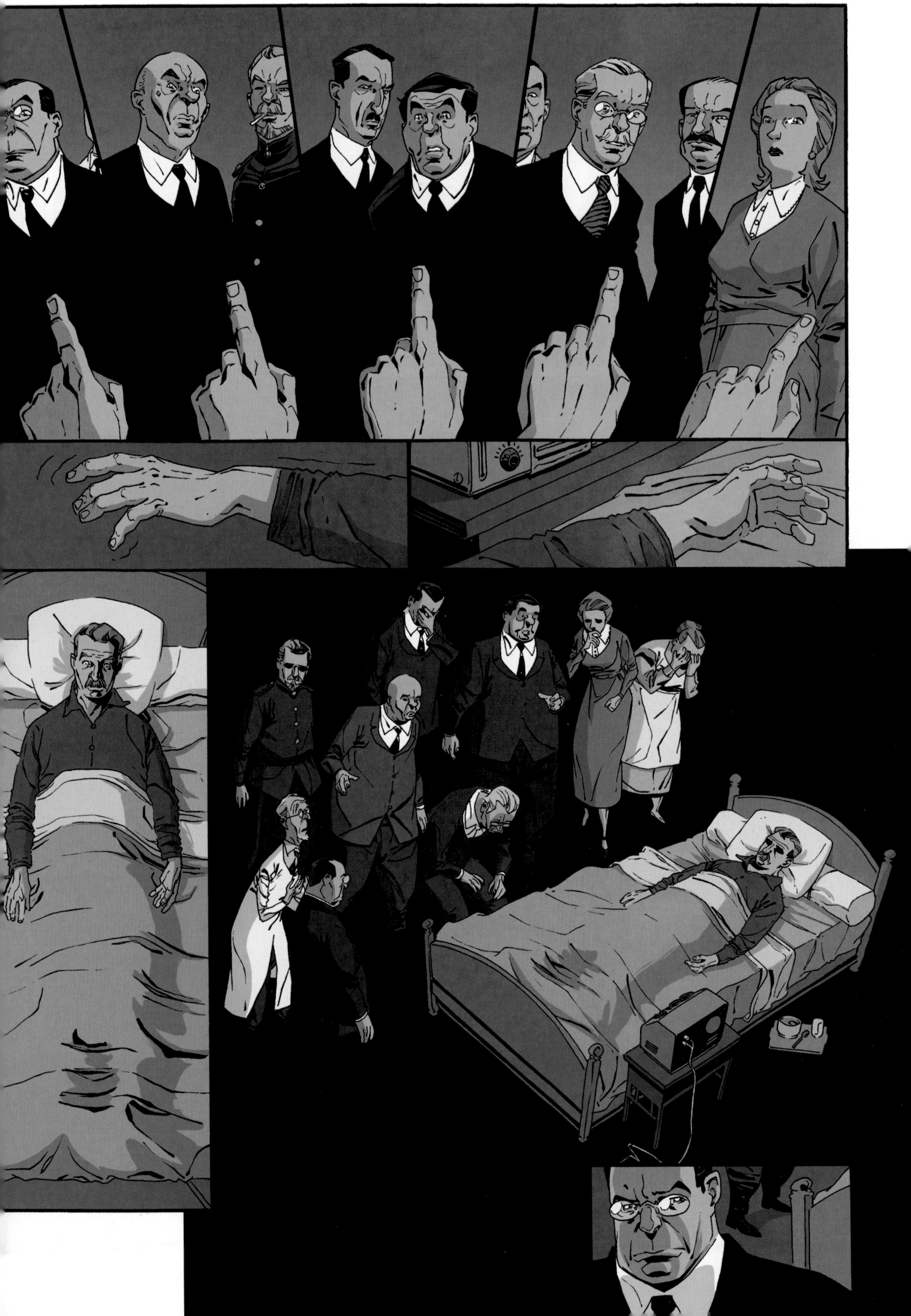

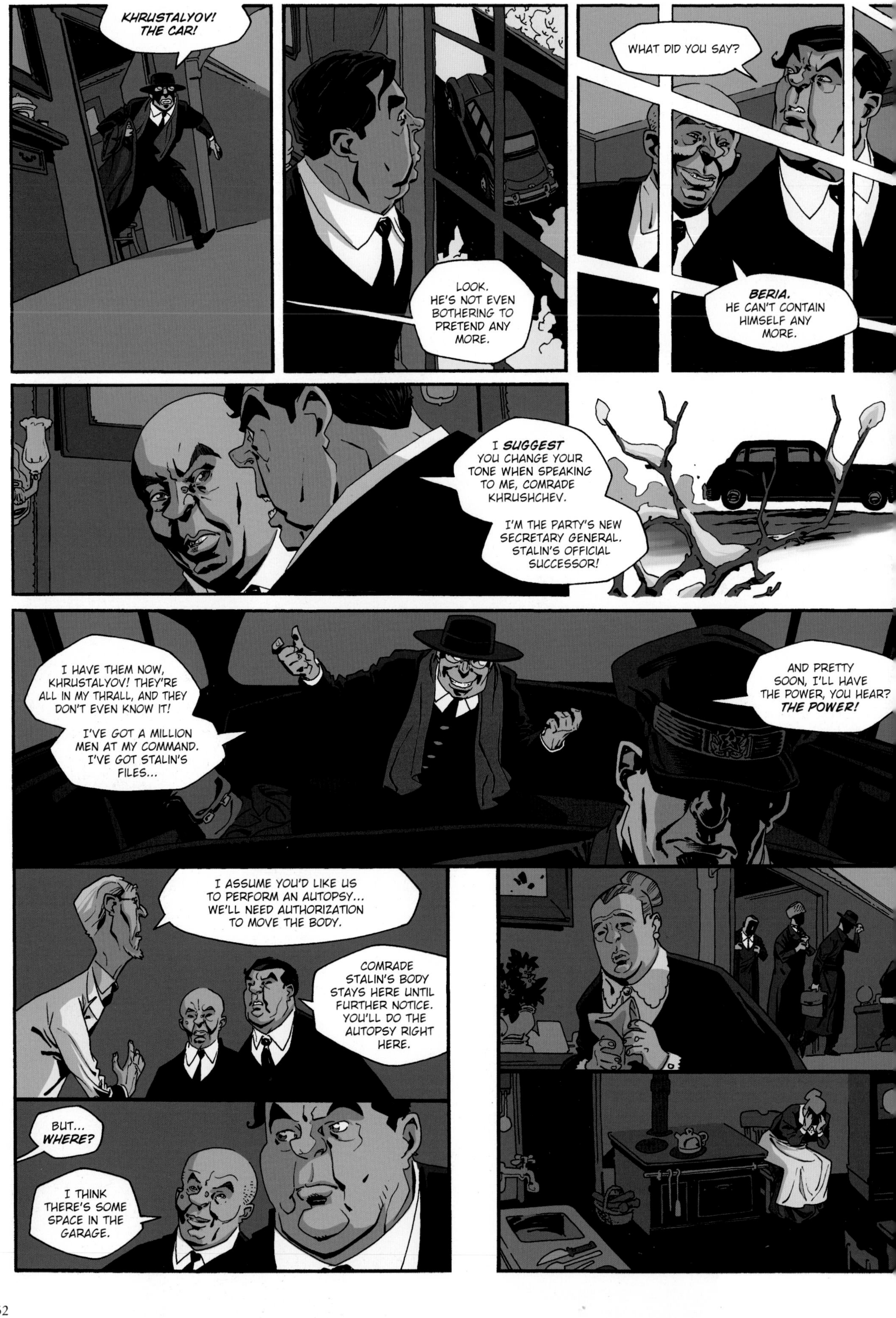
KHRUSTALYOV! THE CAR!
LOOK. HE'S NOT EVEN BOTHERING TO PRETEND ANY MORE.
WHAT DID YOU SAY?
BERIA. HE CAN'T CONTAIN HIMSELF ANY MORE.
I SUGGEST YOU CHANGE YOUR TONE WHEN SPEAKING TO ME, COMRADE KHRUSHCHEV.
I'M THE PARTY'S NEW SECRETARY GENERAL. STALIN'S OFFICIAL SUCCESSOR!
I HAVE THEM NOW, KHRUSTALYOV! THEY'RE ALL IN MY THRALL, AND THEY DON'T EVEN KNOW IT!
I'VE GOT A MILLION MEN AT MY COMMAND. I'VE GOT STALIN'S FILES...
AND PRETTY SOON, I'LL HAVE THE POWER, YOU HEAR? THE POWER!
I ASSUME YOU'D LIKE US TO PERFORM AN AUTOPSY... WE'LL NEED AUTHORIZATION TO MOVE THE BODY.
COMRADE STALIN'S BODY STAYS HERE UNTIL FURTHER NOTICE. YOU'LL DO THE AUTOPSY RIGHT HERE.
BUT... WHERE?
I THINK THERE'S SOME SPACE IN THE GARAGE.

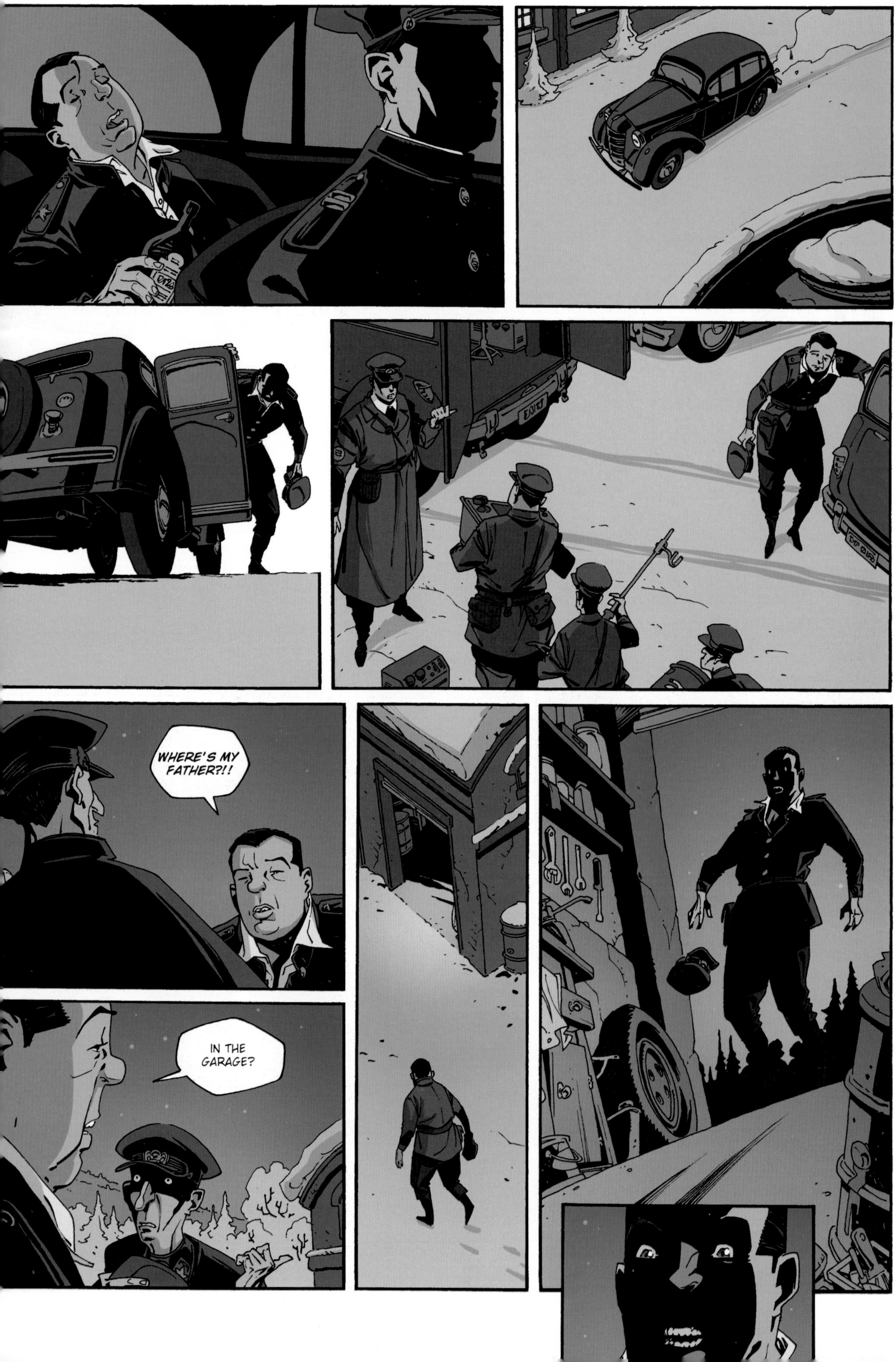
WHERE'S MY FATHER?!!
IN THE GARAGE?

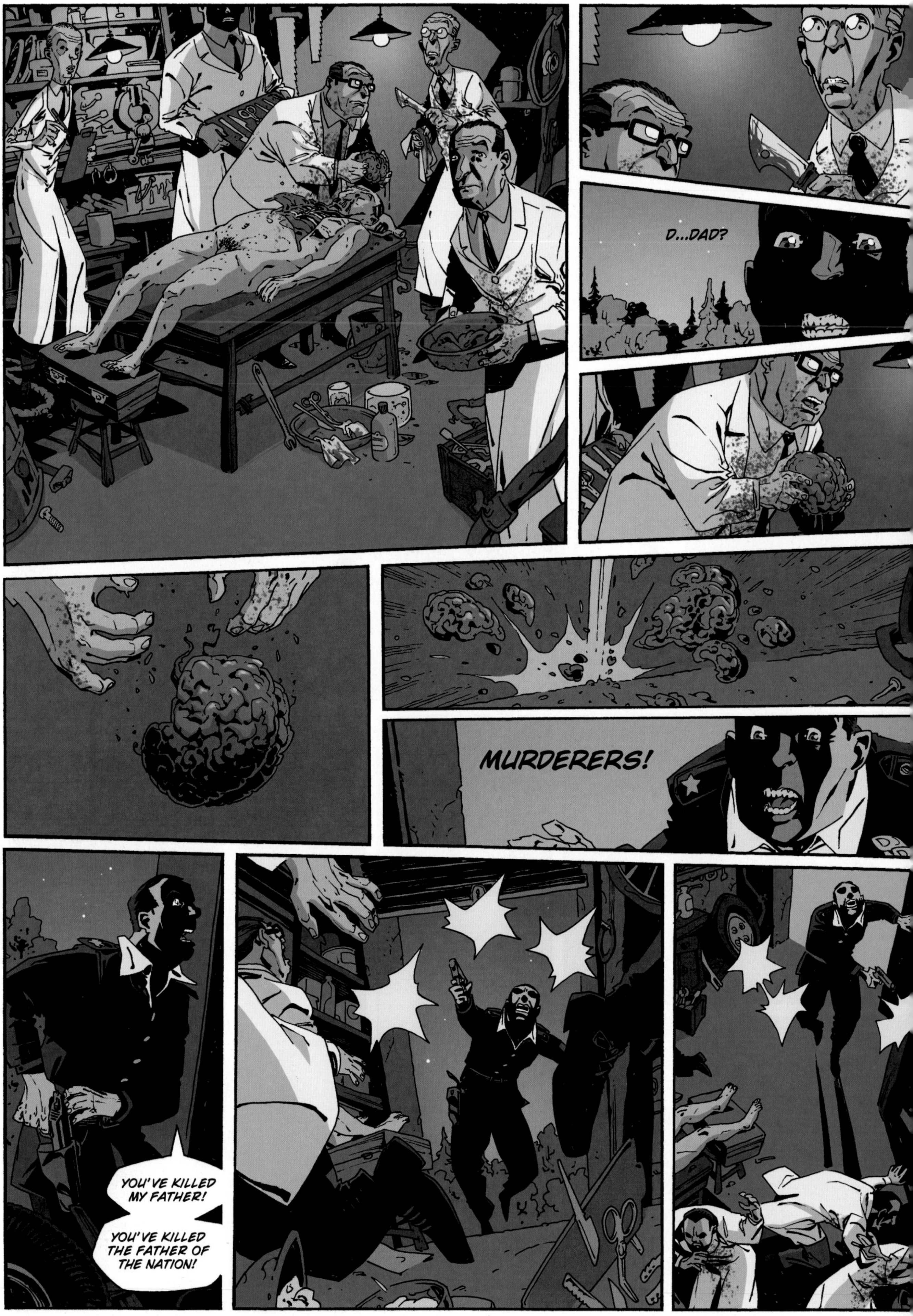
D...DAD?
MURDERERS!
YOU'VE KILLED MY FATHER!
YOU'VE KILLED THE FATHER OF THE NATION!

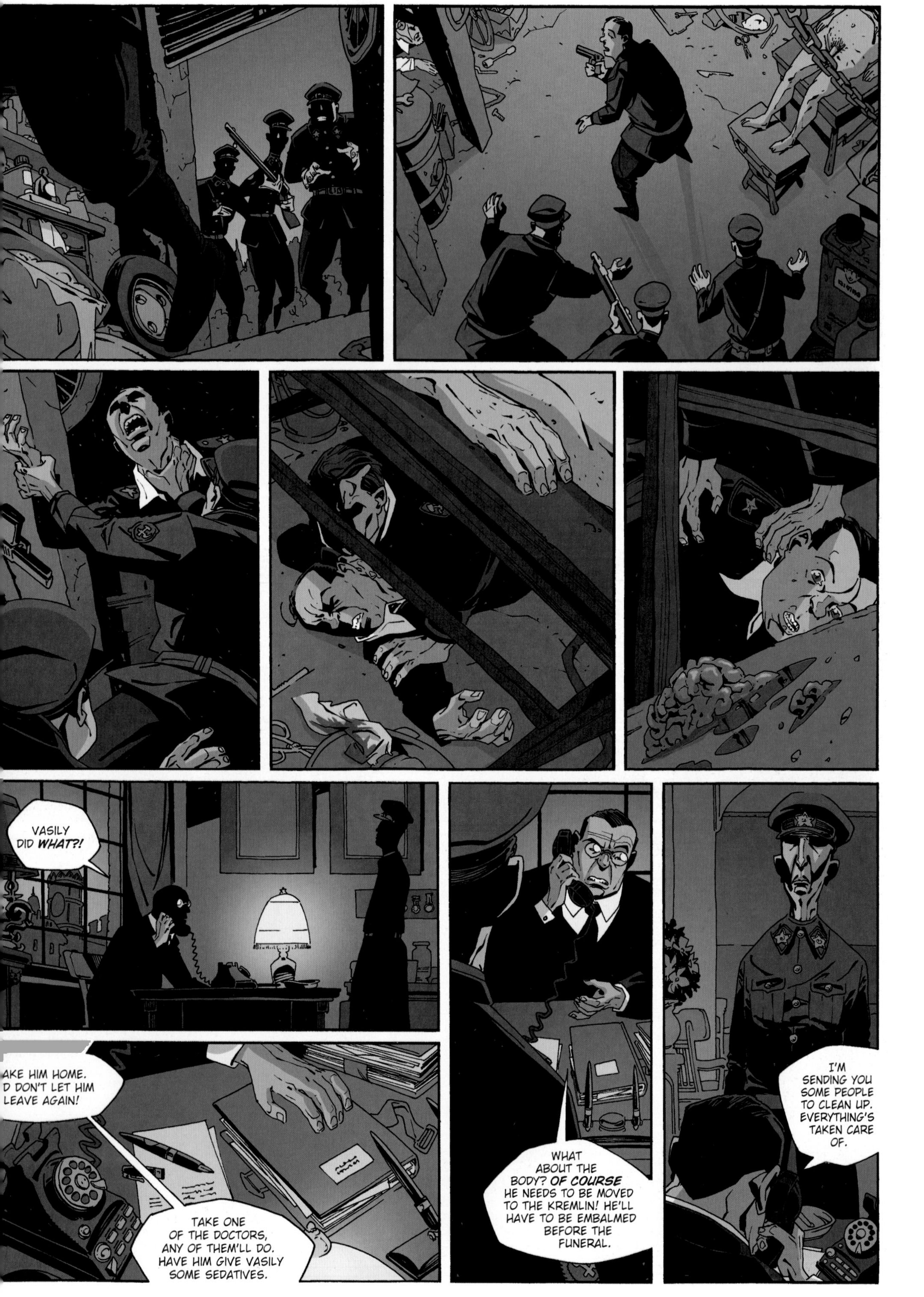
VASILY DID WHAT?!
AKE HIM HOME. D DON'T LET HIM LEAVE AGAIN!
TAKE ONE OF THE DOCTORS, ANY OF THEM'LL DO. HAVE HIM GIVE VASILY SOME SEDATIVES.
WHAT ABOUT THE BODY? OF COURSE HE NEEDS TO BE MOVED TO THE KREMLIN! HE'LL HAVE TO BE EMBALMED BEFORE THE FUNERAL.
I'M SENDING YOU SOME PEOPLE TO CLEAN UP. EVERYTHING'S TAKEN CARE OF.

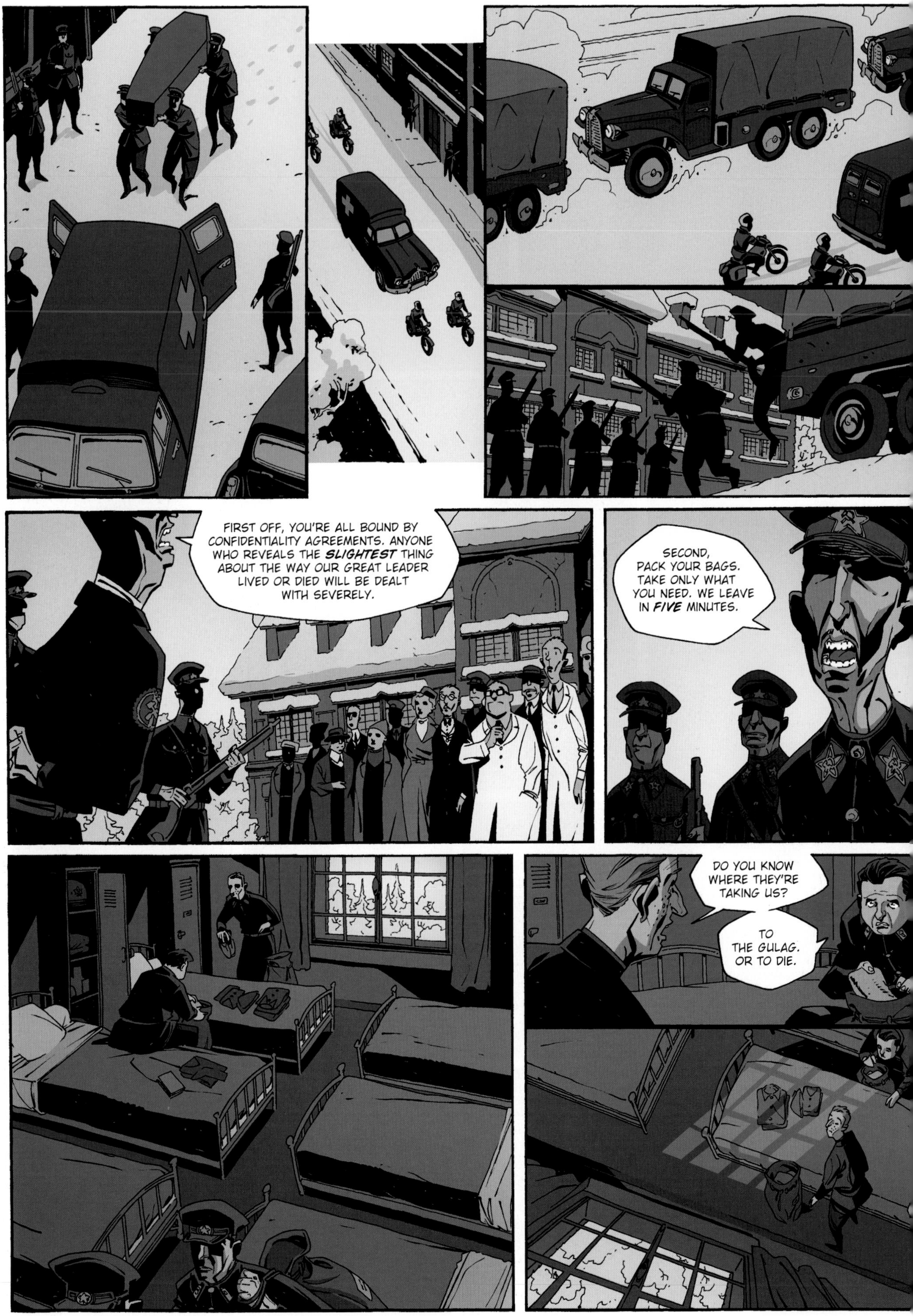
FIRST OFF, YOU'RE ALL BOUND BY CONFIDENTIALITY AGREEMENTS. ANYONE WHO REVEALS THE SLIGHTEST THING ABOUT THE WAY OUR GREAT LEADER LIVED OR DIED WILL BE DEALT WITH SEVERELY.
SECOND, PACK YOUR BAGS. TAKE ONLY WHAT YOU NEED. WE LEAVE IN FIVE MINUTES.
DO YOU KNOW WHERE THEY'RE TAKING US?
TO THE GULAG. OR TO DIE.

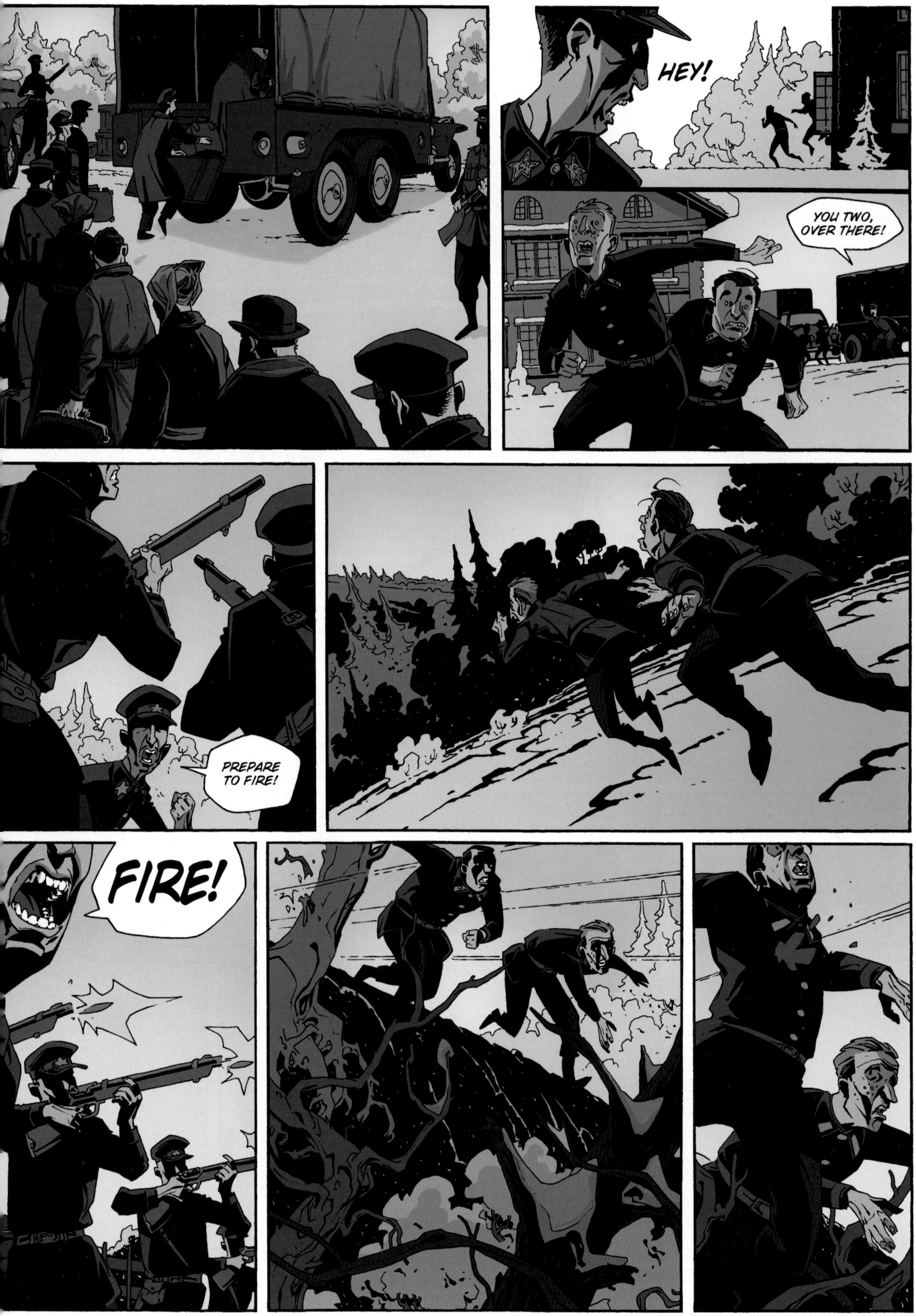
HEY!
YOU TWO, OVER THERE!
PREPARE TO FIRE!
FIRE!

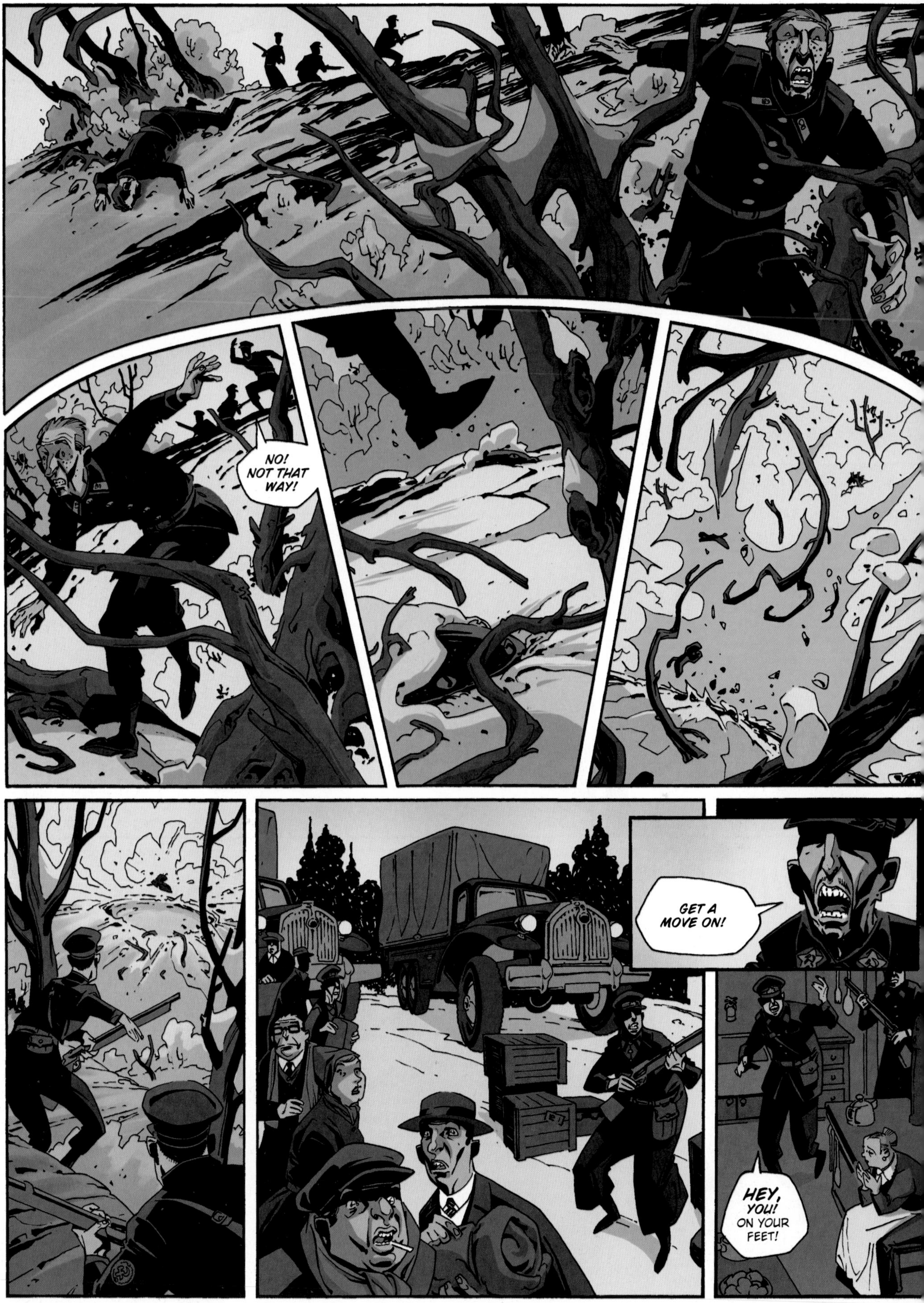
NO! NOT THAT WAY!
GET A MOVE ON!
HEY, YOU! ON YOUR FEET!

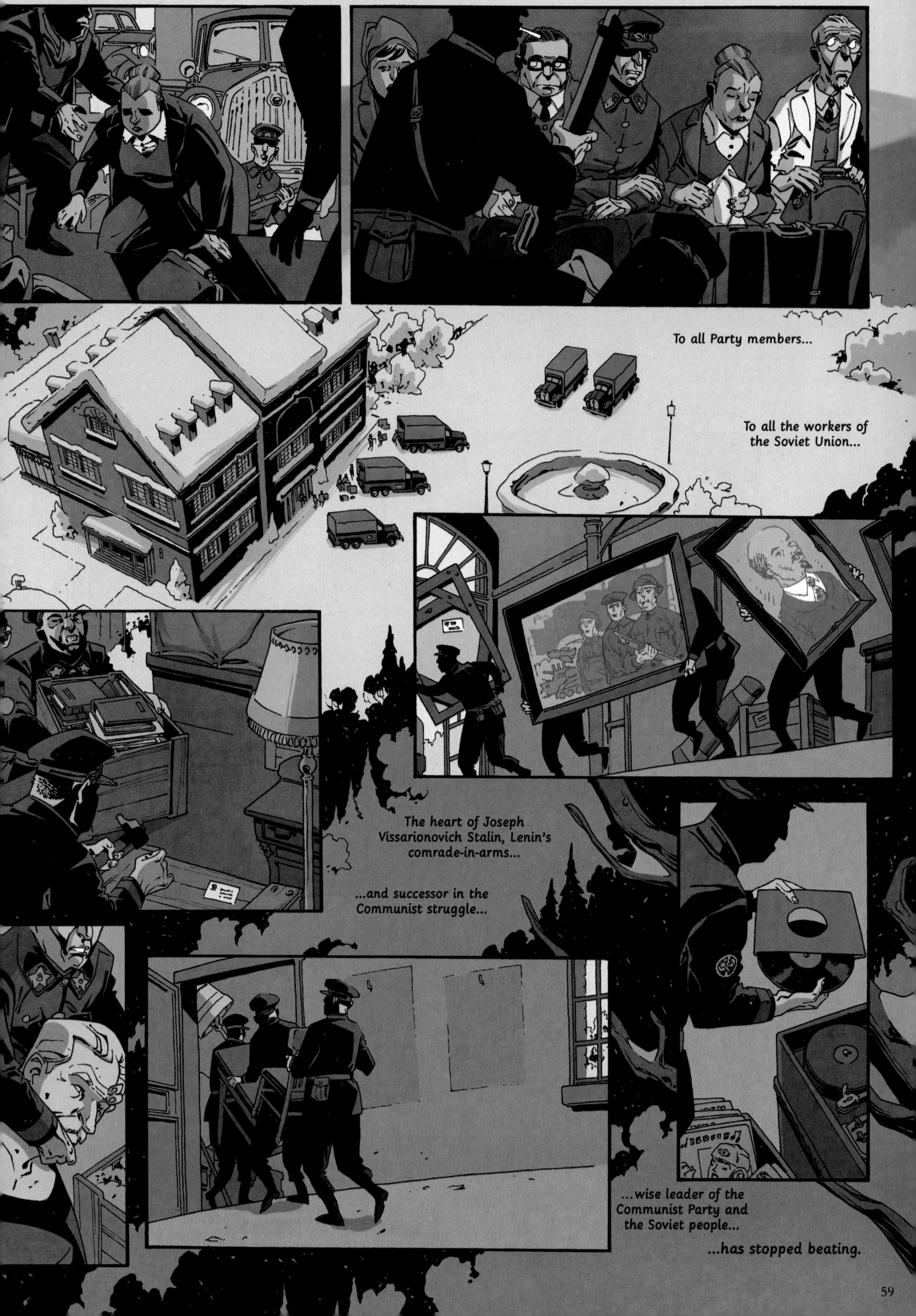
To all Party members...
To all the workers of the Soviet Union...
The heart of Joseph Vissarionovich Stalin, Lenin's comrade-in-arms...
...and successor in the Communist struggle...
...wise leader of the Communist Party and the Soviet people...
...has stopped beating.

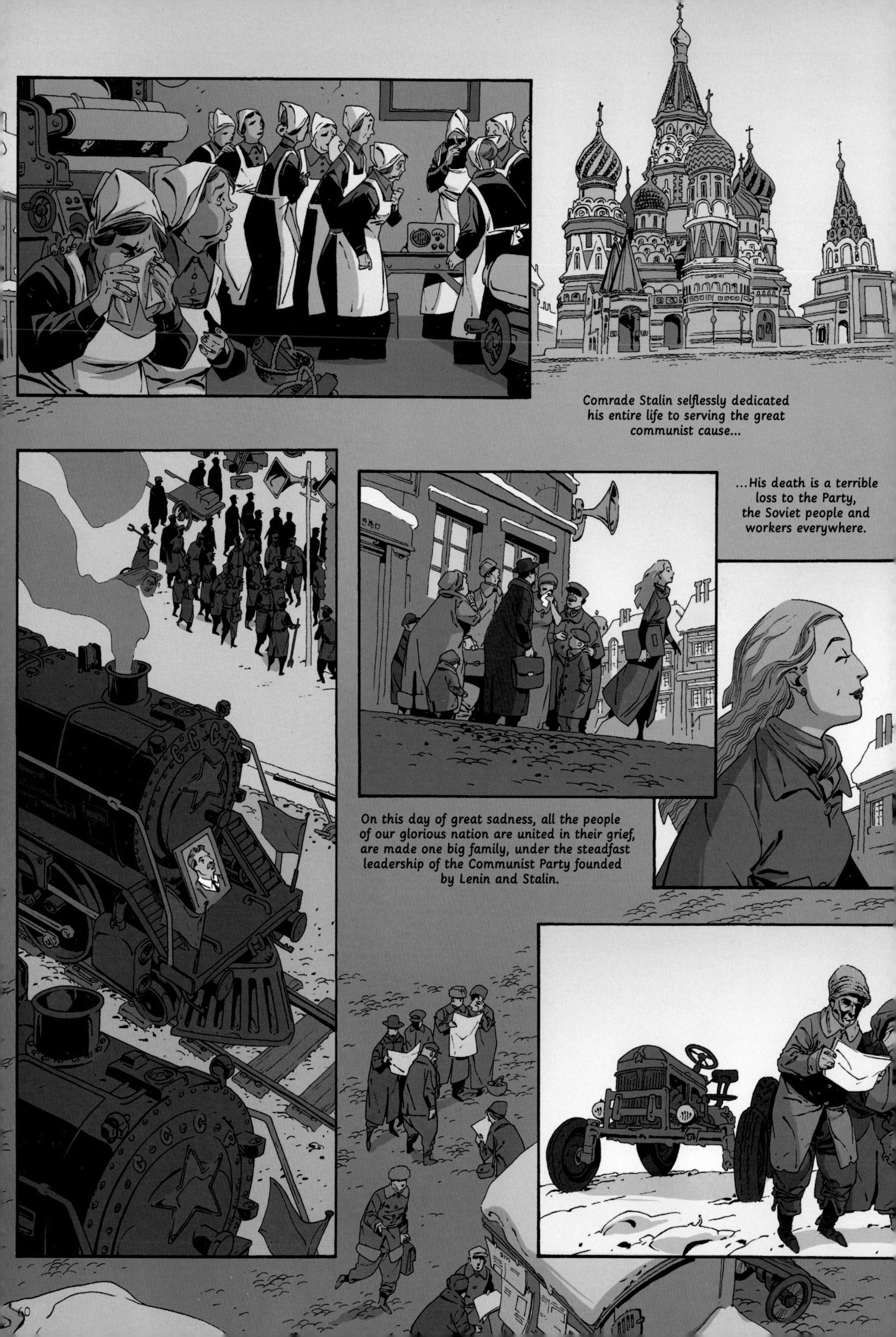
Comrade Stalin selflessly dedicated his entire life to serving the great communist cause...
...His death is a terrible loss to the Party, the Soviet people and workers everywhere.
On this day of great sadness, all the people of our glorious nation are united in their grief, are made one big family, under the steadfast leadership of the Communist Party founded by Lenin and Stalin.

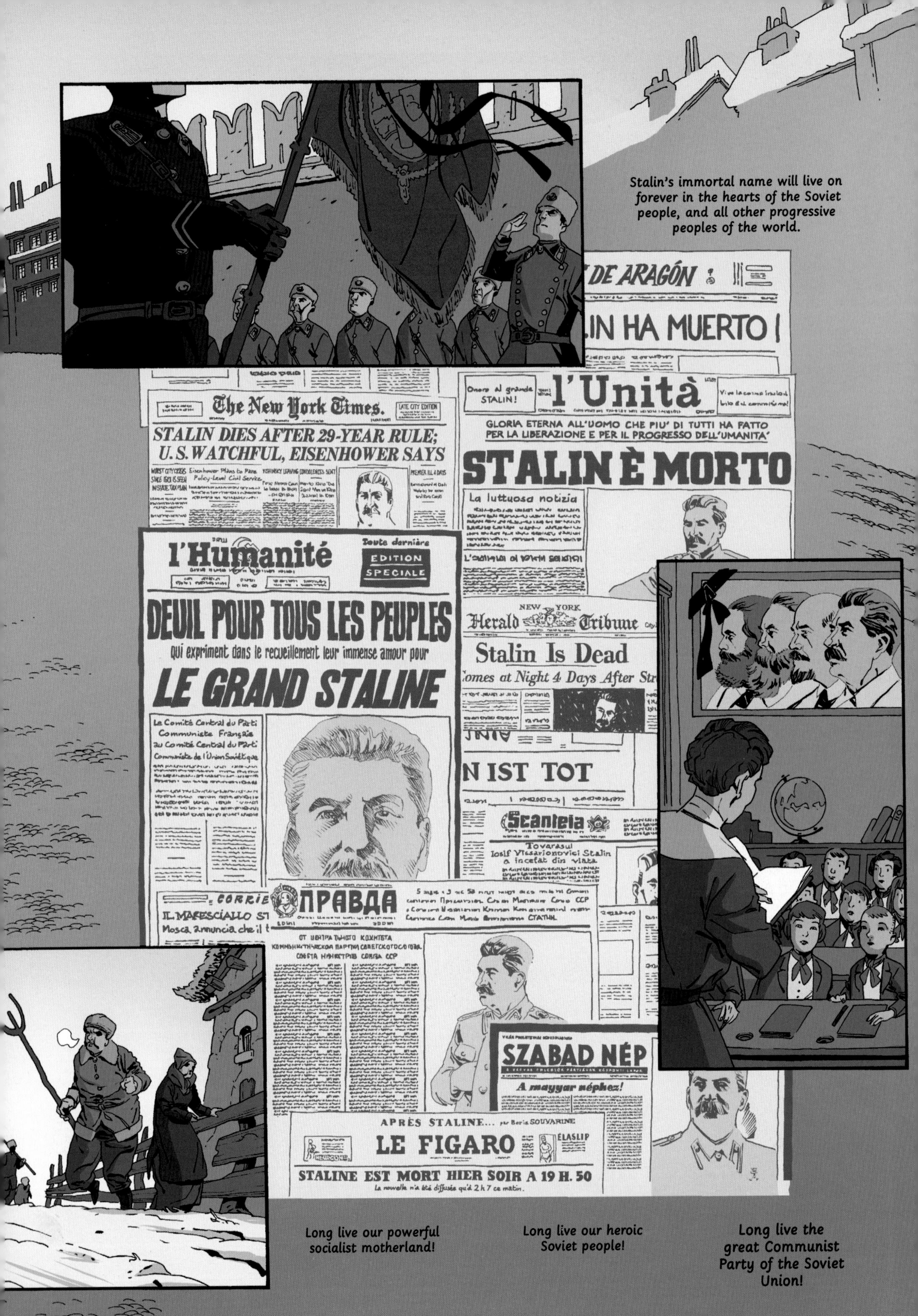
Stalin's immortal name will live on forever in the hearts of the Soviet people, and all other progressive peoples of the world.
DE ARAGÓN
LIN HA MUERTO !
The New York Times.
STALIN DIES AFTER 29-YEAR RULE; U.S. WATCHFUL, EISENHOWER SAYS
l'Unità
Onore al grande STALIN!
GLORIA ETERNA ALL'UOMO CHE PIU' DI TUTTI HA FATTO PER LA LIBERAZIONE E PER IL PROGRESSO DELL'UMANITA'
STALIN È MORTO
La luttuosa notizia
l'Humanité
Toute dernière
EDITION SPECIALE
DEUIL POUR TOUS LES PEUPLES
qui expriment dans le recueillement leur immense amour pour
LE GRAND STALINE
Le Comité Central du Parti Communiste Français au Comité Central du Parti Communiste de l'Union Soviétique
New York Herald Tribune
Stalin Is Dead
Comes at Night 4 Days After Str
N IST TOT
Scanteia
Tovarasul Iosif Vissarionovici Stalin a incetat din viata
CORRIE
IL MARESCIALLO ST
Mosca annuncia che il
ПРАВДА
SZABAD NÉP
A magyar néphez!
APRÈS STALINE...
LE FIGARO
STALINE EST MORT HIER SOIR A 19 H. 50
La nouvelle n'a été diffusée qu'à 2 h 7 ce matin.
Long live our powerful socialist motherland!
Long live our heroic Soviet people!
Long live the great Communist Party of the Soviet Union!

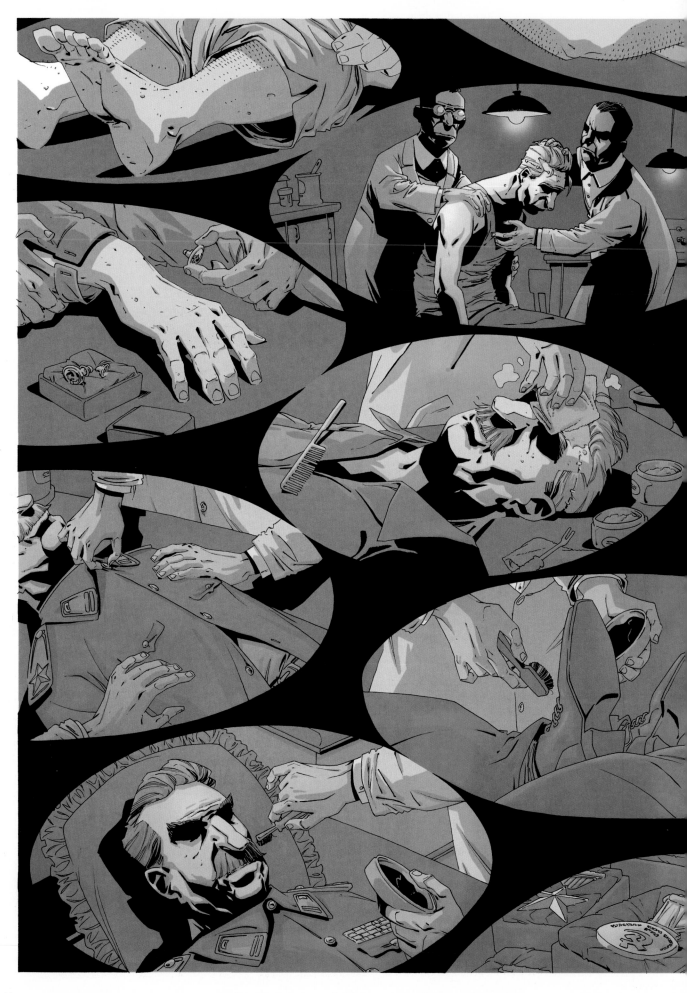

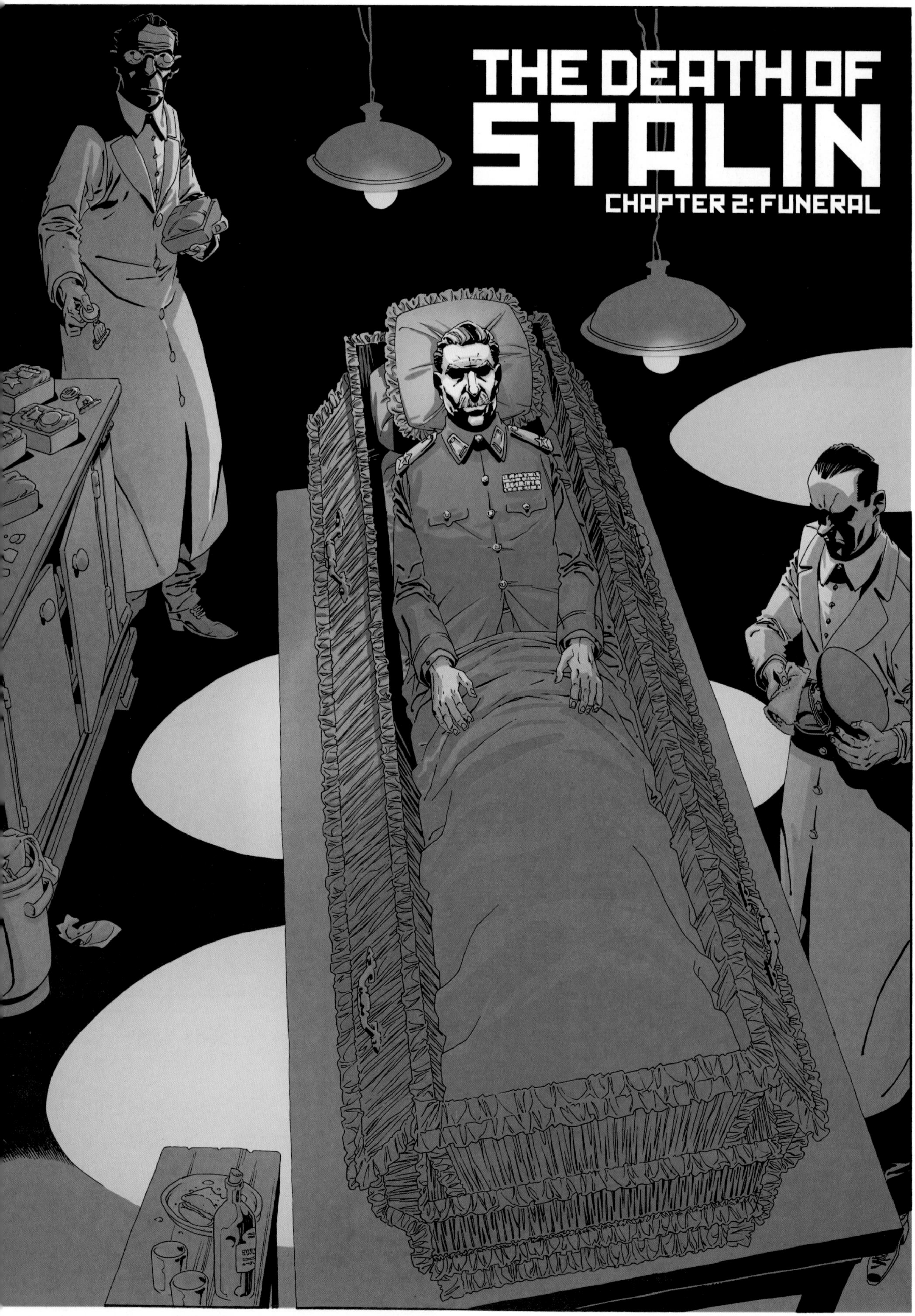
THE DEATH OF
STALIN
CHAPTER 2: FUNERAL

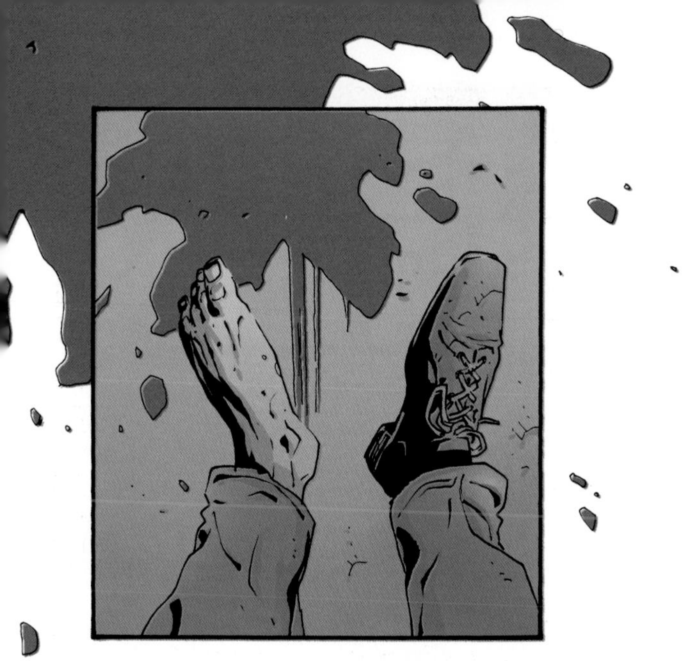

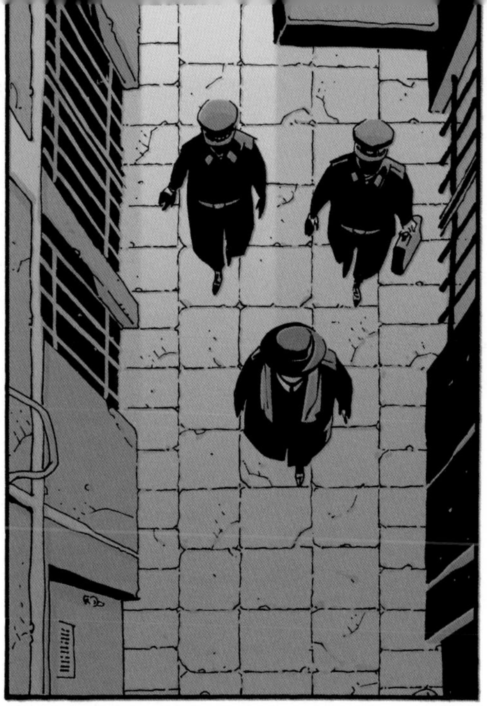

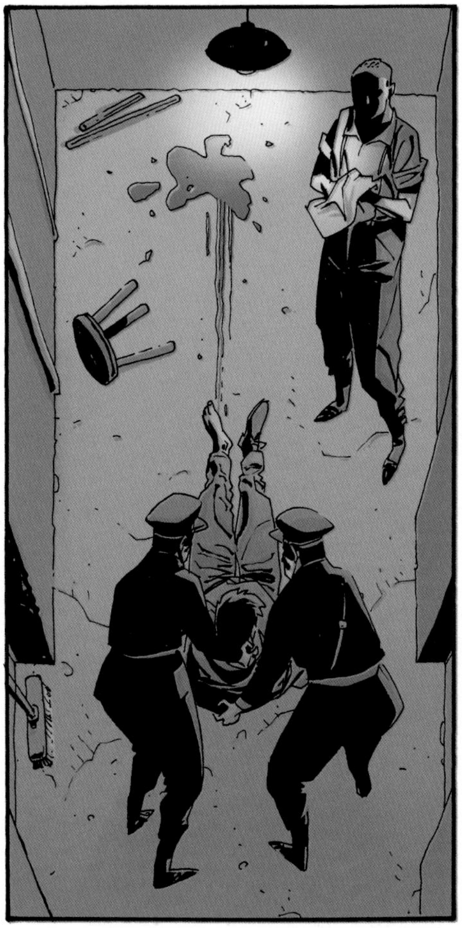

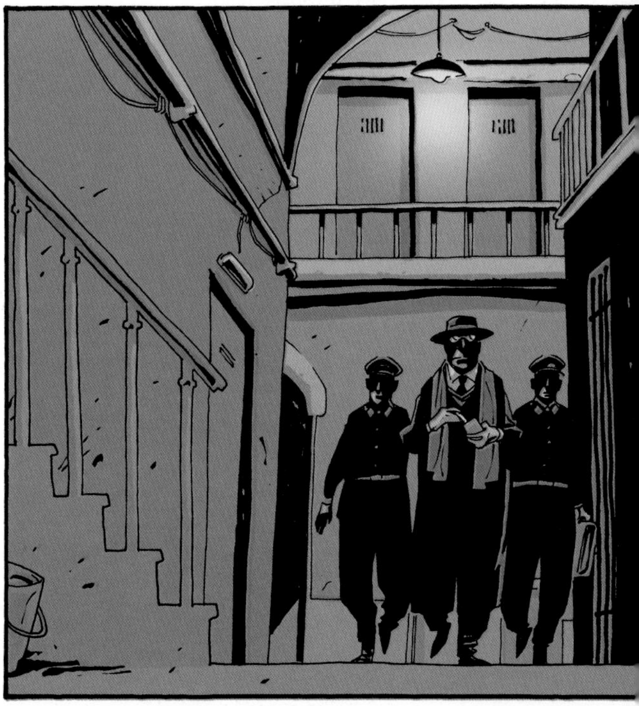

Lubyanka Prison.
March 6, 1953.

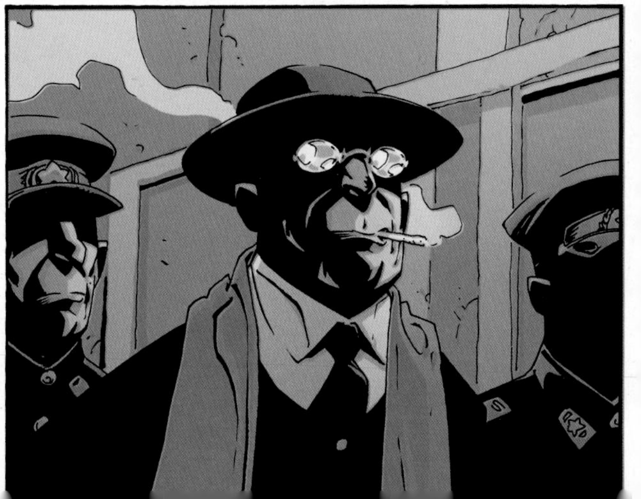

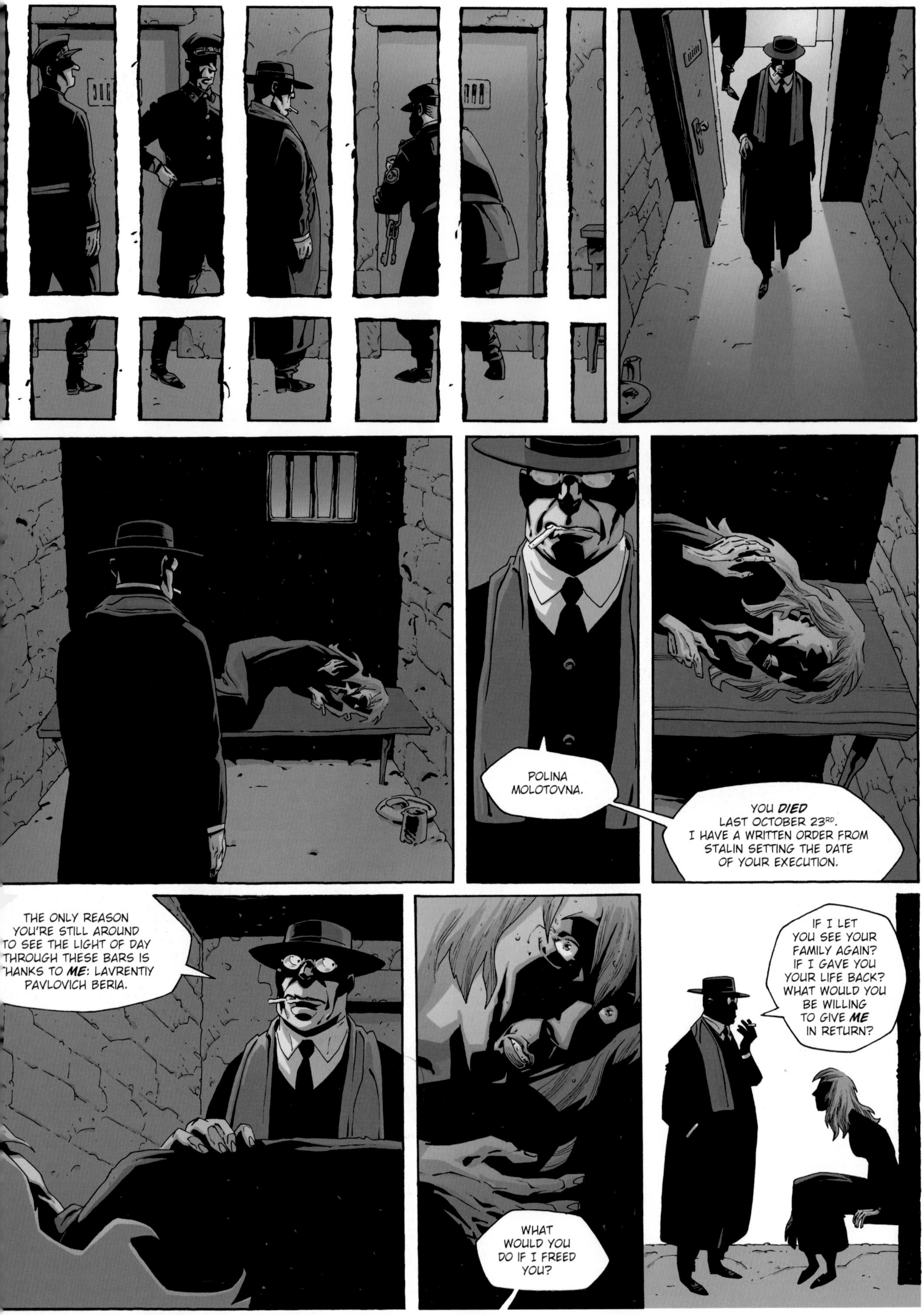
POLINA MOLOTOVNA.
YOU DIED LAST OCTOBER 23RD. I HAVE A WRITTEN ORDER FROM STALIN SETTING THE DATE OF YOUR EXECUTION.
THE ONLY REASON YOU'RE STILL AROUND TO SEE THE LIGHT OF DAY THROUGH THESE BARS IS THANKS TO ME: LAVRENTIY PAVLOVICH BERIA.
WHAT WOULD YOU DO IF I FREED YOU?
IF I LET YOU SEE YOUR FAMILY AGAIN? IF I GAVE YOU YOUR LIFE BACK? WHAT WOULD YOU BE WILLING TO GIVE ME IN RETURN?

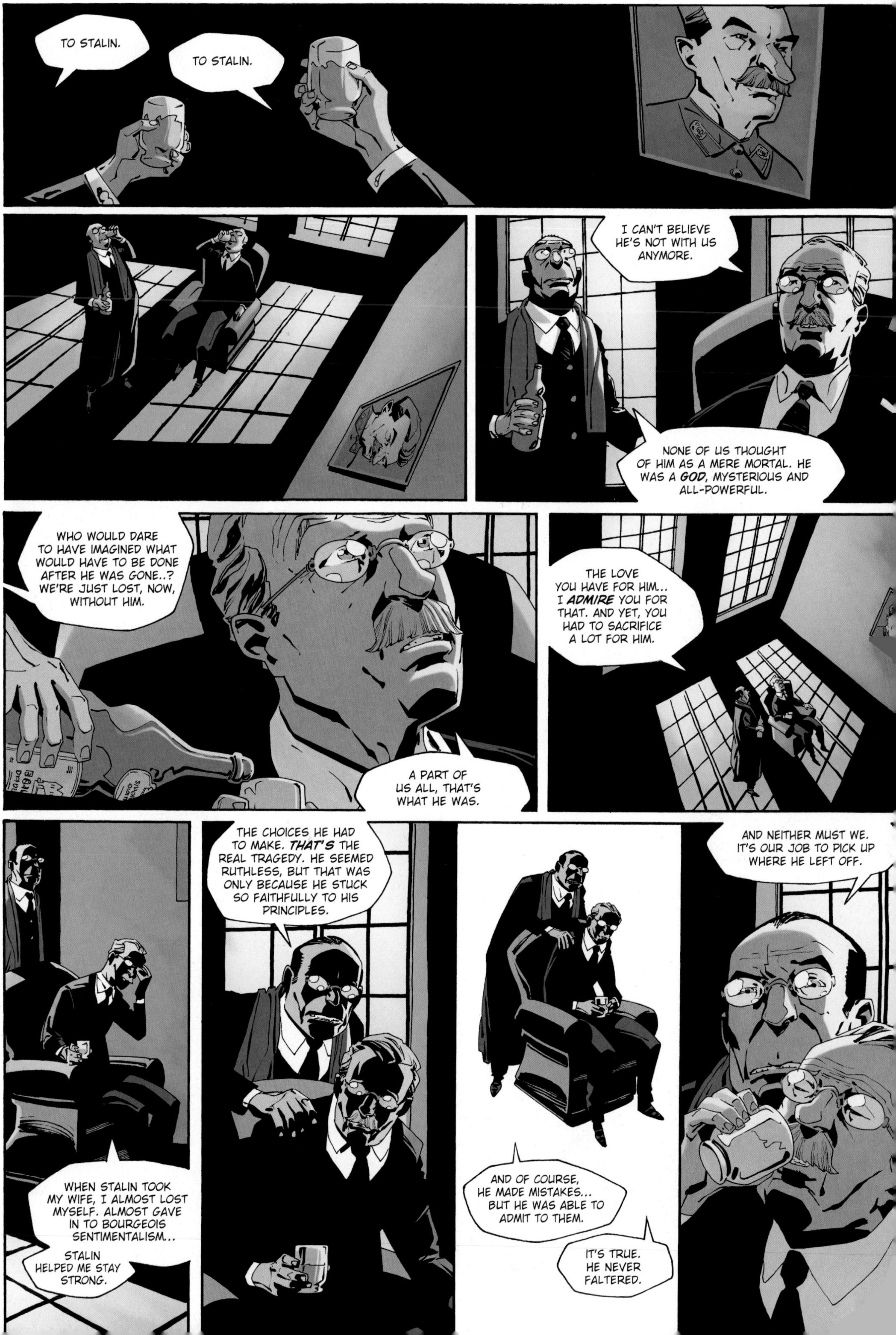
TO STALIN.
TO STALIN.
I CAN'T BELIEVE HE'S NOT WITH US ANYMORE.
NONE OF US THOUGHT OF HIM AS A MERE MORTAL. HE WAS A ***GOD***, MYSTERIOUS AND ALL-POWERFUL.
WHO WOULD DARE TO HAVE IMAGINED WHAT WOULD HAVE TO BE DONE AFTER HE WAS GONE..? WE'RE JUST LOST, NOW, WITHOUT HIM.
A PART OF US ALL, THAT'S WHAT HE WAS.
THE LOVE YOU HAVE FOR HIM... I ***ADMIRE*** YOU FOR THAT. AND YET, YOU HAD TO SACRIFICE A LOT FOR HIM.
WHEN STALIN TOOK MY WIFE, I ALMOST LOST MYSELF. ALMOST GAVE IN TO BOURGEOIS SENTIMENTALISM...
STALIN HELPED ME STAY STRONG.
THE CHOICES HE HAD TO MAKE. ***THAT'S*** THE REAL TRAGEDY. HE SEEMED RUTHLESS, BUT THAT WAS ONLY BECAUSE HE STUCK SO FAITHFULLY TO HIS PRINCIPLES.
AND OF COURSE, HE MADE MISTAKES... BUT HE WAS ABLE TO ADMIT TO THEM.
IT'S TRUE. HE NEVER FALTERED.
AND NEITHER MUST WE. IT'S OUR JOB TO PICK UP WHERE HE LEFT OFF.

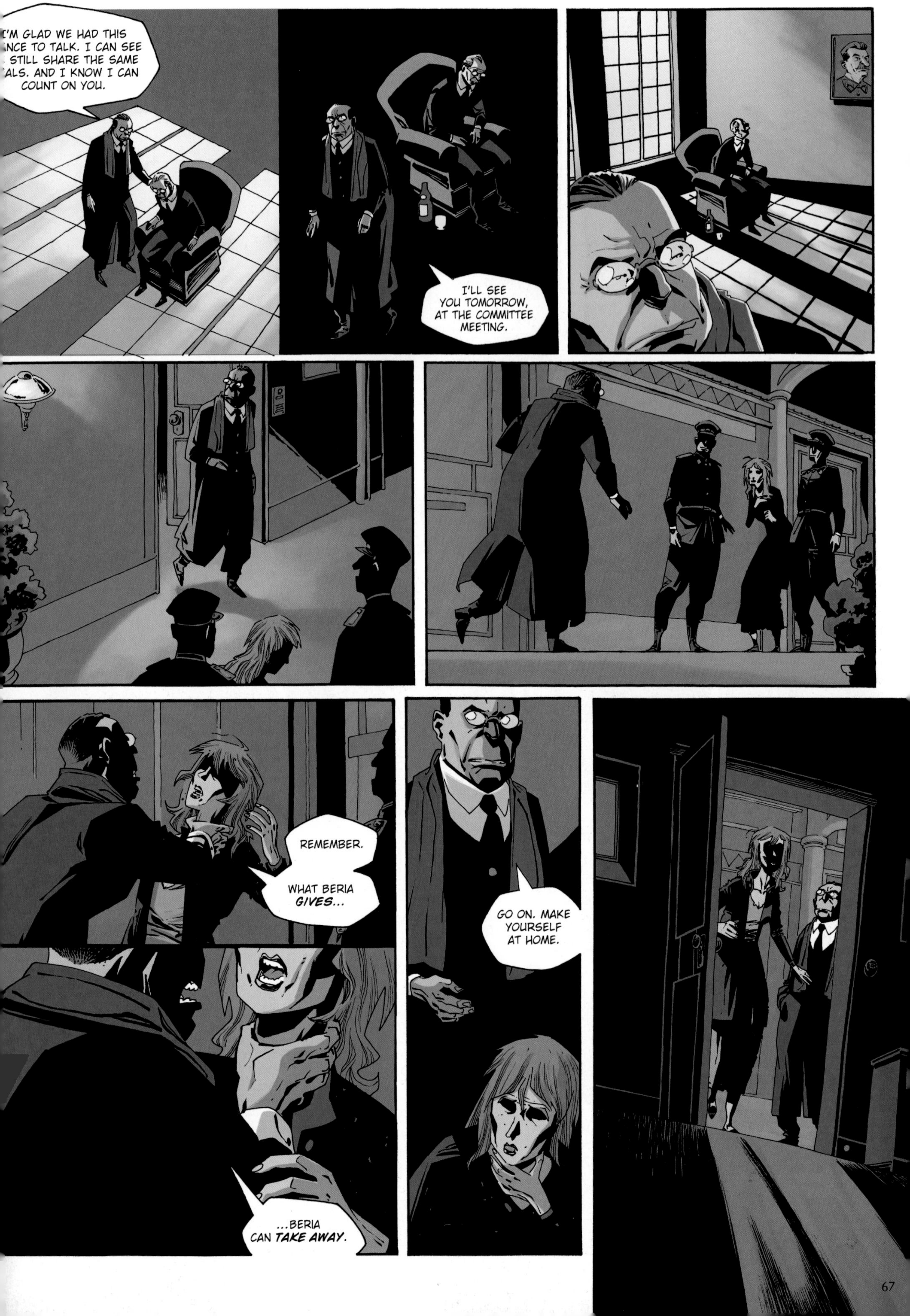
'M GLAD WE HAD THIS NCE TO TALK. I CAN SEE STILL SHARE THE SAME ALS. AND I KNOW I CAN COUNT ON YOU.
I'LL SEE YOU TOMORROW, AT THE COMMITTEE MEETING.
REMEMBER.
WHAT BERIA *GIVES*...
...BERIA CAN *TAKE AWAY*.
GO ON. MAKE YOURSELF AT HOME.

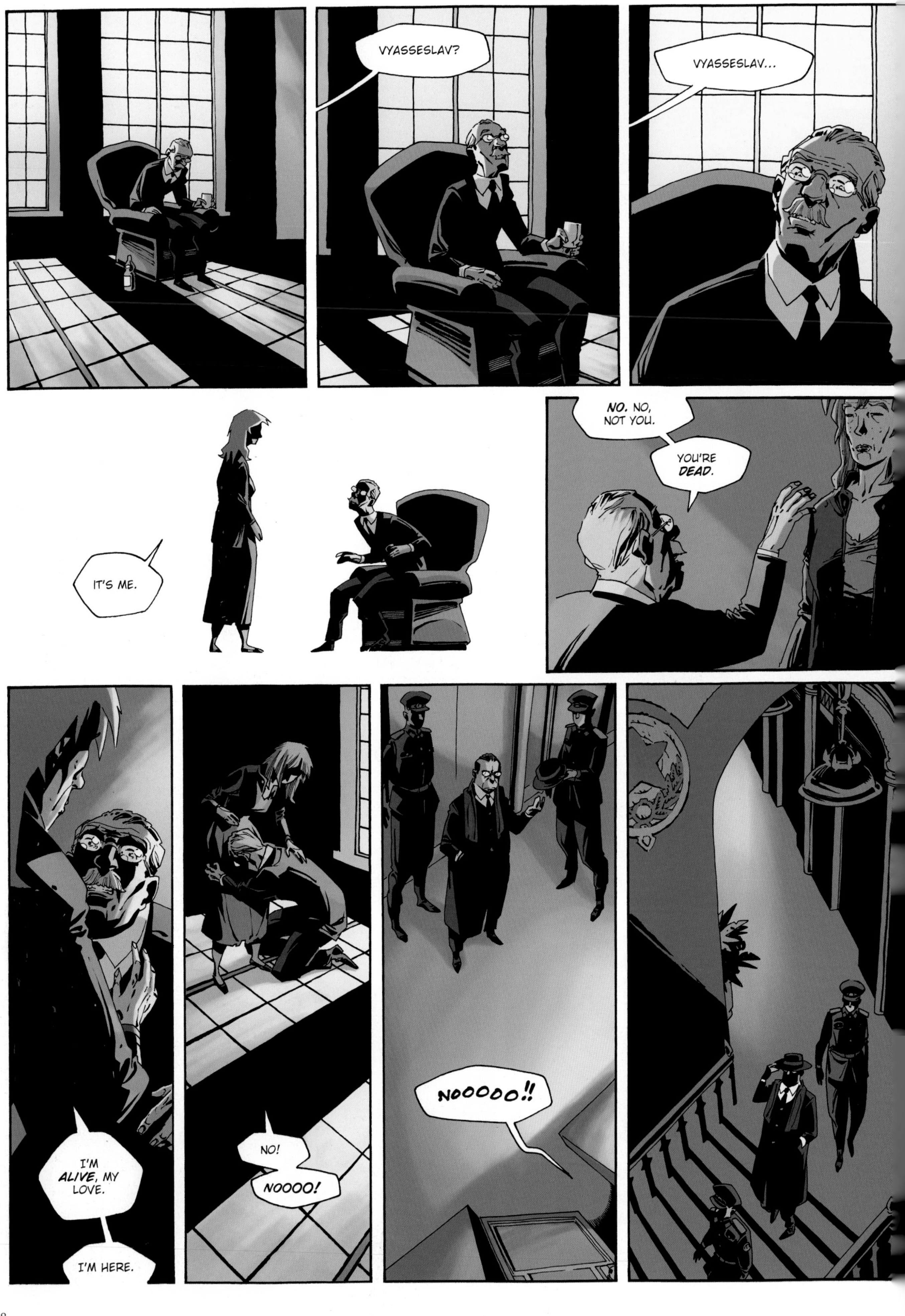
VYASSESLAV?
VYASSESLAV...
IT'S ME.
NO. NO, NOT YOU.
YOU'RE DEAD.
I'M ALIVE, MY LOVE.
I'M HERE.
NO!
NOOOO!
NOOOOO!!

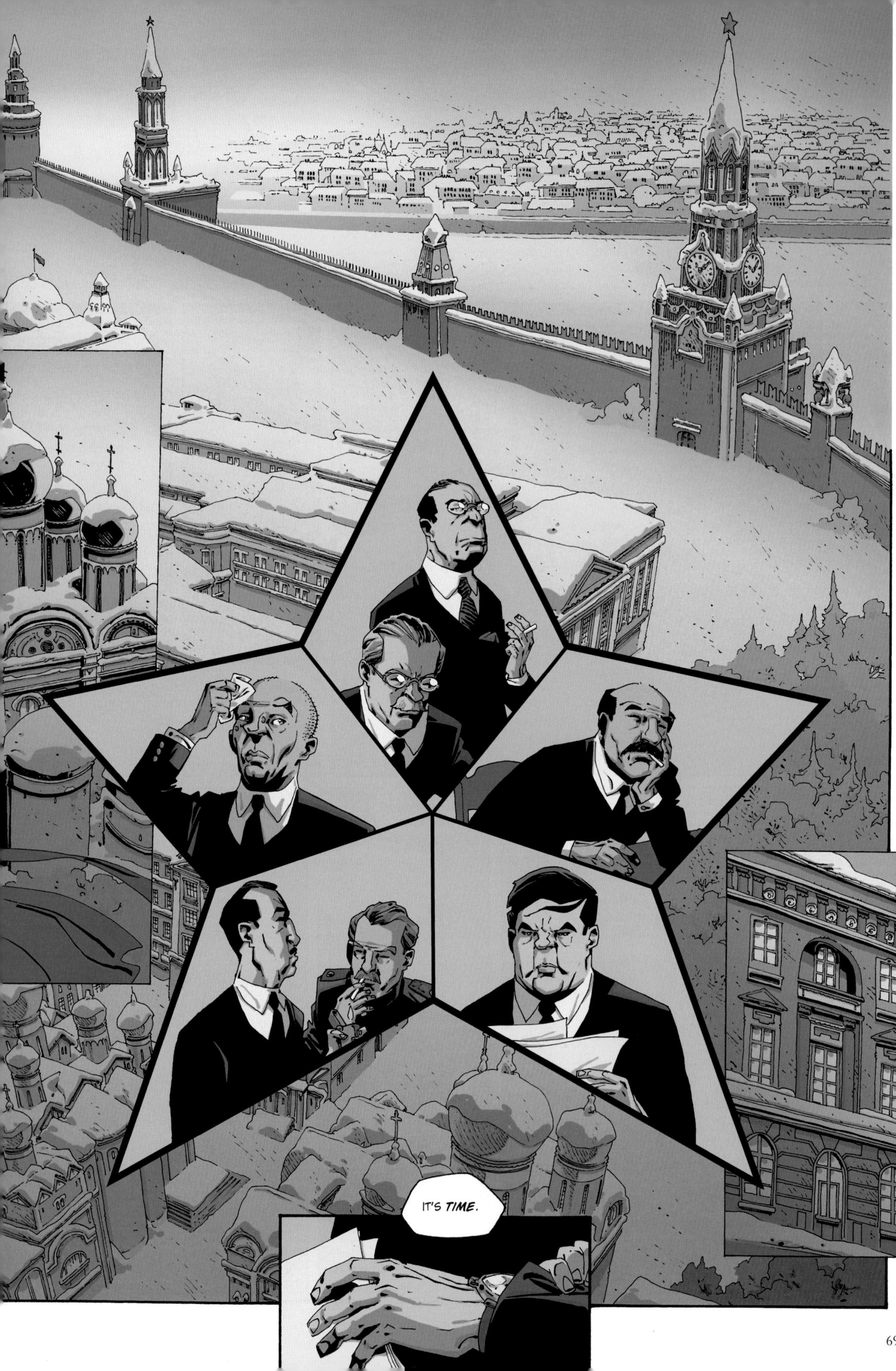
IT'S TIME.

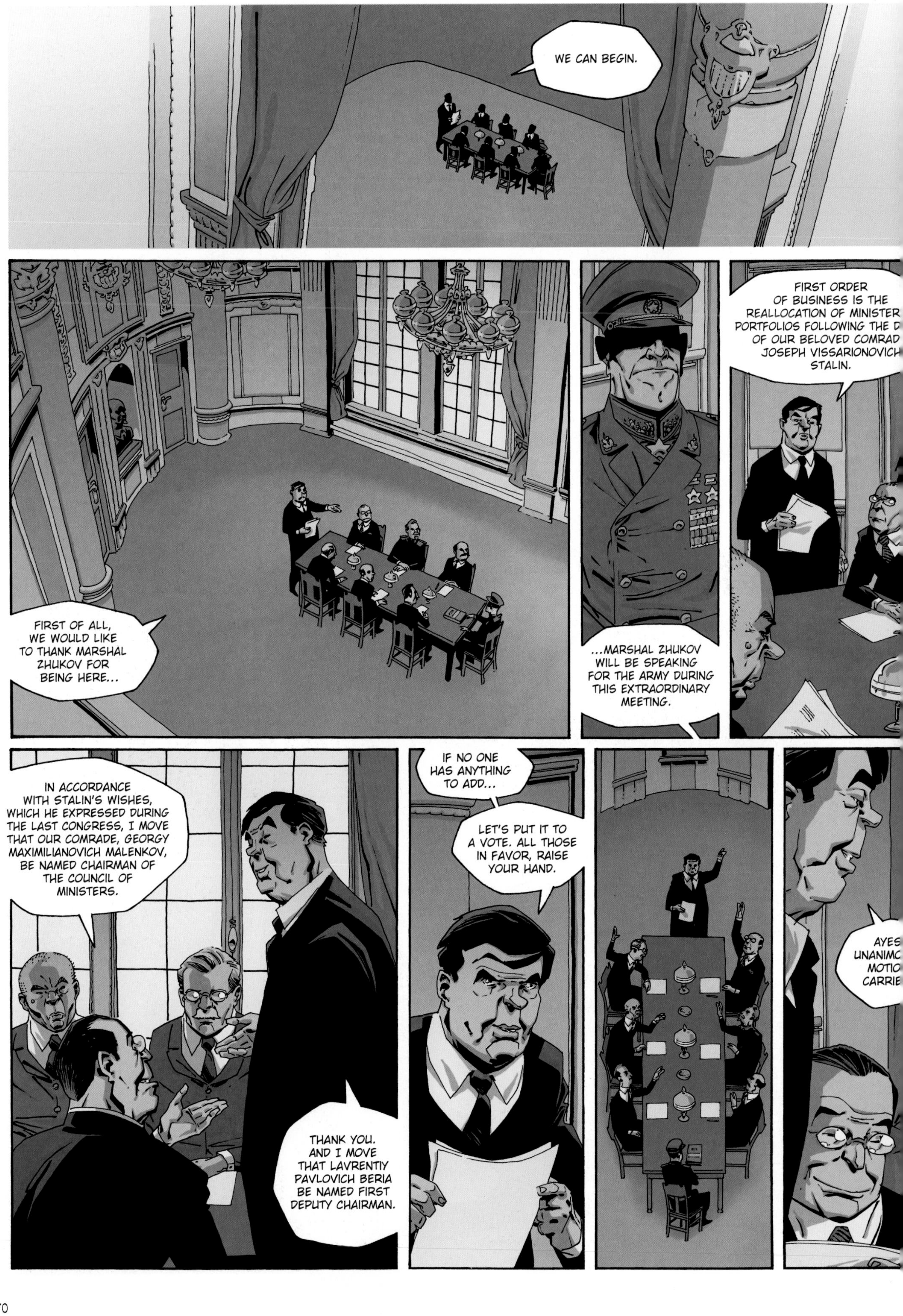
WE CAN BEGIN.
FIRST OF ALL, WE WOULD LIKE TO THANK MARSHAL ZHUKOV FOR BEING HERE...
...MARSHAL ZHUKOV WILL BE SPEAKING FOR THE ARMY DURING THIS EXTRAORDINARY MEETING.
FIRST ORDER OF BUSINESS IS THE REALLOCATION OF MINISTER PORTFOLIOS FOLLOWING THE D OF OUR BELOVED COMRAD JOSEPH VISSARIONOVICH STALIN.
IN ACCORDANCE WITH STALIN'S WISHES, WHICH HE EXPRESSED DURING THE LAST CONGRESS, I MOVE THAT OUR COMRADE, GEORGY MAXIMILIANOVICH MALENKOV, BE NAMED CHAIRMAN OF THE COUNCIL OF MINISTERS.
THANK YOU. AND I MOVE THAT LAVRENTIY PAVLOVICH BERIA BE NAMED FIRST DEPUTY CHAIRMAN.
IF NO ONE HAS ANYTHING TO ADD...
LET'S PUT IT TO A VOTE. ALL THOSE IN FAVOR, RAISE YOUR HAND.
AYES UNANIMO MOTIO CARRIE

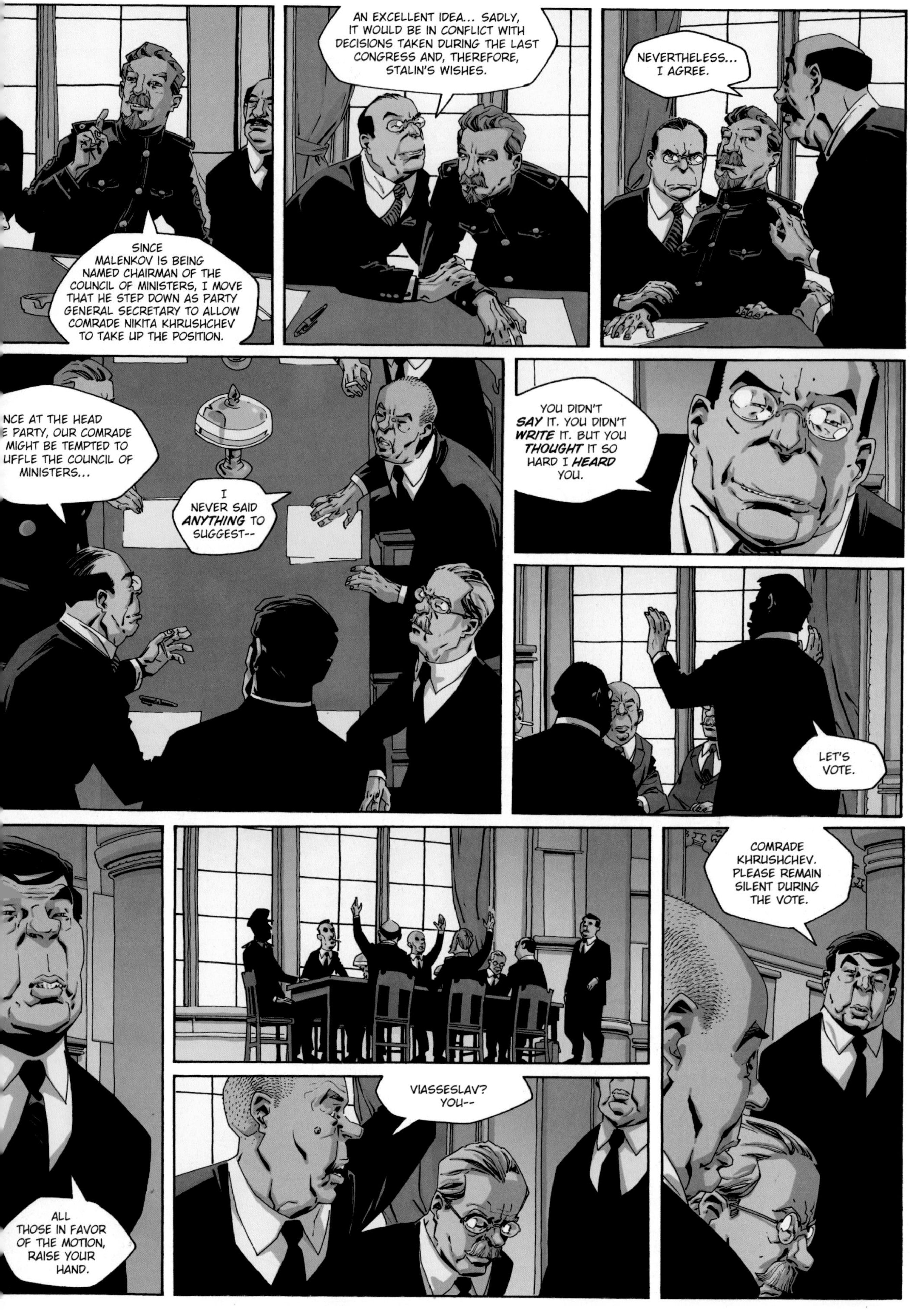

SINCE MALENKOV IS BEING NAMED CHAIRMAN OF THE COUNCIL OF MINISTERS, I MOVE THAT HE STEP DOWN AS PARTY GENERAL SECRETARY TO ALLOW COMRADE NIKITA KHRUSHCHEV TO TAKE UP THE POSITION.
AN EXCELLENT IDEA... SADLY, IT WOULD BE IN CONFLICT WITH DECISIONS TAKEN DURING THE LAST CONGRESS AND, THEREFORE, STALIN'S WISHES.
NEVERTHELESS... I AGREE.
NCE AT THE HEAD E PARTY, OUR COMRADE MIGHT BE TEMPTED TO UFFLE THE COUNCIL OF MINISTERS...
I NEVER SAID ANYTHING TO SUGGEST--
YOU DIDN'T SAY IT. YOU DIDN'T WRITE IT. BUT YOU THOUGHT IT SO HARD I HEARD YOU.
LET'S VOTE.
ALL THOSE IN FAVOR OF THE MOTION, RAISE YOUR HAND.
VIASSESLAV? YOU--
COMRADE KHRUSHCHEV. PLEASE REMAIN SILENT DURING THE VOTE.

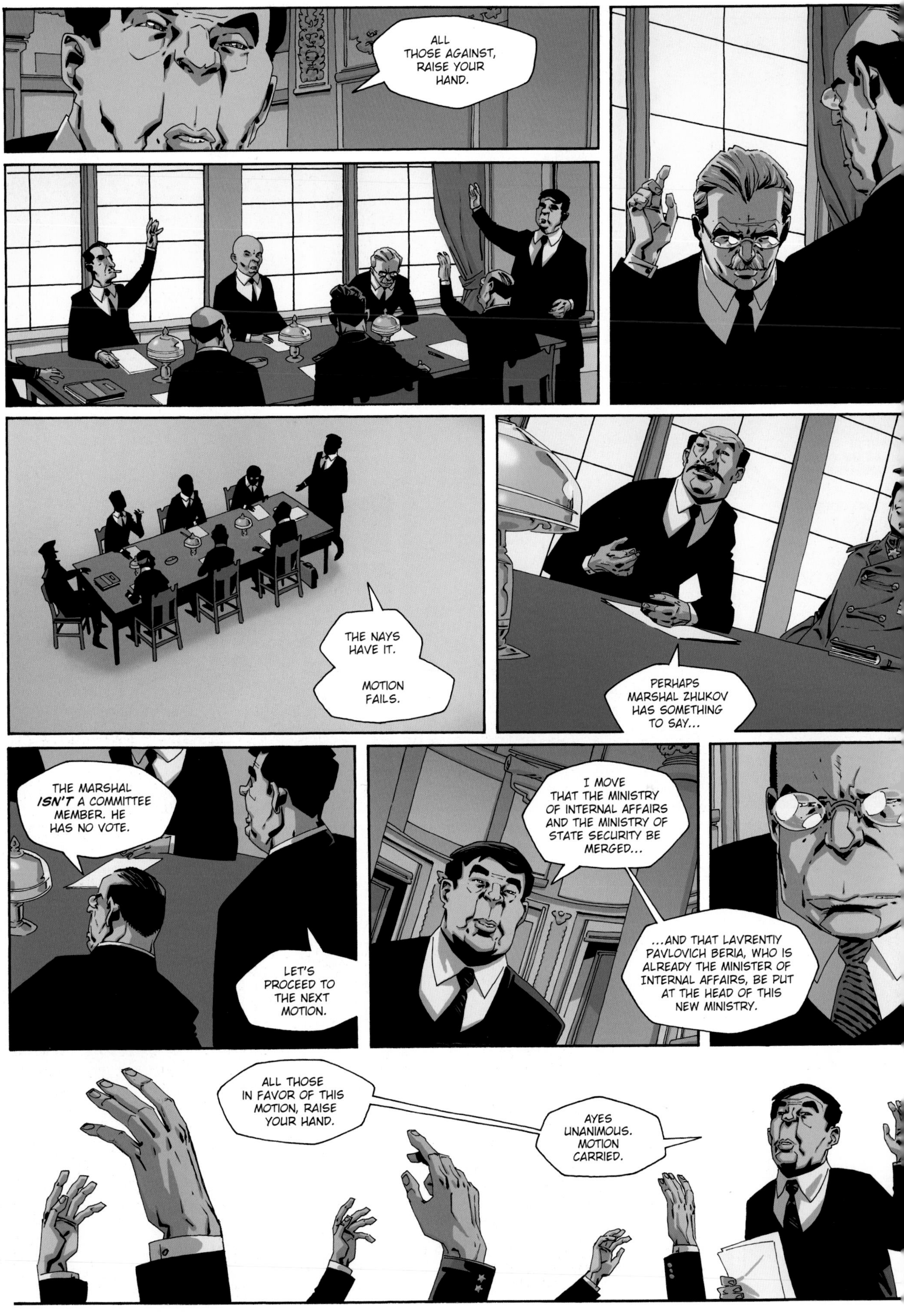
ALL THOSE AGAINST, RAISE YOUR HAND.
THE NAYS HAVE IT.
MOTION FAILS.
PERHAPS MARSHAL ZHUKOV HAS SOMETHING TO SAY...
THE MARSHAL *ISN'T* A COMMITTEE MEMBER. HE HAS NO VOTE.
LET'S PROCEED TO THE NEXT MOTION.
I MOVE THAT THE MINISTRY OF INTERNAL AFFAIRS AND THE MINISTRY OF STATE SECURITY BE MERGED...
...AND THAT LAVRENTIY PAVLOVICH BERIA, WHO IS ALREADY THE MINISTER OF INTERNAL AFFAIRS, BE PUT AT THE HEAD OF THIS NEW MINISTRY.
ALL THOSE IN FAVOR OF THIS MOTION, RAISE YOUR HAND.
AYES UNANIMOUS. MOTION CARRIED.

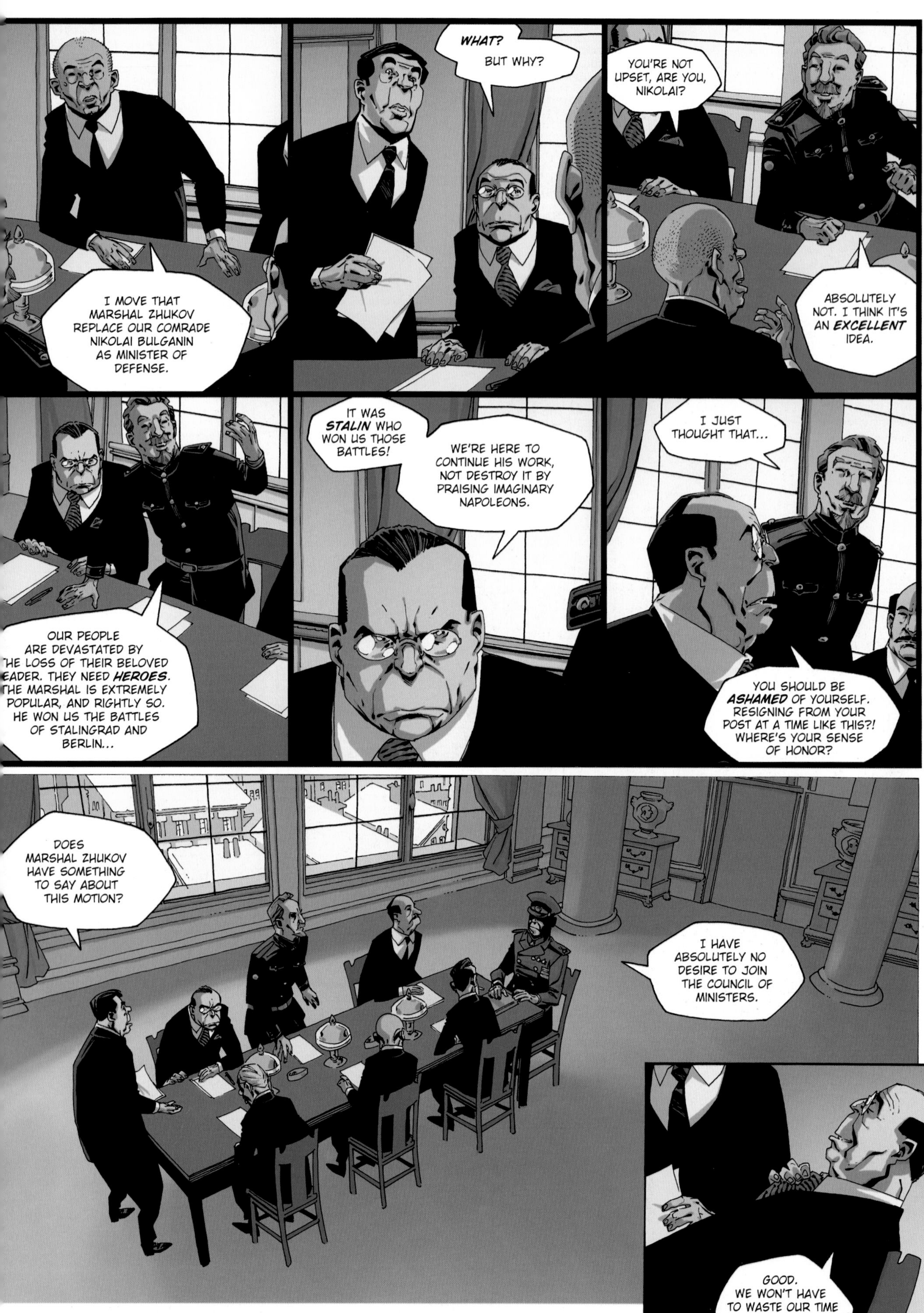
I MOVE THAT MARSHAL ZHUKOV REPLACE OUR COMRADE NIKOLAI BULGANIN AS MINISTER OF DEFENSE.
WHAT? BUT WHY?
YOU'RE NOT UPSET, ARE YOU, NIKOLAI?
ABSOLUTELY NOT. I THINK IT'S AN EXCELLENT IDEA.
OUR PEOPLE ARE DEVASTATED BY THE LOSS OF THEIR BELOVED LEADER. THEY NEED HEROES. THE MARSHAL IS EXTREMELY POPULAR, AND RIGHTLY SO. HE WON US THE BATTLES OF STALINGRAD AND BERLIN...
IT WAS STALIN WHO WON US THOSE BATTLES!
WE'RE HERE TO CONTINUE HIS WORK, NOT DESTROY IT BY PRAISING IMAGINARY NAPOLEONS.
I JUST THOUGHT THAT...
YOU SHOULD BE ASHAMED OF YOURSELF. RESIGNING FROM YOUR POST AT A TIME LIKE THIS?! WHERE'S YOUR SENSE OF HONOR?
DOES MARSHAL ZHUKOV HAVE SOMETHING TO SAY ABOUT THIS MOTION?
I HAVE ABSOLUTELY NO DESIRE TO JOIN THE COUNCIL OF MINISTERS.
GOOD. WE WON'T HAVE TO WASTE OUR TIME VOTING, THEN.

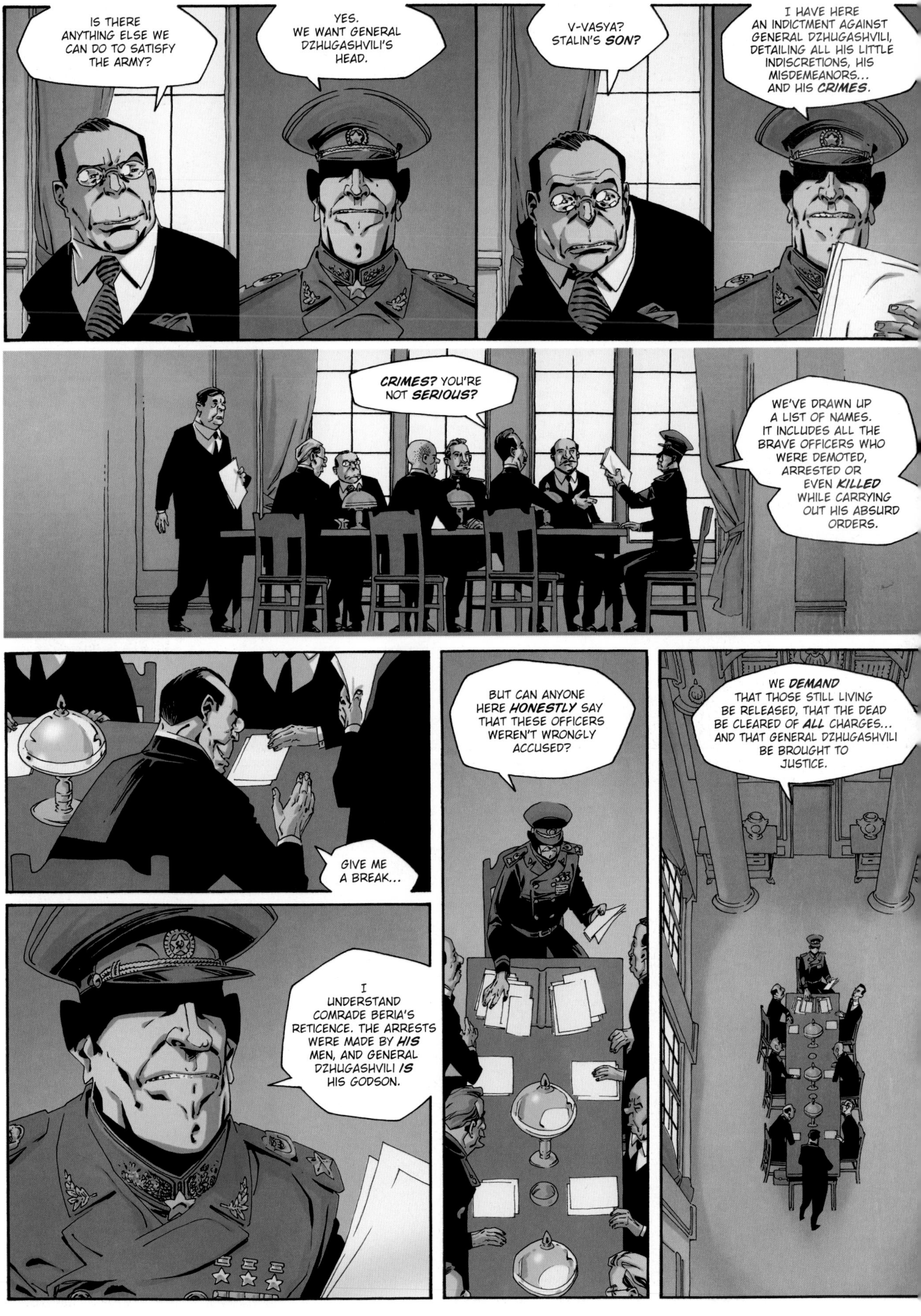
IS THERE ANYTHING ELSE WE CAN DO TO SATISFY THE ARMY?
YES. WE WANT GENERAL DZHUGASHVILI'S HEAD.
V-VASYA? STALIN'S SON?
I HAVE HERE AN INDICTMENT AGAINST GENERAL DZHUGASHVILI, DETAILING ALL HIS LITTLE INDISCRETIONS, HIS MISDEMEANORS... AND HIS CRIMES.
CRIMES? YOU'RE NOT SERIOUS?
WE'VE DRAWN UP A LIST OF NAMES. IT INCLUDES ALL THE BRAVE OFFICERS WHO WERE DEMOTED, ARRESTED OR EVEN KILLED WHILE CARRYING OUT HIS ABSURD ORDERS.
GIVE ME A BREAK...
I UNDERSTAND COMRADE BERIA'S RETICENCE. THE ARRESTS WERE MADE BY HIS MEN, AND GENERAL DZHUGASHVILI IS HIS GODSON.
BUT CAN ANYONE HERE HONESTLY SAY THAT THESE OFFICERS WEREN'T WRONGLY ACCUSED?
WE DEMAND THAT THOSE STILL LIVING BE RELEASED, THAT THE DEAD BE CLEARED OF ALL CHARGES... AND THAT GENERAL DZHUGASHVILI BE BROUGHT TO JUSTICE.

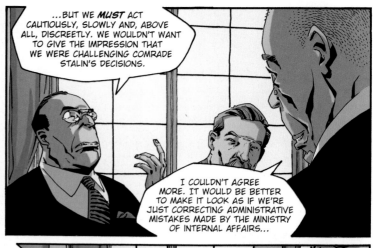

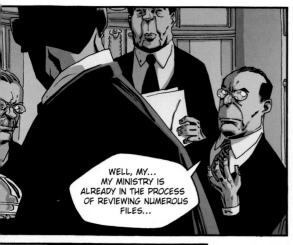

WELL, MY... MY MINISTRY IS ALREADY IN THE PROCESS OF REVIEWING NUMEROUS FILES...
...BUT WE MUST ACT CAUTIOUSLY, SLOWLY AND, ABOVE ALL, DISCREETLY. WE WOULDN'T WANT TO GIVE THE IMPRESSION THAT WE WERE CHALLENGING COMRADE STALIN'S DECISIONS.
I COULDN'T AGREE MORE. IT WOULD BE BETTER TO MAKE IT LOOK AS IF WE'RE JUST CORRECTING ADMINISTRATIVE MISTAKES MADE BY THE MINISTRY OF INTERNAL AFFAIRS...
WHAT ARE YOU IMPLYING? THAT I'M THE ONLY ONE AT FAULT HERE?
COME ON, LAVRENTIY... WOULD YOU HAVE US BELIEVE YOU DIDN'T ARREST ANYONE?
VERY WELL...
I HAVE HERE PROOF THAT NONE OF THE ARRESTS CAME FROM ME. EACH OF THESE WARRANTS WAS SIGNED BY STALIN HIMSELF... AND COUNTERSIGNED BY AT LEAST ONE OF YOU.
WHERE DID YOU GET THEM?
YOU STOLE THEM FROM STALIN!

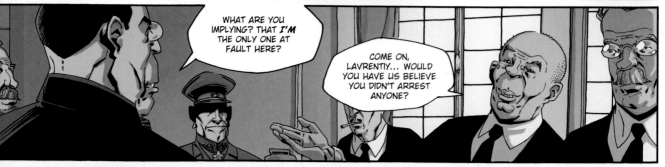

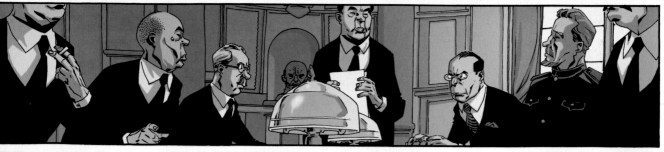

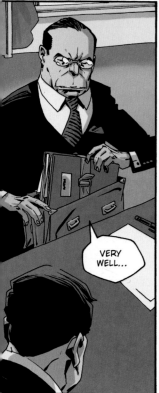

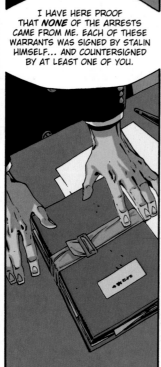

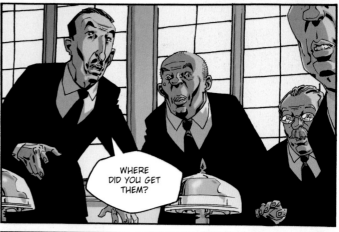

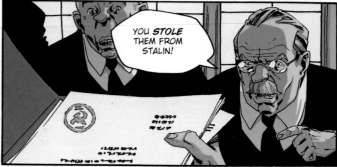

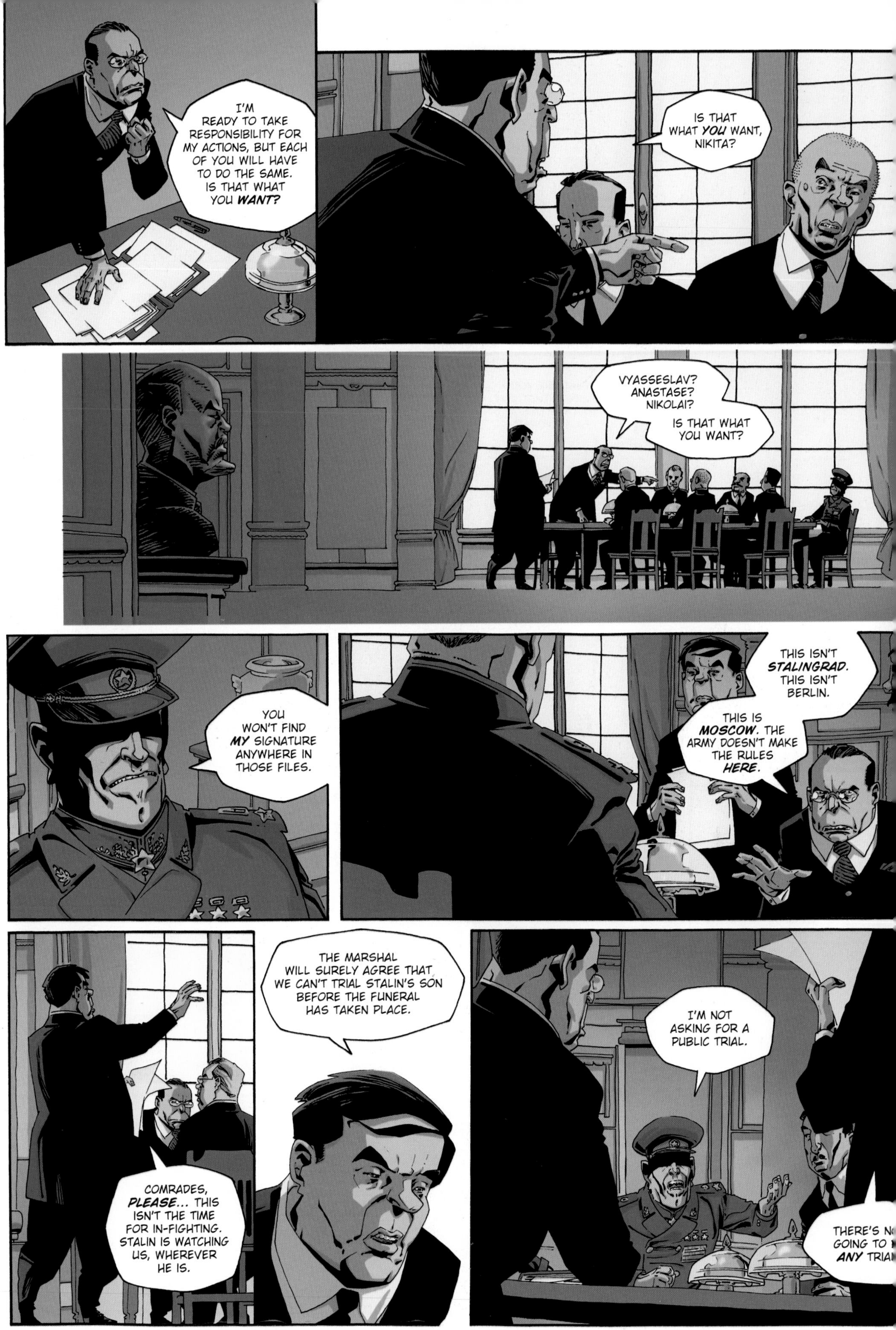
I'M READY TO TAKE RESPONSIBILITY FOR MY ACTIONS, BUT EACH OF YOU WILL HAVE TO DO THE SAME. IS THAT WHAT YOU *WANT?*
IS THAT WHAT *YOU* WANT, NIKITA?
VYASSESLAV? ANASTASE? NIKOLAI?
IS THAT WHAT YOU WANT?
YOU WON'T FIND *MY* SIGNATURE ANYWHERE IN THOSE FILES.
THIS ISN'T *STALINGRAD.* THIS ISN'T BERLIN.
THIS IS *MOSCOW.* THE ARMY DOESN'T MAKE THE RULES *HERE.*
COMRADES, *PLEASE...* THIS ISN'T THE TIME FOR IN-FIGHTING. STALIN IS WATCHING US, WHEREVER HE IS.
THE MARSHAL WILL SURELY AGREE THAT WE CAN'T TRIAL STALIN'S SON BEFORE THE FUNERAL HAS TAKEN PLACE.
I'M NOT ASKING FOR A PUBLIC TRIAL.

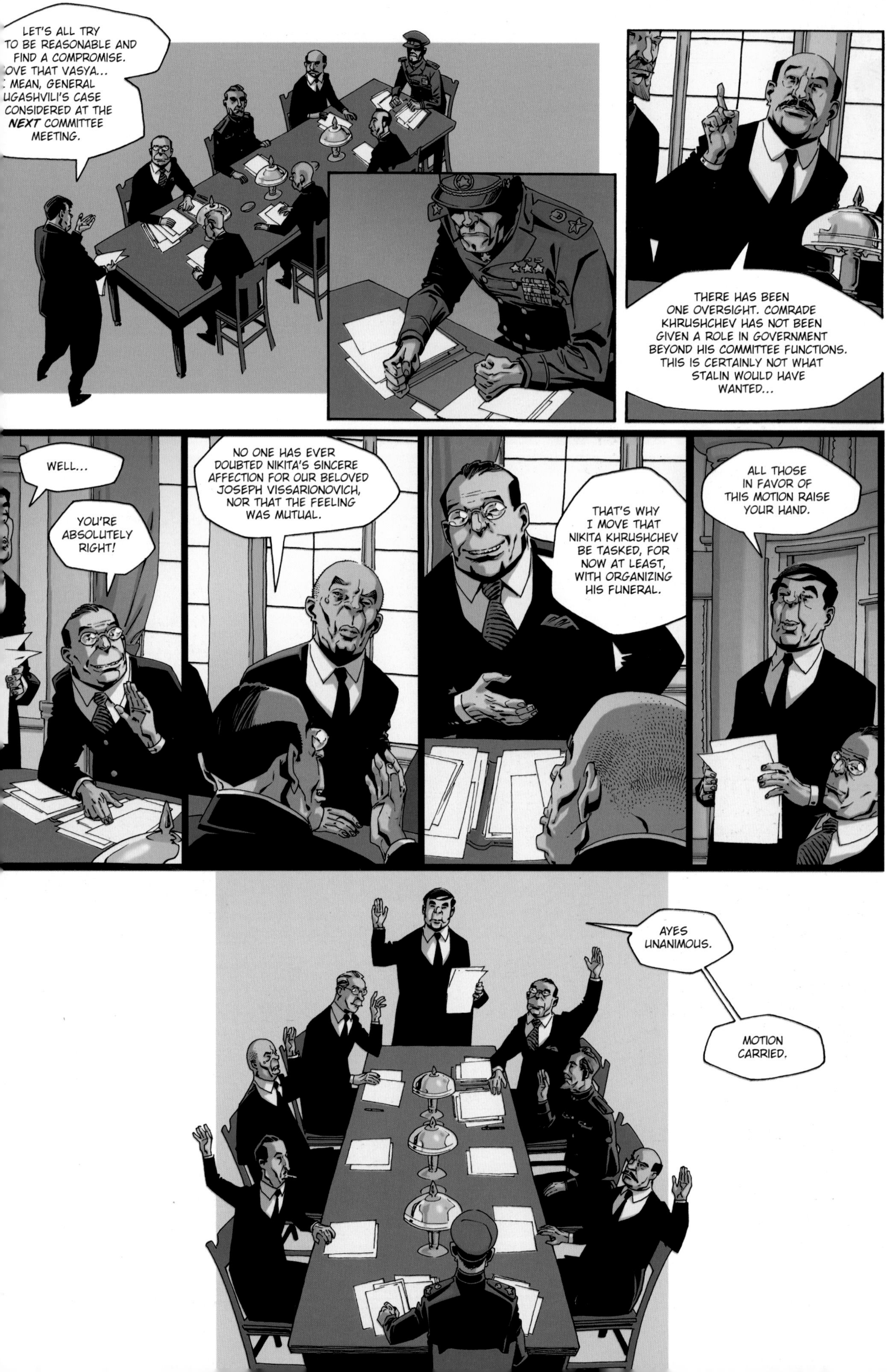
LET'S ALL TRY TO BE REASONABLE AND FIND A COMPROMISE. OVE THAT VASYA... MEAN, GENERAL UGASHVILI'S CASE CONSIDERED AT THE NEXT COMMITTEE MEETING.
THERE HAS BEEN ONE OVERSIGHT. COMRADE KHRUSHCHEV HAS NOT BEEN GIVEN A ROLE IN GOVERNMENT BEYOND HIS COMMITTEE FUNCTIONS. THIS IS CERTAINLY NOT WHAT STALIN WOULD HAVE WANTED...
WELL...
YOU'RE ABSOLUTELY RIGHT!
NO ONE HAS EVER DOUBTED NIKITA'S SINCERE AFFECTION FOR OUR BELOVED JOSEPH VISSARIONOVICH, NOR THAT THE FEELING WAS MUTUAL.
THAT'S WHY I MOVE THAT NIKITA KHRUSHCHEV BE TASKED, FOR NOW AT LEAST, WITH ORGANIZING HIS FUNERAL.
ALL THOSE IN FAVOR OF THIS MOTION RAISE YOUR HAND.
AYES UNANIMOUS.
MOTION CARRIED.

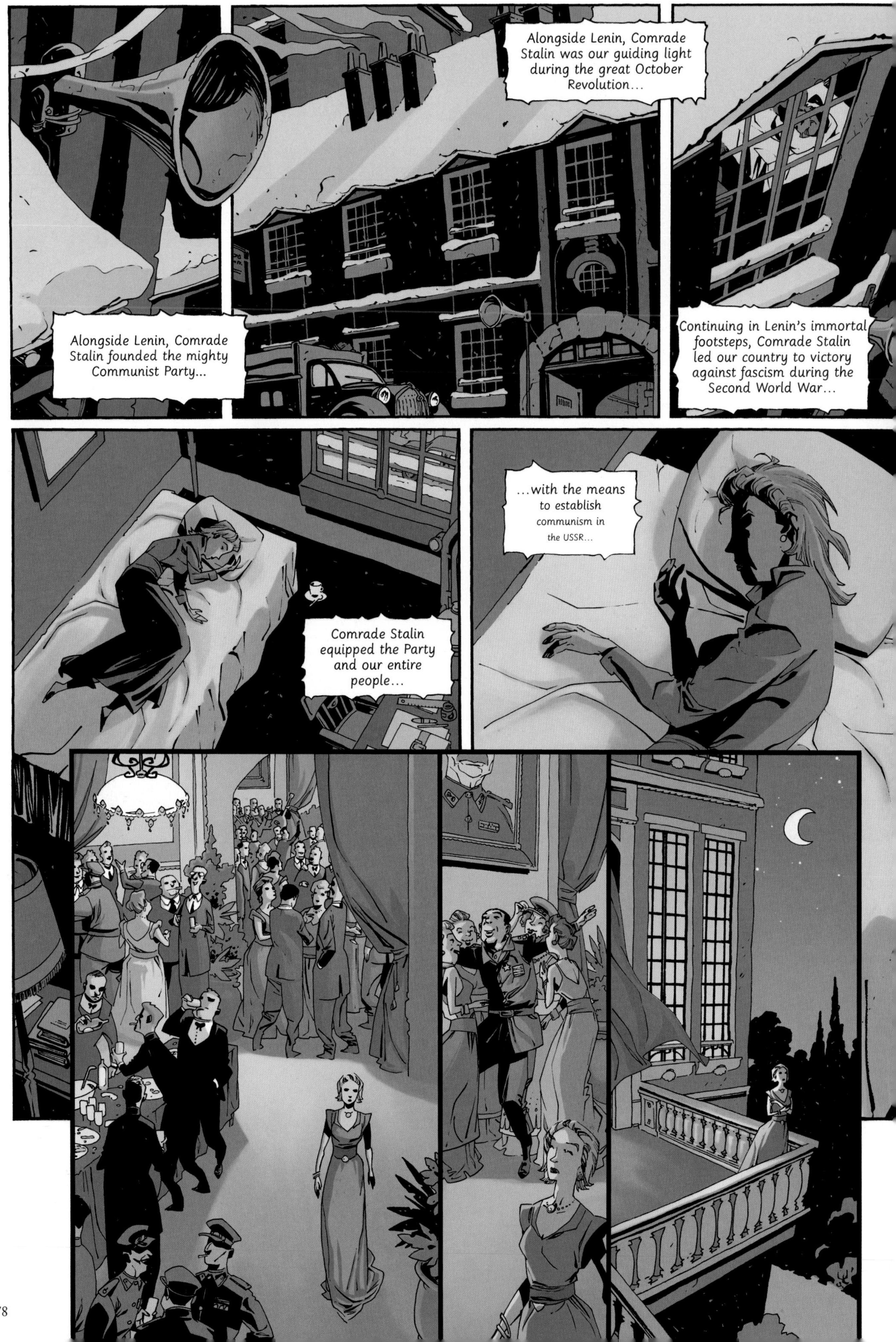
Alongside Lenin, Comrade Stalin founded the mighty Communist Party...
Alongside Lenin, Comrade Stalin was our guiding light during the great October Revolution...
Continuing in Lenin's immortal footsteps, Comrade Stalin led our country to victory against fascism during the Second World War...
Comrade Stalin equipped the Party and our entire people...
...with the means to establish communism in the USSR...

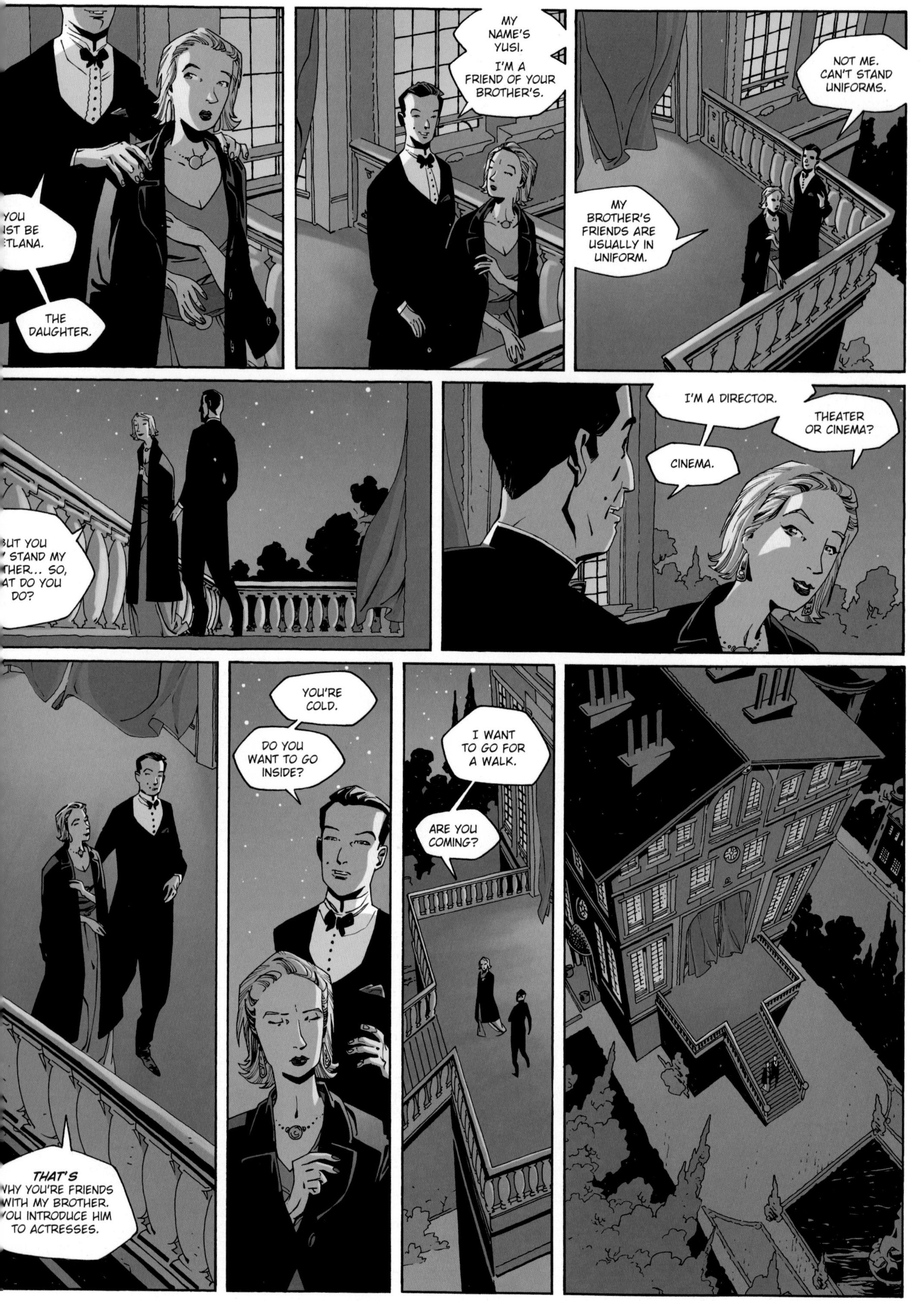
YOU IST BE TLANA.
THE DAUGHTER.
MY NAME'S YUSI.
I'M A FRIEND OF YOUR BROTHER'S.
MY BROTHER'S FRIENDS ARE USUALLY IN UNIFORM.
NOT ME. CAN'T STAND UNIFORMS.
UT YOU STAND MY THER... SO, AT DO YOU DO?
I'M A DIRECTOR.
THEATER OR CINEMA?
CINEMA.
THAT'S WHY YOU'RE FRIENDS WITH MY BROTHER. YOU INTRODUCE HIM TO ACTRESSES.
YOU'RE COLD.
DO YOU WANT TO GO INSIDE?
I WANT TO GO FOR A WALK.
ARE YOU COMING?

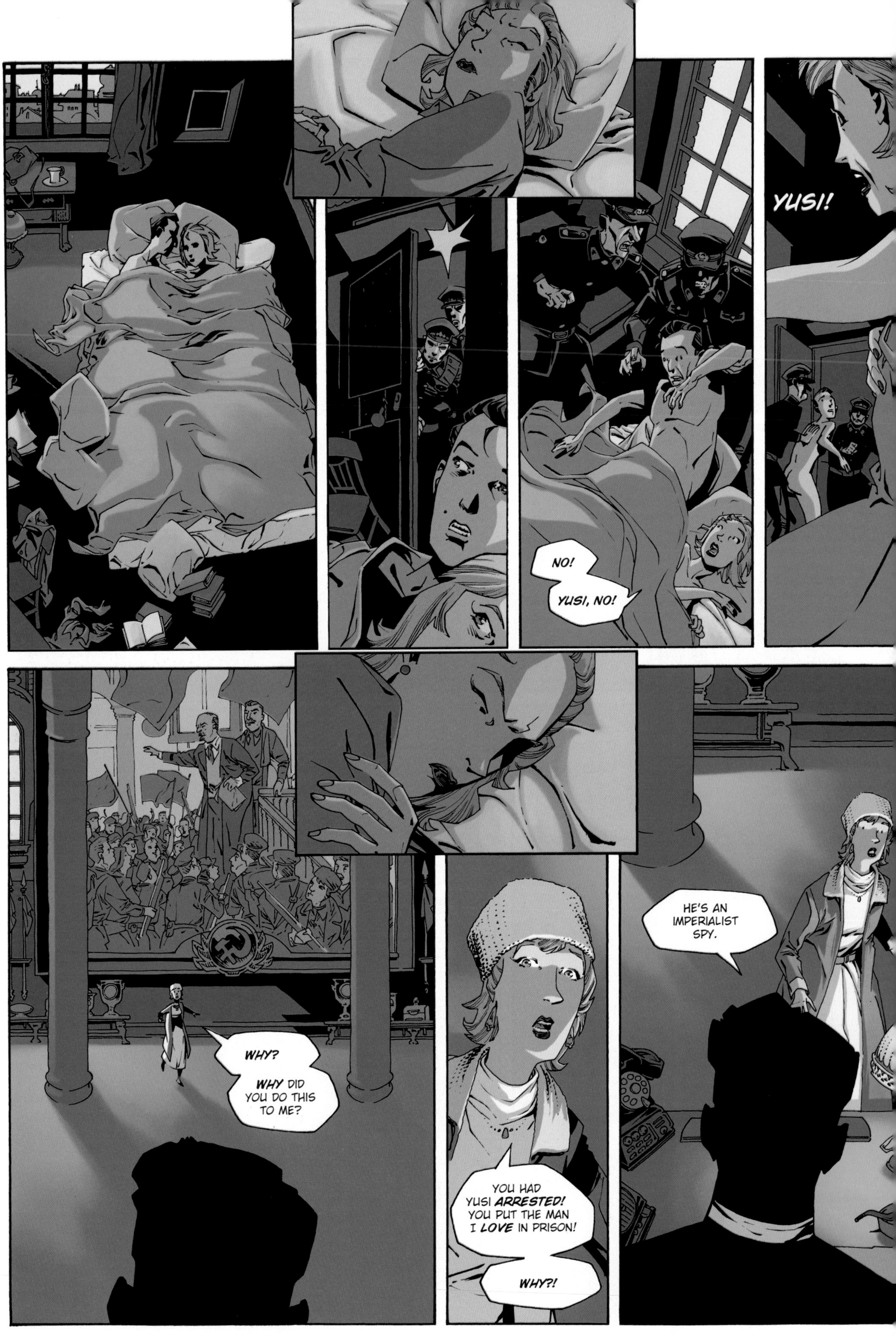
YUSI!
NO!
YUSI, NO!
WHY?
WHY DID YOU DO THIS TO ME?
YOU HAD YUSI ARRESTED! YOU PUT THE MAN I LOVE IN PRISON!
WHY?!
HE'S AN IMPERIALIST SPY.

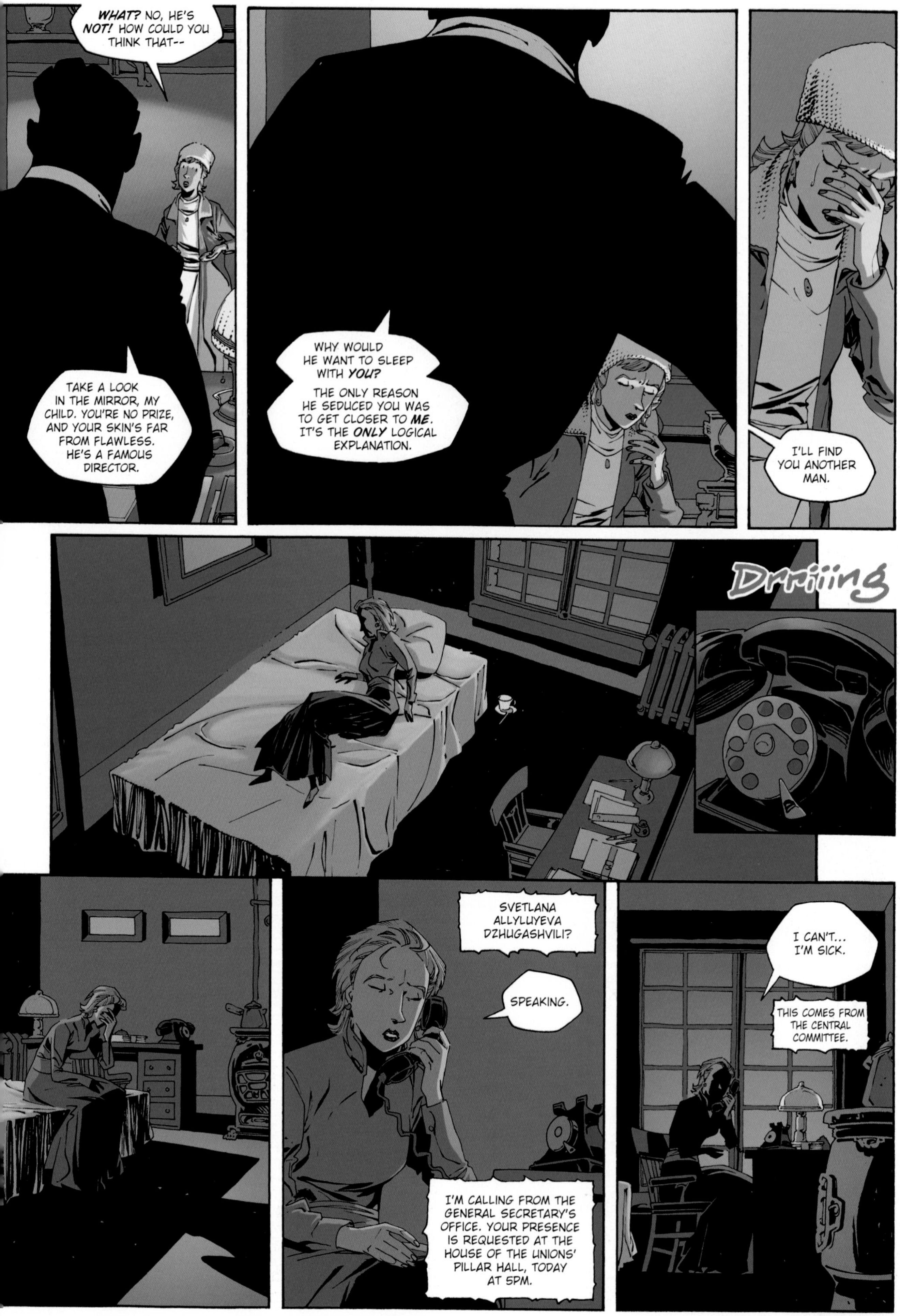
WHAT? NO, HE'S NOT! HOW COULD YOU THINK THAT--
TAKE A LOOK IN THE MIRROR, MY CHILD. YOU'RE NO PRIZE, AND YOUR SKIN'S FAR FROM FLAWLESS. HE'S A FAMOUS DIRECTOR.
WHY WOULD HE WANT TO SLEEP WITH YOU?
THE ONLY REASON HE SEDUCED YOU WAS TO GET CLOSER TO ME. IT'S THE ONLY LOGICAL EXPLANATION.
I'LL FIND YOU ANOTHER MAN.
Drriiing
SVETLANA ALLYLUYEVA DZHUGASHVILI?
SPEAKING.
I'M CALLING FROM THE GENERAL SECRETARY'S OFFICE. YOUR PRESENCE IS REQUESTED AT THE HOUSE OF THE UNIONS' PILLAR HALL, TODAY AT 5PM.
I CAN'T... I'M SICK.
THIS COMES FROM THE CENTRAL COMMITTEE.

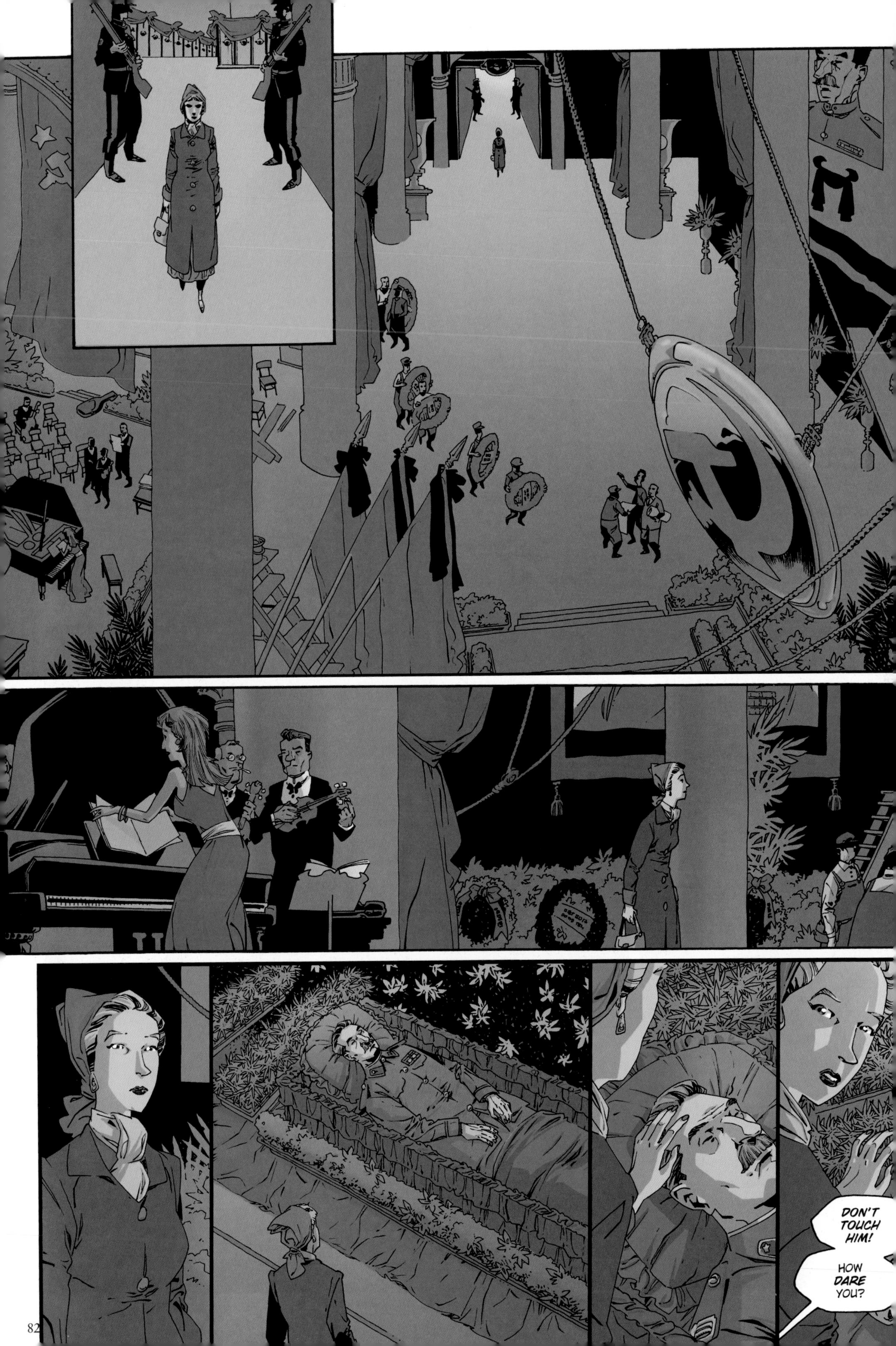
DON'T TOUCH HIM!
HOW DARE YOU?

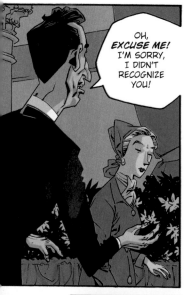

OH, **EXCUSE ME!** I'M SORRY, I DIDN'T RECOGNIZE YOU!

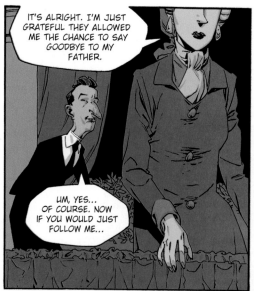

IT'S ALRIGHT. I'M JUST GRATEFUL THEY ALLOWED ME THE CHANCE TO SAY GOODBYE TO MY FATHER.

UM, YES... OF COURSE. NOW IF YOU WOULD JUST FOLLOW ME...

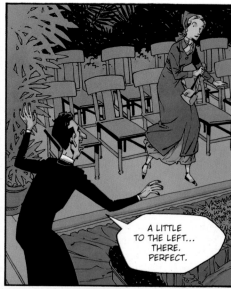

A LITTLE TO THE LEFT... THERE. PERFECT.

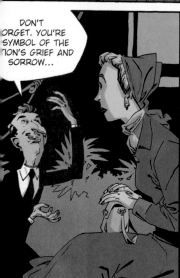

DON'T FORGET. YOU'RE SYMBOL OF THE NATION'S GRIEF AND SORROW...

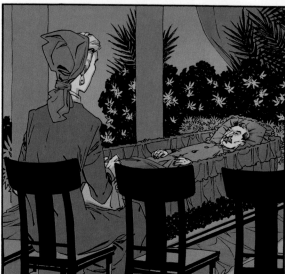

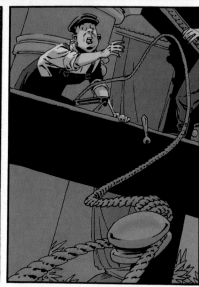

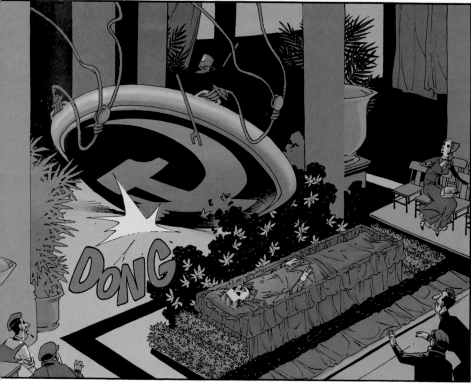

DONG

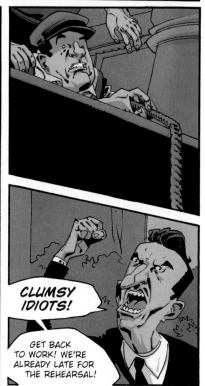

CLUMSY IDIOTS!

GET BACK TO WORK! WE'RE ALREADY LATE FOR THE REHEARSAL!

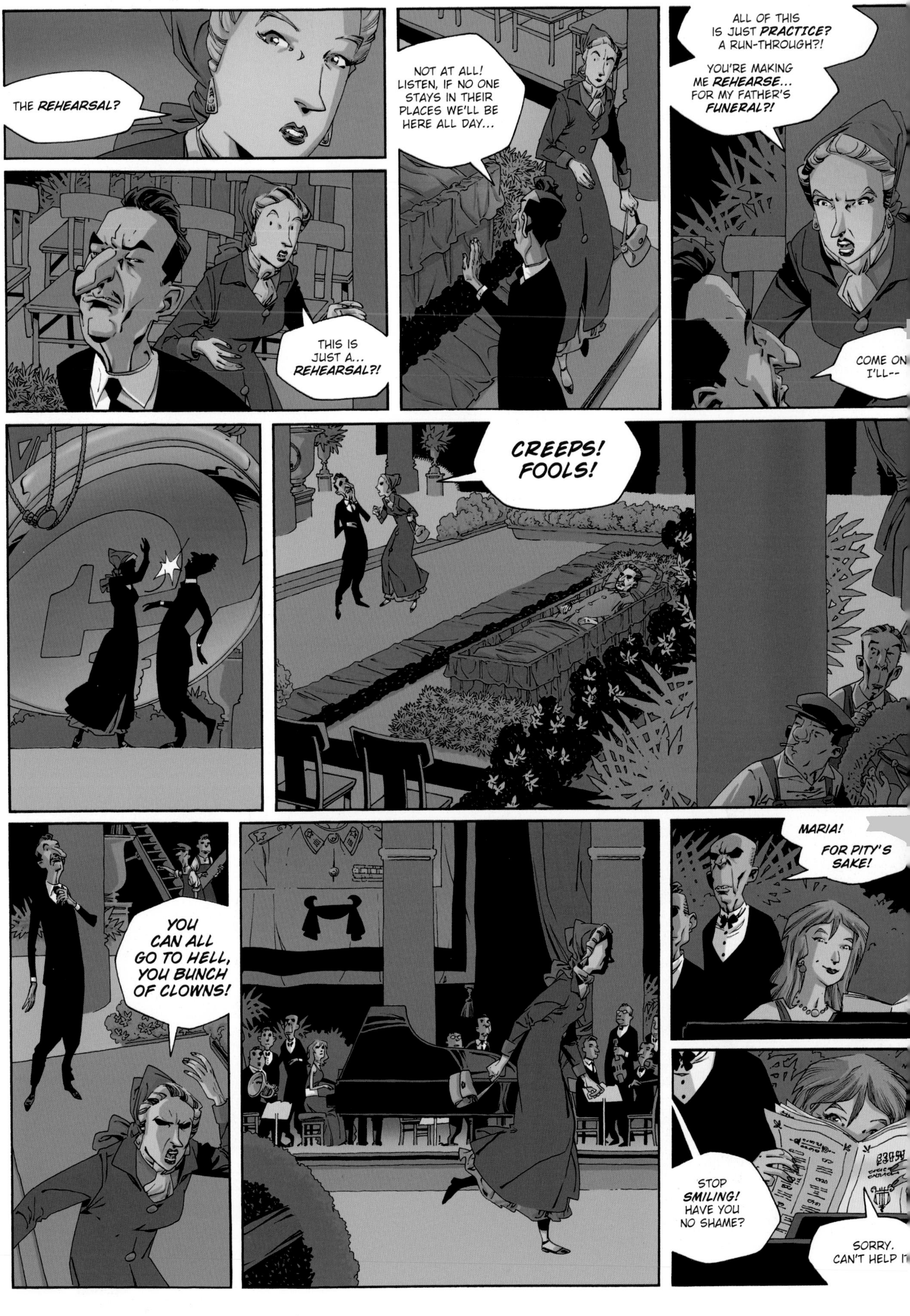
THE REHEARSAL?
THIS IS JUST A... REHEARSAL?!
NOT AT ALL! LISTEN, IF NO ONE STAYS IN THEIR PLACES WE'LL BE HERE ALL DAY...
ALL OF THIS IS JUST PRACTICE? A RUN-THROUGH?!
YOU'RE MAKING ME REHEARSE... FOR MY FATHER'S FUNERAL?!
COME ON I'LL--
CREEPS! FOOLS!
YOU CAN ALL GO TO HELL, YOU BUNCH OF CLOWNS!
MARIA!
FOR PITY'S SAKE!
STOP SMILING! HAVE YOU NO SHAME?
SORRY. CAN'T HELP IT

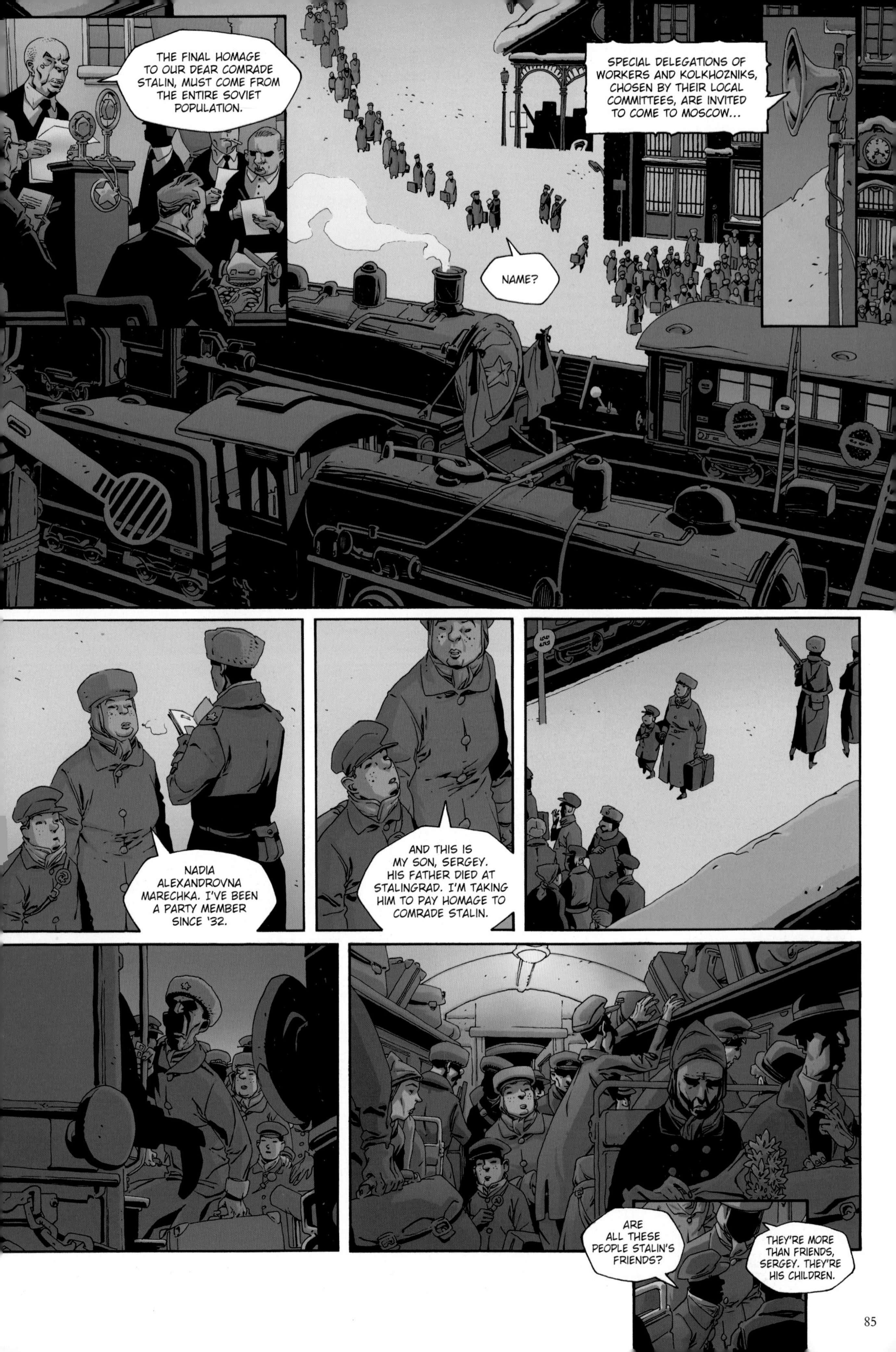
THE FINAL HOMAGE TO OUR DEAR COMRADE STALIN, MUST COME FROM THE ENTIRE SOVIET POPULATION.
SPECIAL DELEGATIONS OF WORKERS AND KOLKHOZNIKS, CHOSEN BY THEIR LOCAL COMMITTEES, ARE INVITED TO COME TO MOSCOW...
NAME?
NADIA ALEXANDROVNA MARECHKA. I'VE BEEN A PARTY MEMBER SINCE '32.
AND THIS IS MY SON, SERGEY. HIS FATHER DIED AT STALINGRAD. I'M TAKING HIM TO PAY HOMAGE TO COMRADE STALIN.
ARE ALL THESE PEOPLE STALIN'S FRIENDS?
THEY'RE MORE THAN FRIENDS, SERGEY. THEY'RE HIS CHILDREN.

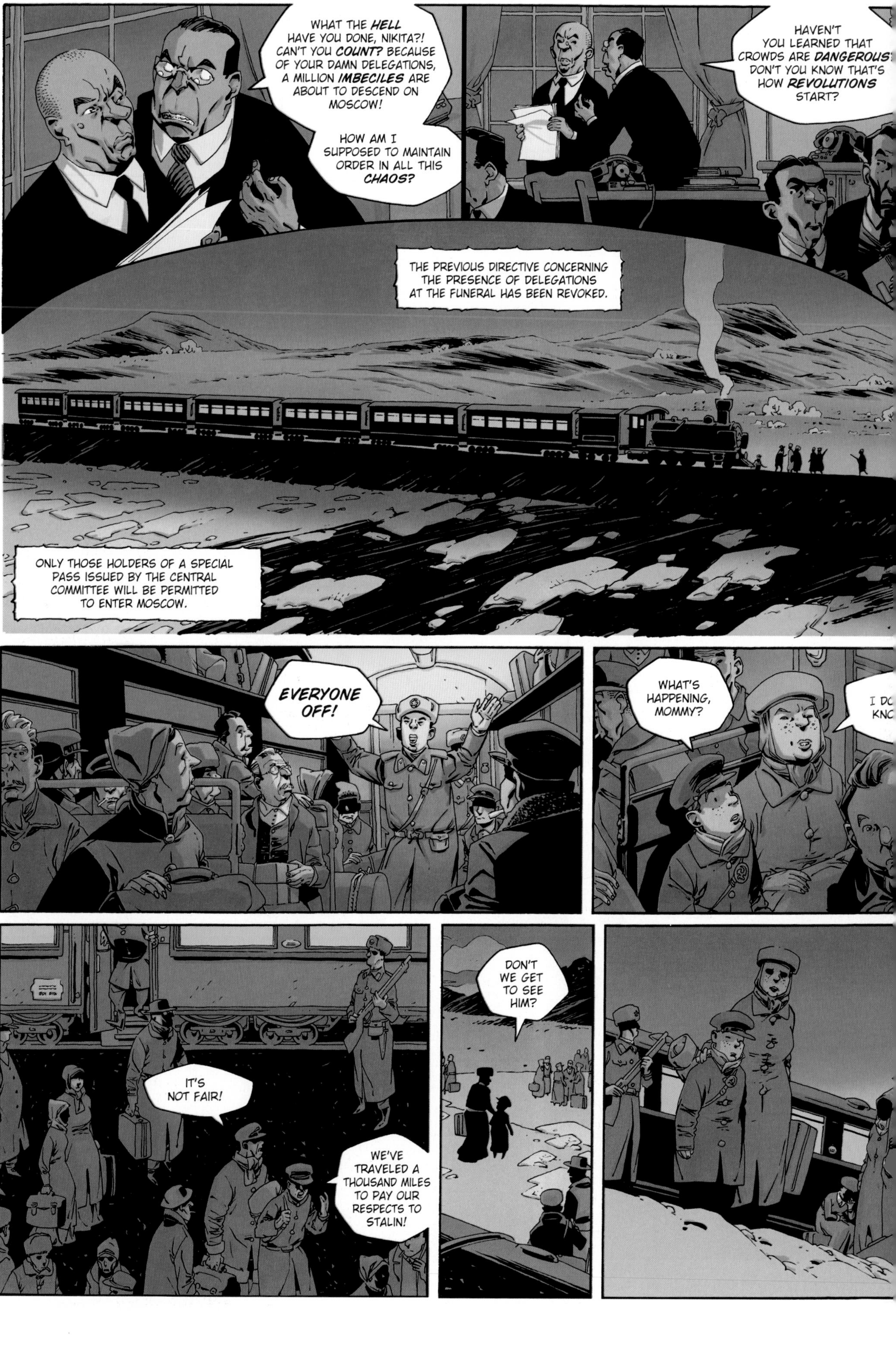
WHAT THE ***HELL*** HAVE YOU DONE, NIKITA?! CAN'T YOU ***COUNT?*** BECAUSE OF YOUR DAMN DELEGATIONS, A MILLION ***IMBECILES*** ARE ABOUT TO DESCEND ON MOSCOW!
HOW AM I SUPPOSED TO MAINTAIN ORDER IN ALL THIS ***CHAOS?***
HAVEN'T YOU LEARNED THAT CROWDS ARE ***DANGEROUS***
DON'T YOU KNOW THAT'S HOW ***REVOLUTIONS*** START?
THE PREVIOUS DIRECTIVE CONCERNING THE PRESENCE OF DELEGATIONS AT THE FUNERAL HAS BEEN REVOKED.
ONLY THOSE HOLDERS OF A SPECIAL PASS ISSUED BY THE CENTRAL COMMITTEE WILL BE PERMITTED TO ENTER MOSCOW.
EVERYONE OFF!
WHAT'S HAPPENING, MOMMY?
IT'S NOT FAIR!
WE'VE TRAVELED A THOUSAND MILES TO PAY OUR RESPECTS TO STALIN!
DON'T WE GET TO SEE HIM?

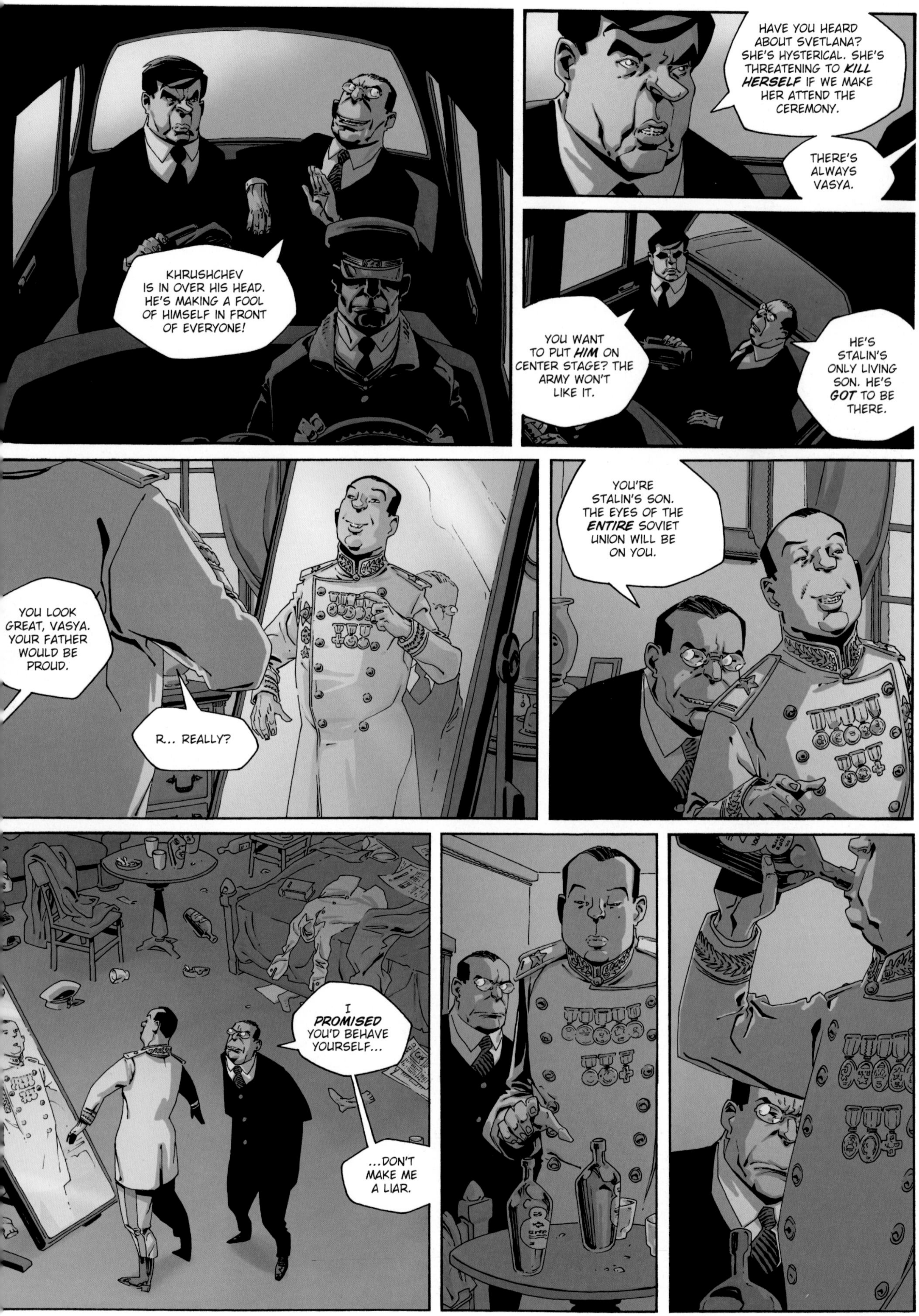
KHRUSHCHEV IS IN OVER HIS HEAD. HE'S MAKING A FOOL OF HIMSELF IN FRONT OF EVERYONE!
HAVE YOU HEARD ABOUT SVETLANA? SHE'S HYSTERICAL. SHE'S THREATENING TO KILL HERSELF IF WE MAKE HER ATTEND THE CEREMONY.
THERE'S ALWAYS VASYA.
YOU WANT TO PUT HIM ON CENTER STAGE? THE ARMY WON'T LIKE IT.
HE'S STALIN'S ONLY LIVING SON. HE'S GOT TO BE THERE.
YOU LOOK GREAT, VASYA. YOUR FATHER WOULD BE PROUD.
R... REALLY?
YOU'RE STALIN'S SON. THE EYES OF THE ENTIRE SOVIET UNION WILL BE ON YOU.
I PROMISED YOU'D BEHAVE YOURSELF...
...DON'T MAKE ME A LIAR.

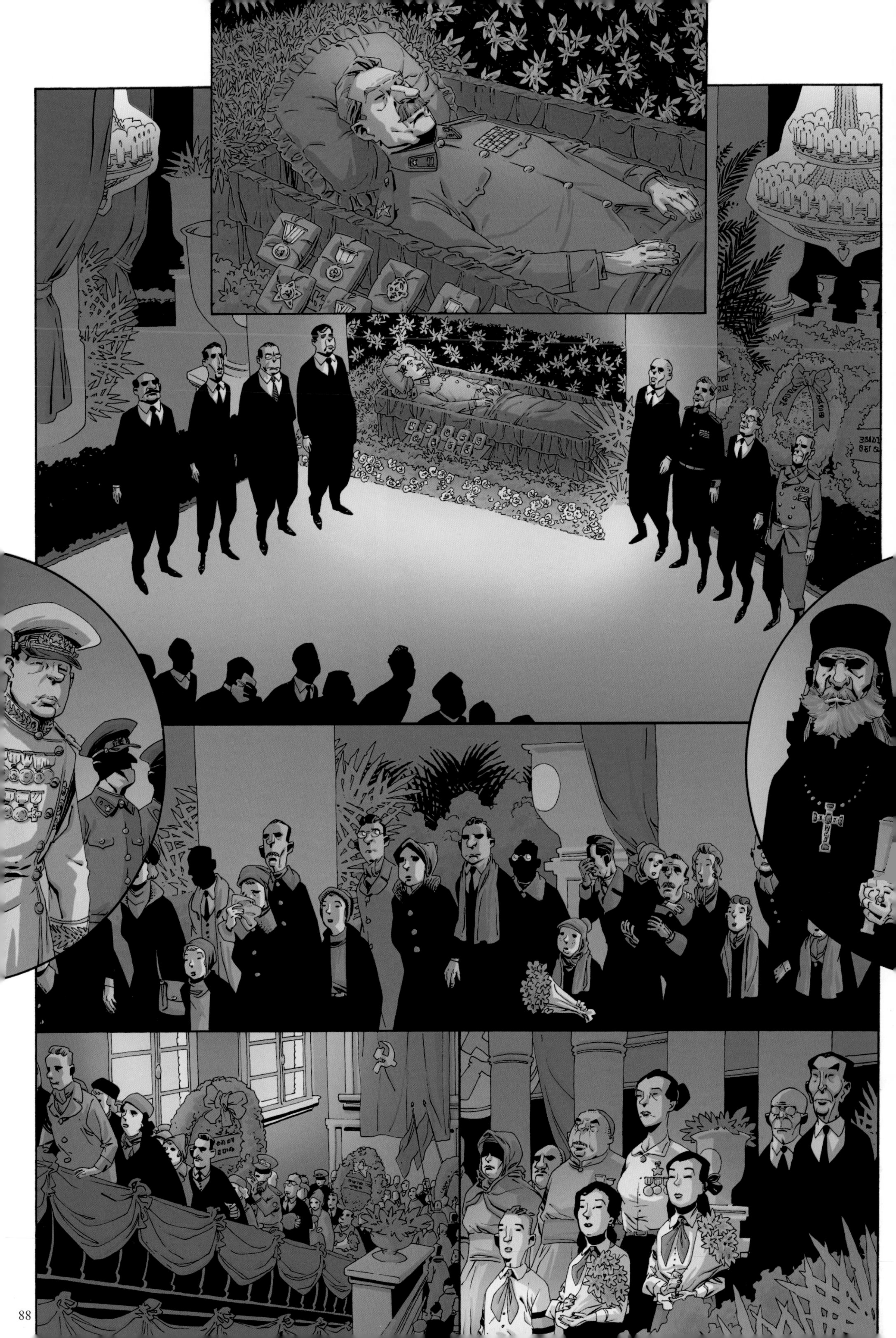

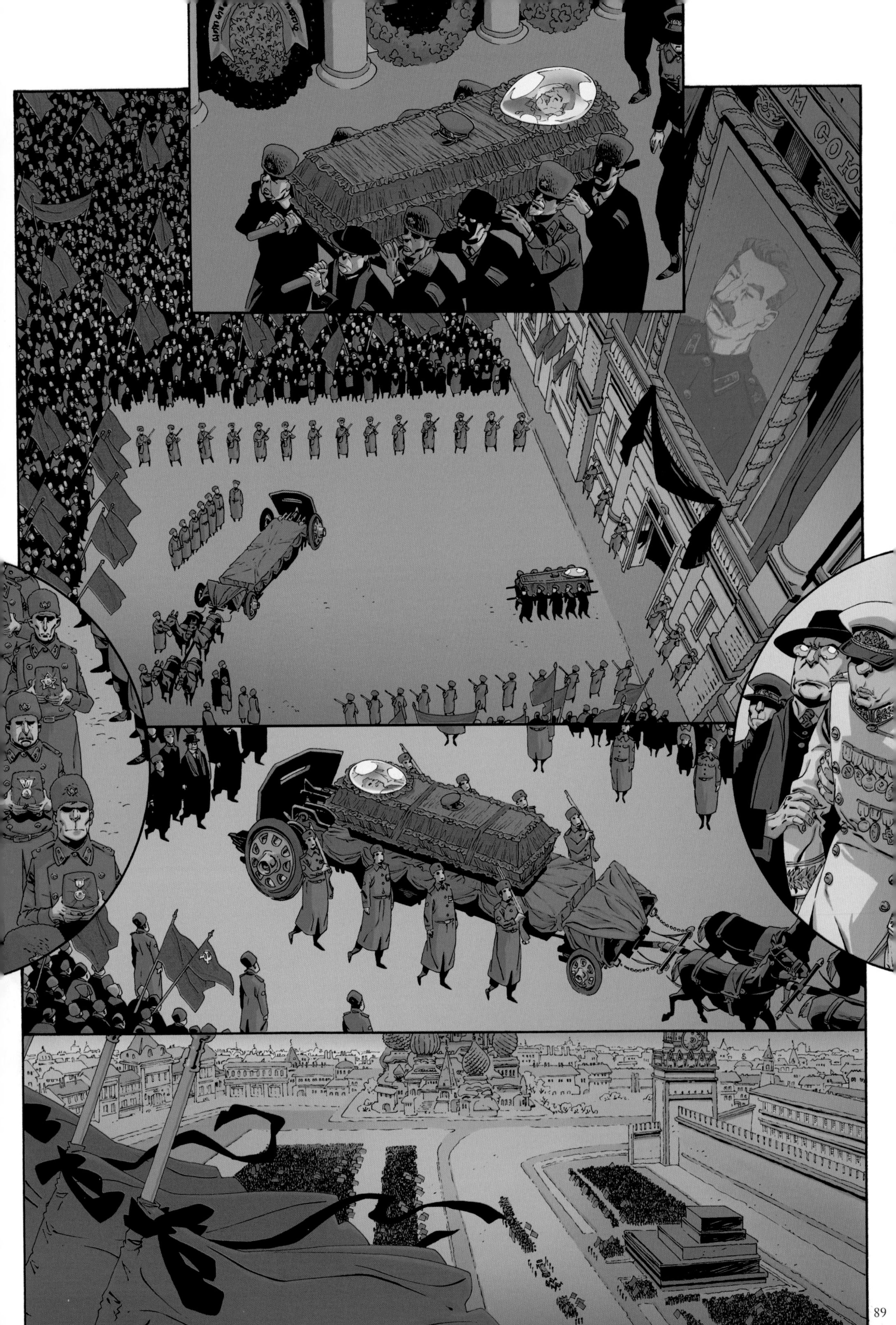

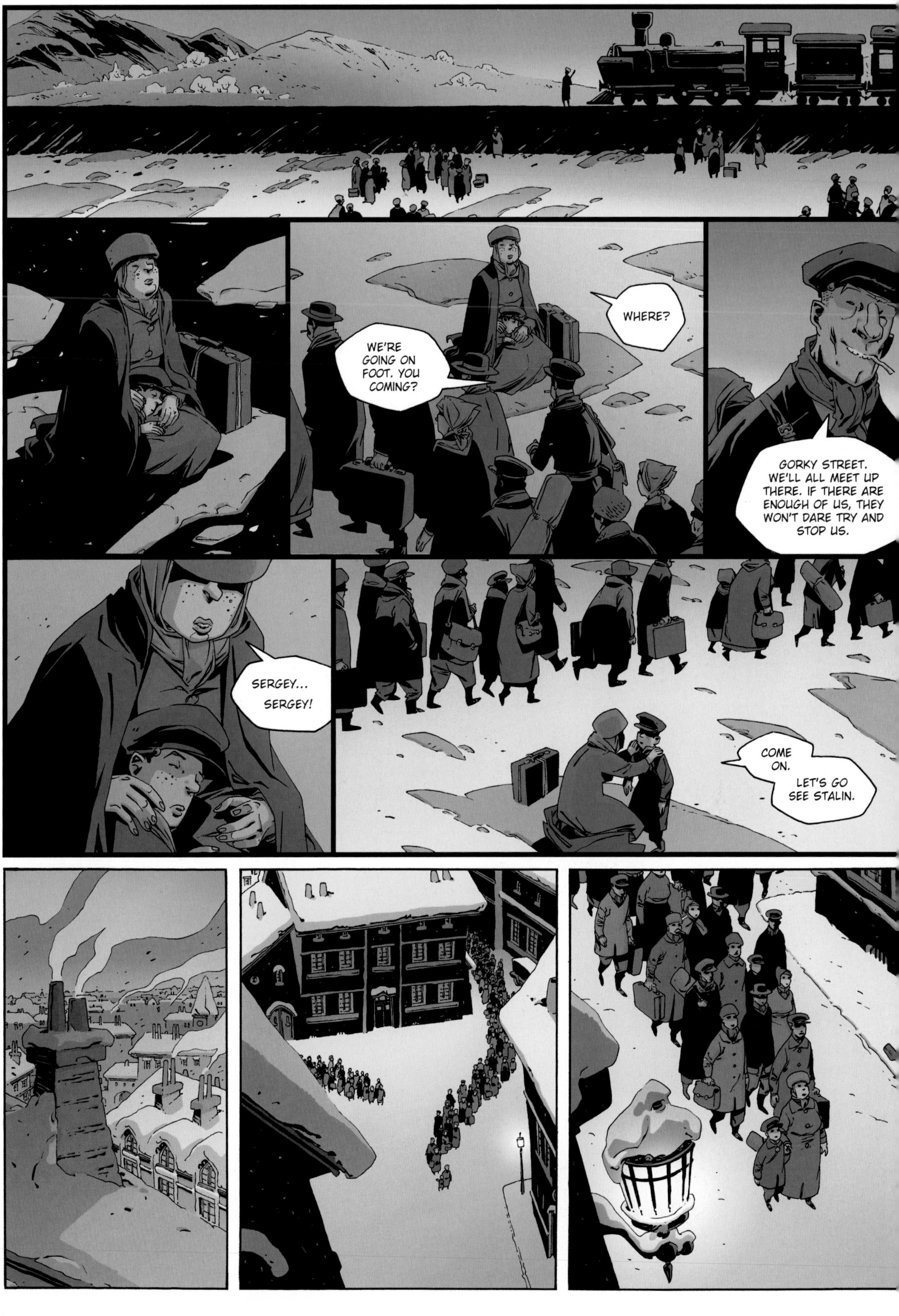
WE'RE GOING ON FOOT. YOU COMING?
WHERE?
GORKY STREET. WE'LL ALL MEET UP THERE. IF THERE ARE ENOUGH OF US, THEY WON'T DARE TRY AND STOP US.
SERGEY... SERGEY!
COME ON.
LET'S GO SEE STALIN.

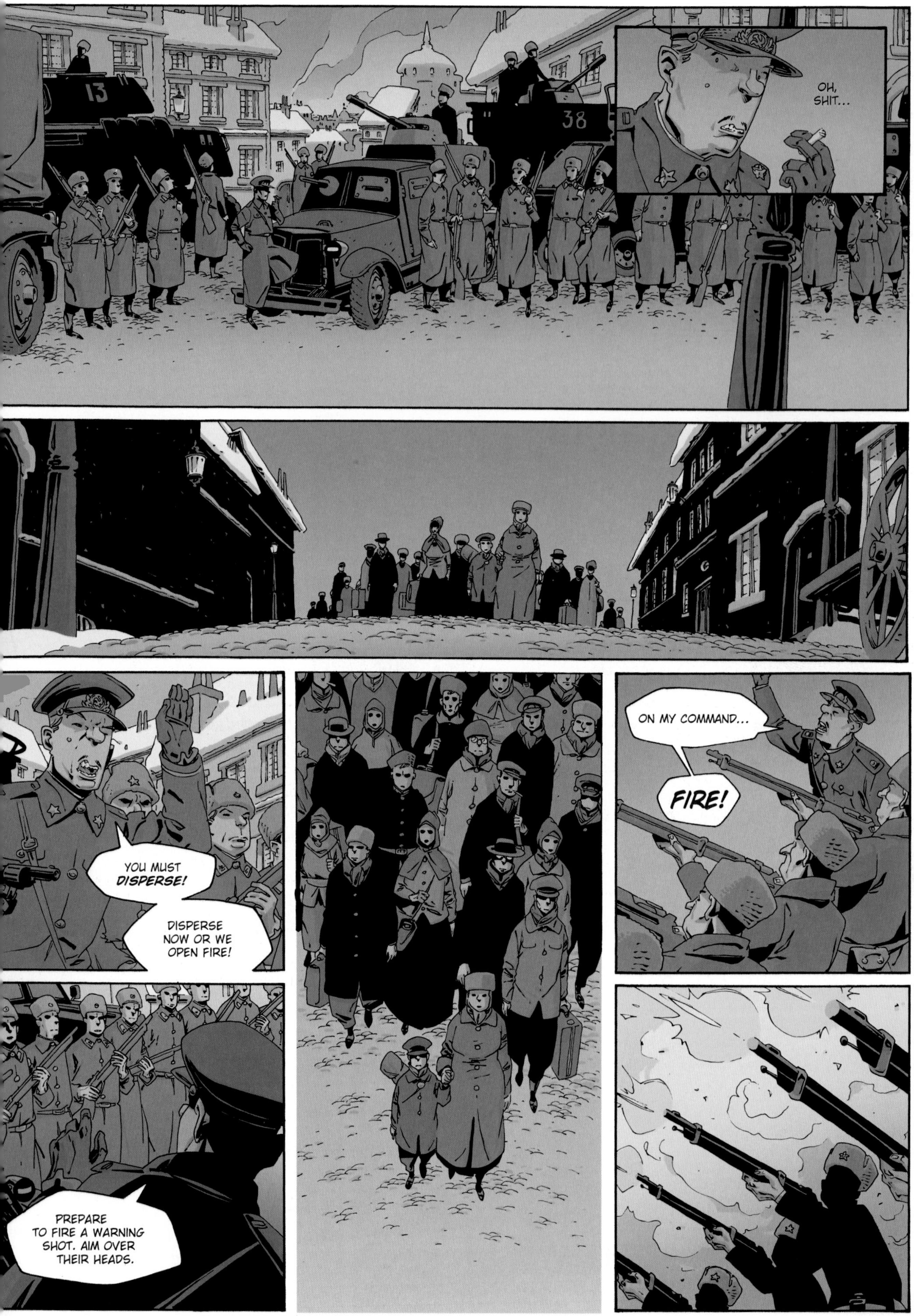
OH, SHIT...
YOU MUST DISPERSE!
DISPERSE NOW OR WE OPEN FIRE!
PREPARE TO FIRE A WARNING SHOT. AIM OVER THEIR HEADS.
ON MY COMMAND...
FIRE!

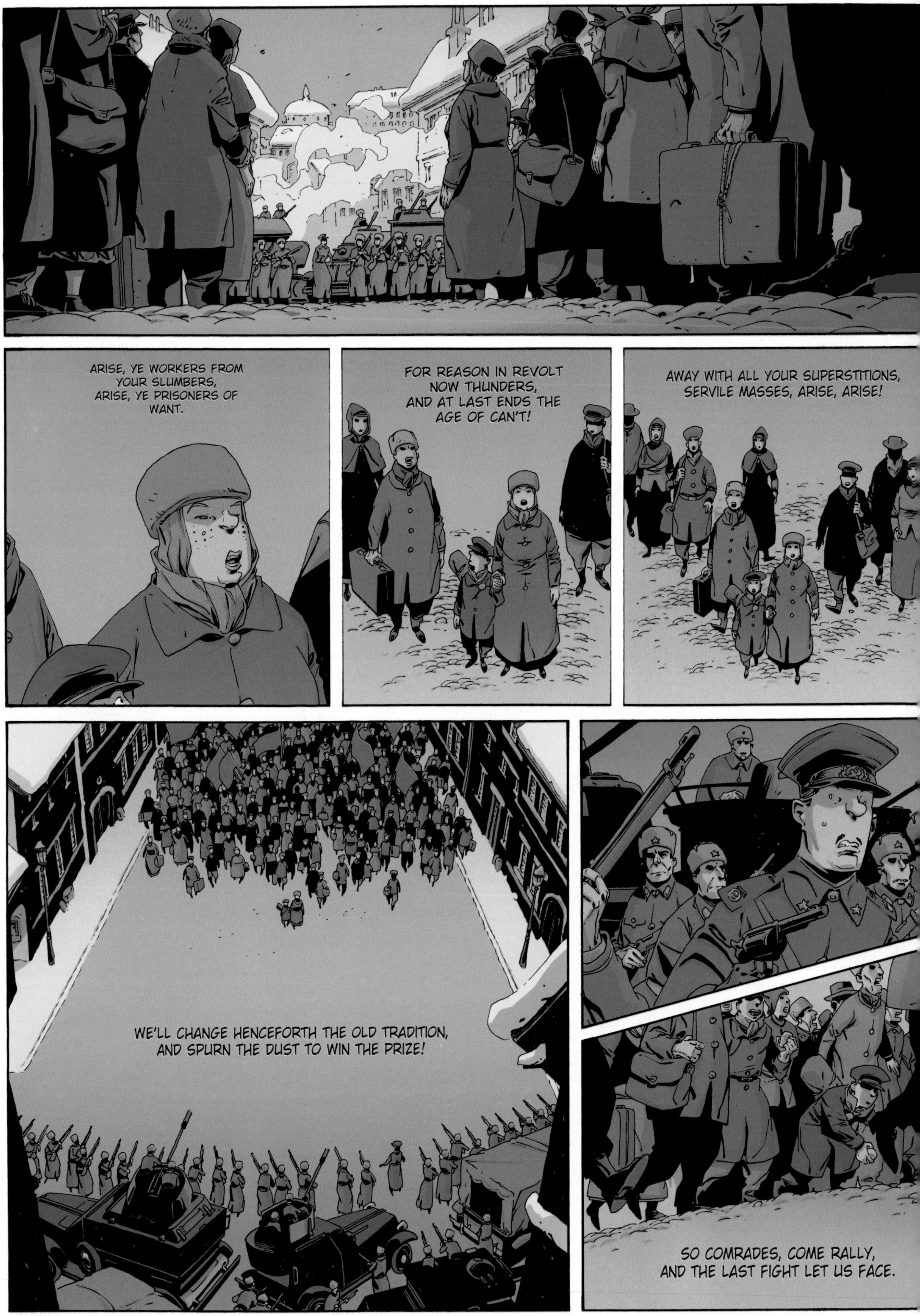

ARISE, YE WORKERS FROM YOUR SLUMBERS, ARISE, YE PRISONERS OF WANT.
FOR REASON IN REVOLT NOW THUNDERS, AND AT LAST ENDS THE AGE OF CAN'T!
AWAY WITH ALL YOUR SUPERSTITIONS, SERVILE MASSES, ARISE, ARISE!
WE'LL CHANGE HENCEFORTH THE OLD TRADITION, AND SPURN THE DUST TO WIN THE PRIZE!
SO COMRADES, COME RALLY, AND THE LAST FIGHT LET US FACE.

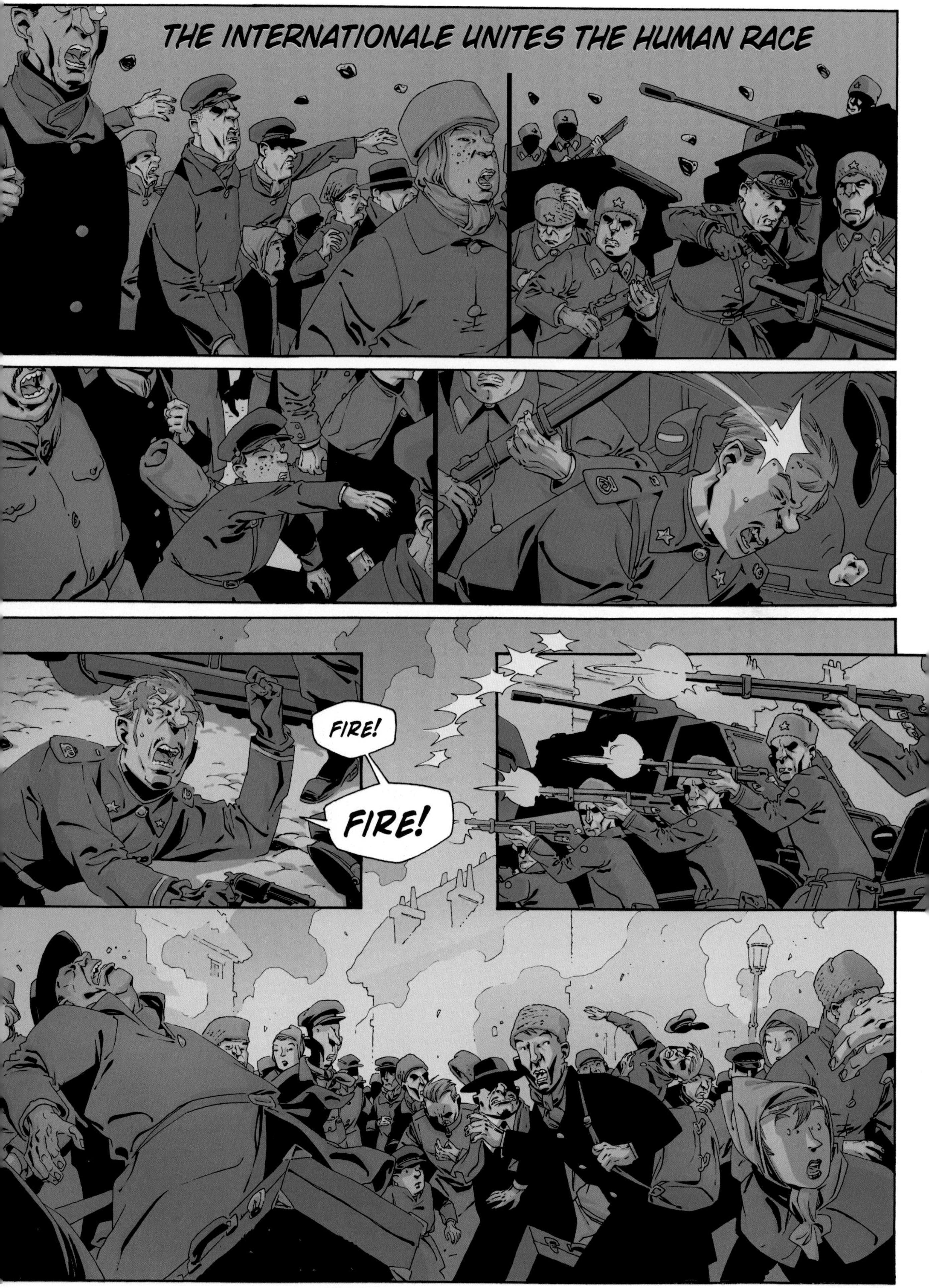
THE INTERNATIONALE UNITES THE HUMAN RACE
FIRE!
FIRE!

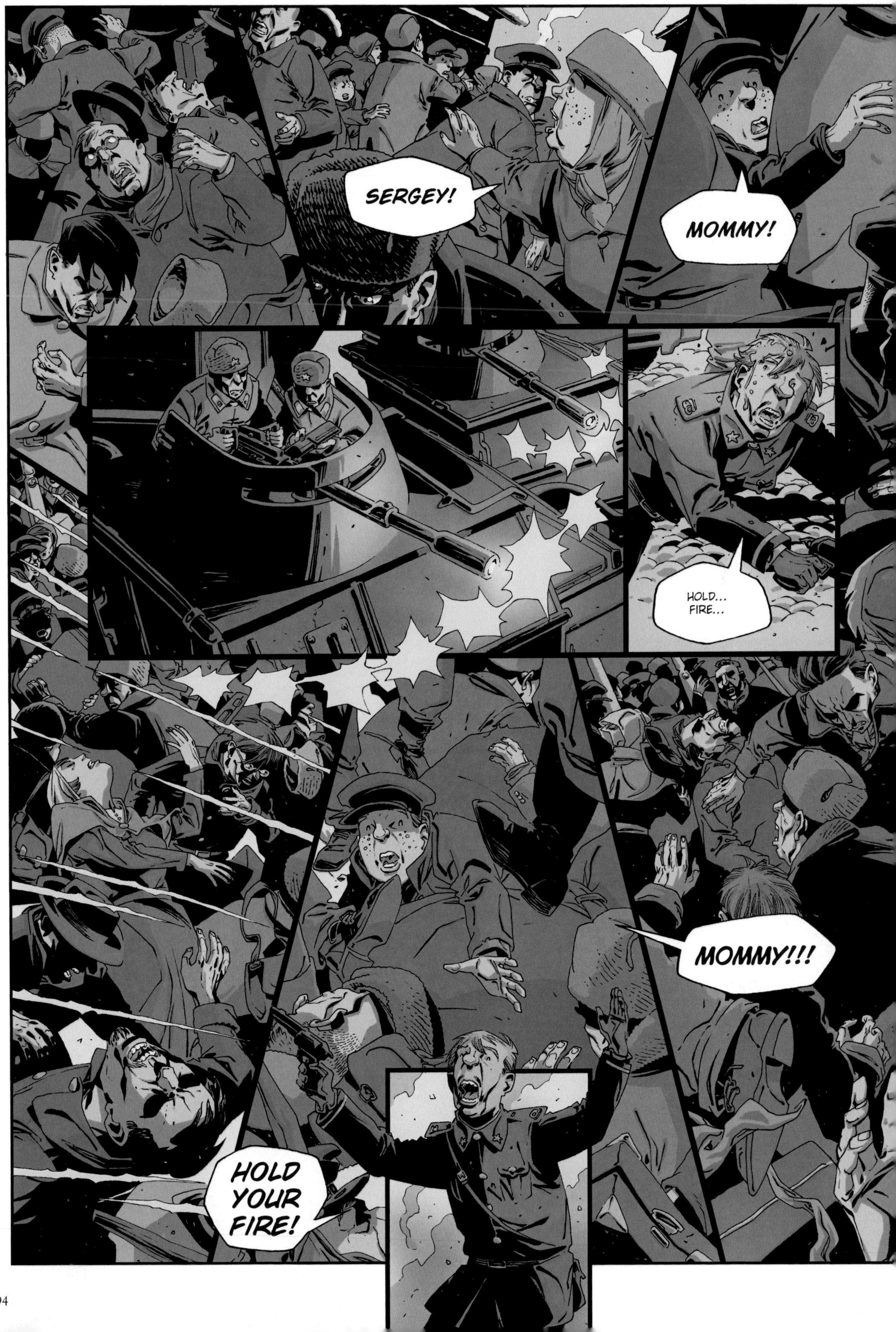
SERGEY!
MOMMY!
HOLD... FIRE...
MOMMY!!!
HOLD YOUR FIRE!

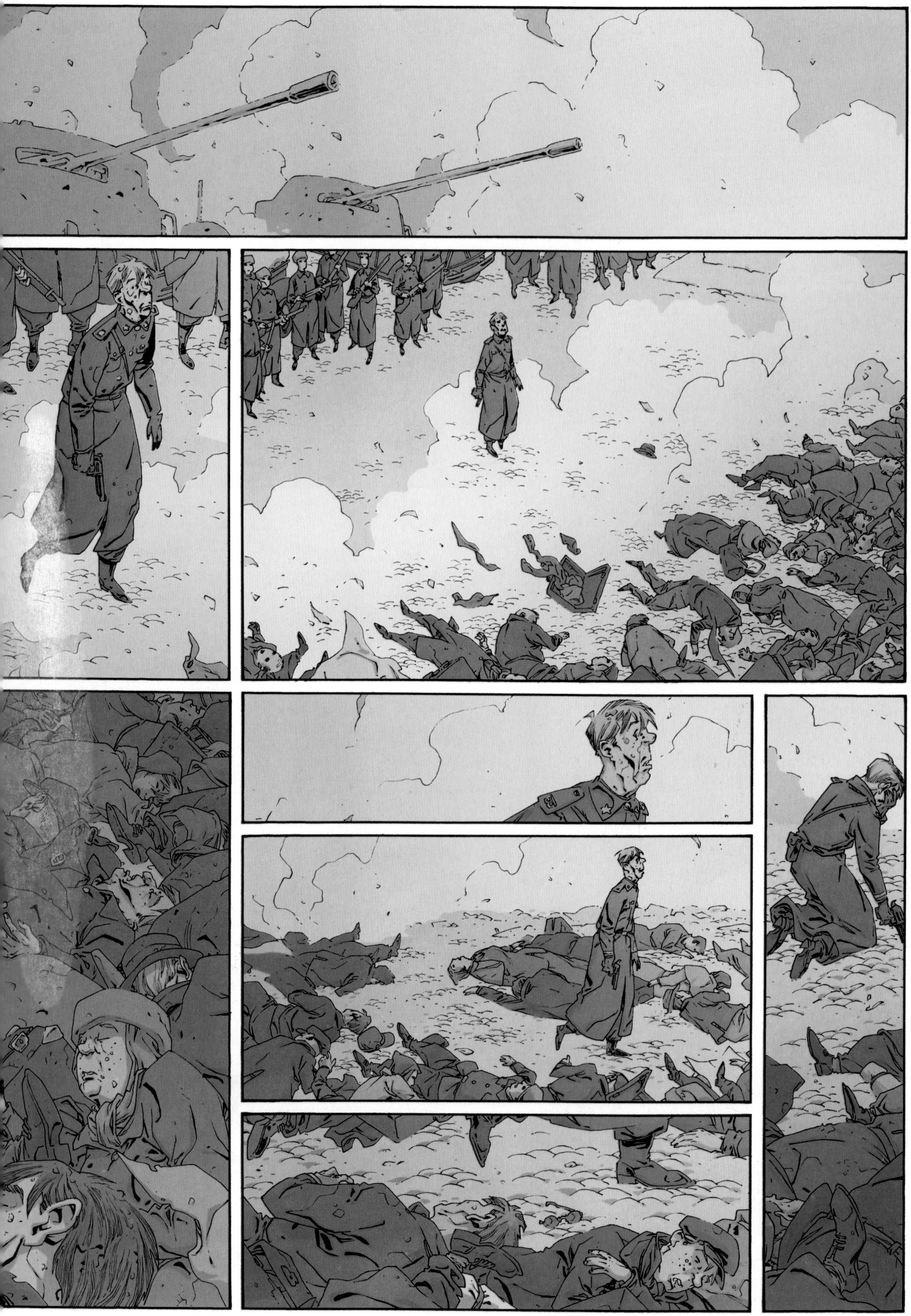

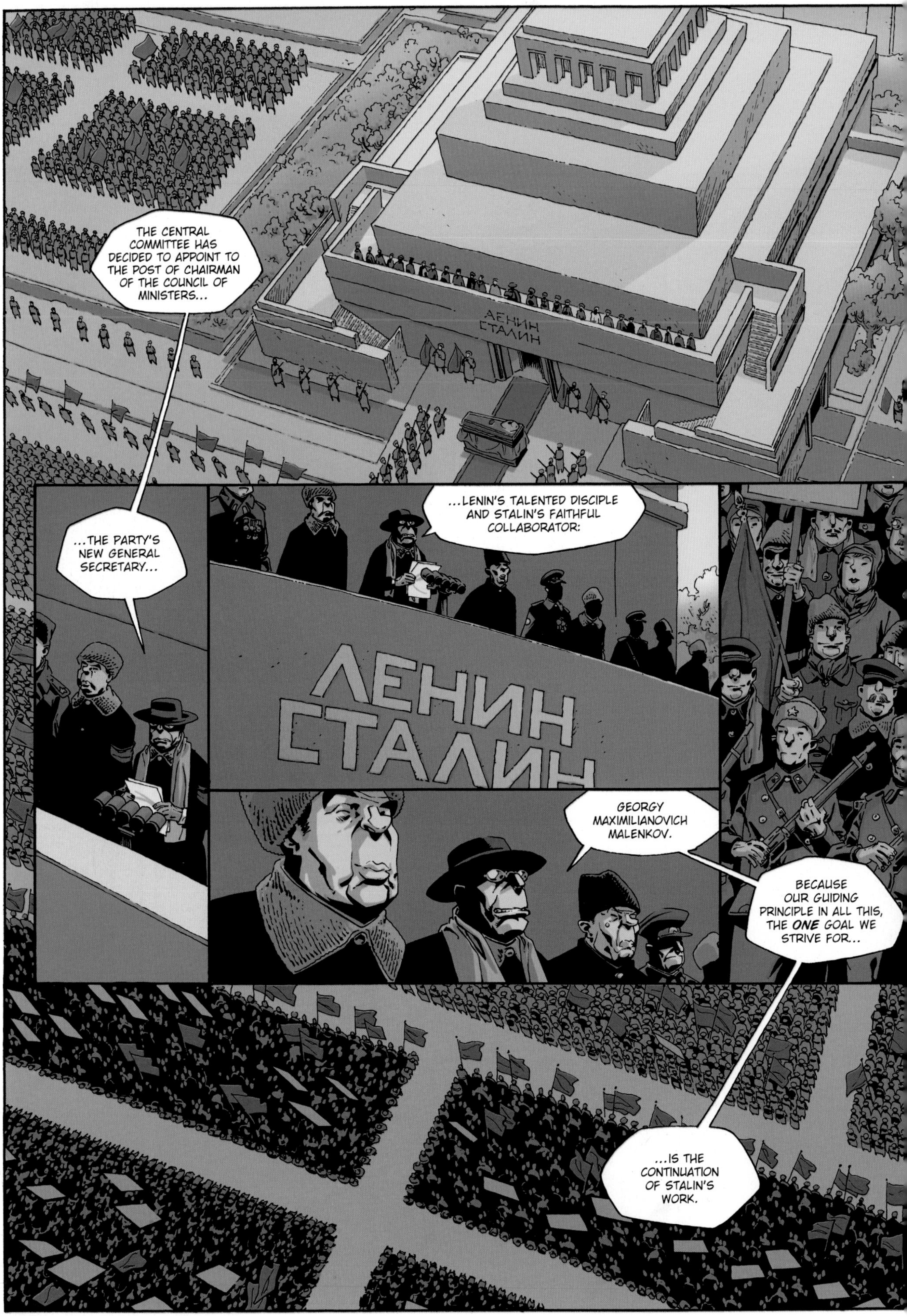
THE CENTRAL COMMITTEE HAS DECIDED TO APPOINT TO THE POST OF CHAIRMAN OF THE COUNCIL OF MINISTERS...
ЛЕНИН СТАЛИН
...THE PARTY'S NEW GENERAL SECRETARY...
...LENIN'S TALENTED DISCIPLE AND STALIN'S FAITHFUL COLLABORATOR:
ЛЕНИН СТАЛИН
GEORGY MAXIMILIANOVICH MALENKOV.
BECAUSE OUR GUIDING PRINCIPLE IN ALL THIS, THE ***ONE*** GOAL WE STRIVE FOR...
...IS THE CONTINUATION OF STALIN'S WORK.

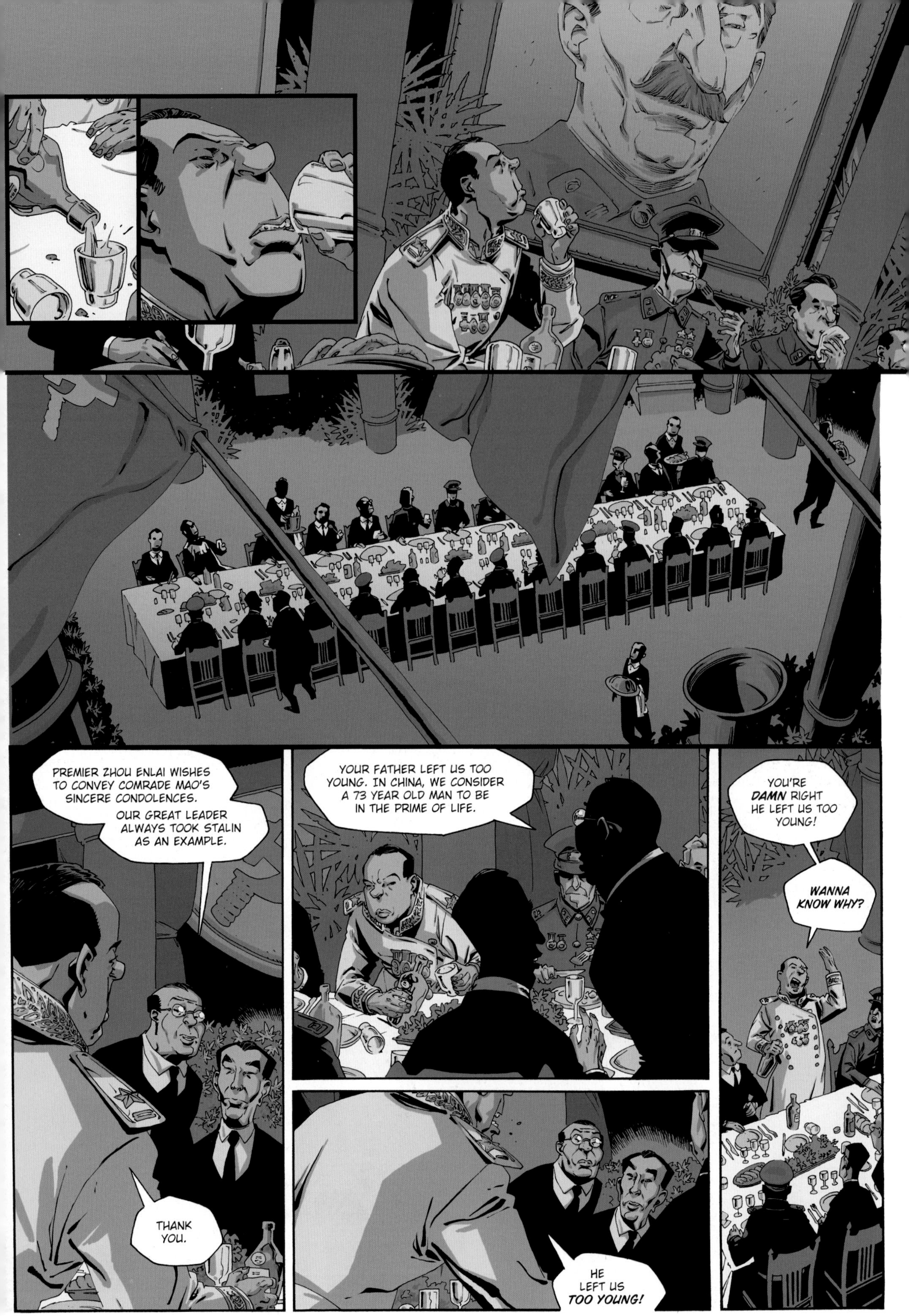
PREMIER ZHOU ENLAI WISHES TO CONVEY COMRADE MAO'S SINCERE CONDOLENCES.
OUR GREAT LEADER ALWAYS TOOK STALIN AS AN EXAMPLE.
THANK YOU.
YOUR FATHER LEFT US TOO YOUNG. IN CHINA, WE CONSIDER A 73 YEAR OLD MAN TO BE IN THE PRIME OF LIFE.
HE LEFT US TOO YOUNG!
YOU'RE DAMN RIGHT HE LEFT US TOO YOUNG!
WANNA KNOW WHY?

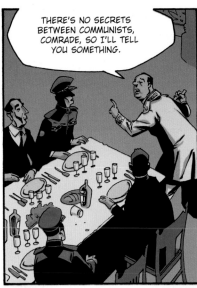

THERE'S NO SECRETS BETWEEN COMMUNISTS, COMRADE, SO I'LL TELL YOU SOMETHING.

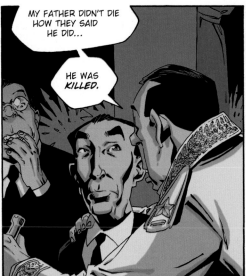

MY FATHER DIDN'T DIE HOW THEY SAID HE DID...

HE WAS *KILLED*.

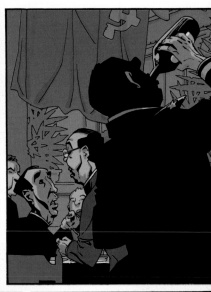

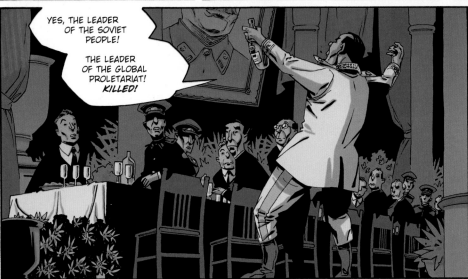

YES, THE LEADER OF THE SOVIET PEOPLE!

THE LEADER OF THE GLOBAL PROLETARIAT! *KILLED!*

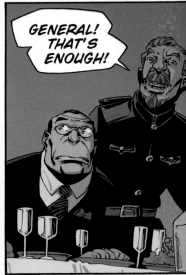

GENERAL! THAT'S ENOUGH!

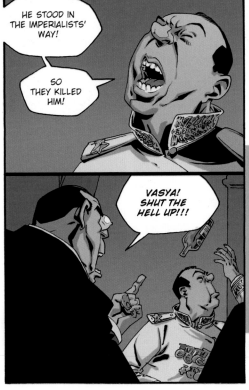

HE STOOD IN THE IMPERIALISTS' WAY!

SO THEY KILLED HIM!

VASYA! SHUT THE HELL UP!!!

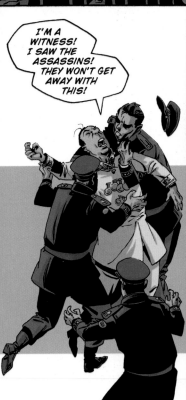

I'M A WITNESS! I SAW THE ASSASSINS! THEY WON'T GET AWAY WITH THIS!

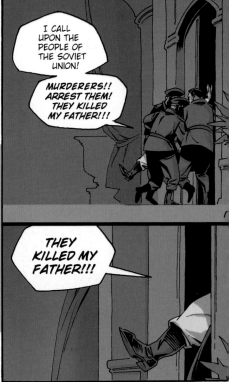

I CALL UPON THE PEOPLE OF THE SOVIET UNION!

MURDERERS!! ARREST THEM! THEY KILLED MY FATHER!!!

THEY KILLED MY FATHER!!!

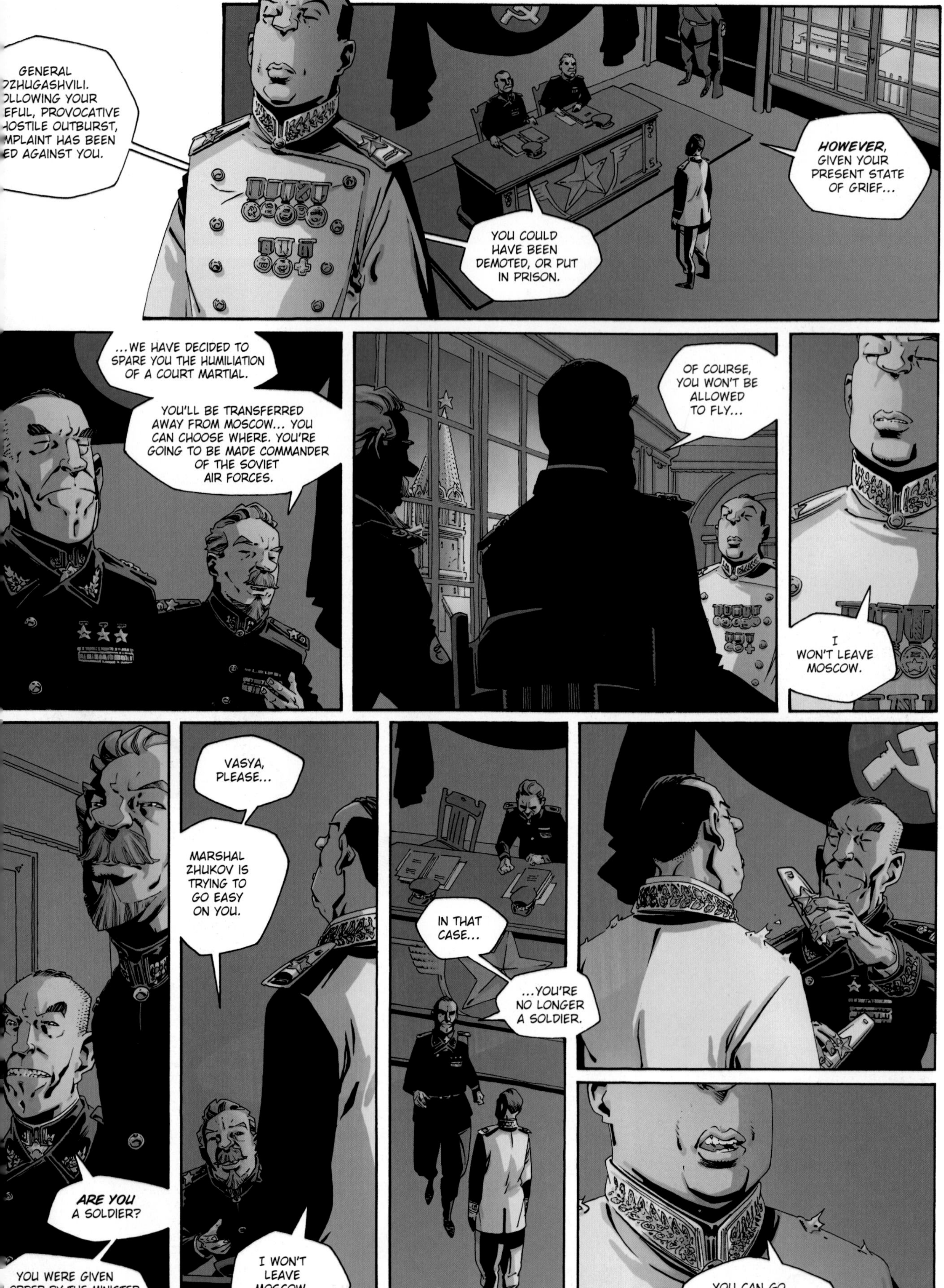
GENERAL
DZHUGASHVILI.
OLLOWING YOUR
EFUL, PROVOCATIVE
HOSTILE OUTBURST,
MPLAINT HAS BEEN
ED AGAINST YOU.
YOU COULD HAVE BEEN DEMOTED, OR PUT IN PRISON.
HOWEVER, GIVEN YOUR PRESENT STATE OF GRIEF...
...WE HAVE DECIDED TO SPARE YOU THE HUMILIATION OF A COURT MARTIAL.
YOU'LL BE TRANSFERRED AWAY FROM MOSCOW... YOU CAN CHOOSE WHERE. YOU'RE GOING TO BE MADE COMMANDER OF THE SOVIET AIR FORCES.
OF COURSE, YOU WON'T BE ALLOWED TO FLY...
I WON'T LEAVE MOSCOW.
ARE YOU A SOLDIER?
YOU WERE GIVEN
ORDER BY THE MINISTER
DEFENSE. IF YOU'RE A
OLDIER, YOU WILL OBEY
THIS ORDER.
VASYA, PLEASE...
MARSHAL ZHUKOV IS TRYING TO GO EASY ON YOU.
I WON'T LEAVE MOSCOW.
IN THAT CASE...
...YOU'RE NO LONGER A SOLDIER.
YOU CAN GO TO HELL, ZHUKOV. I WON'T LEAVE MOSCOW.

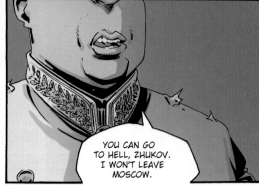

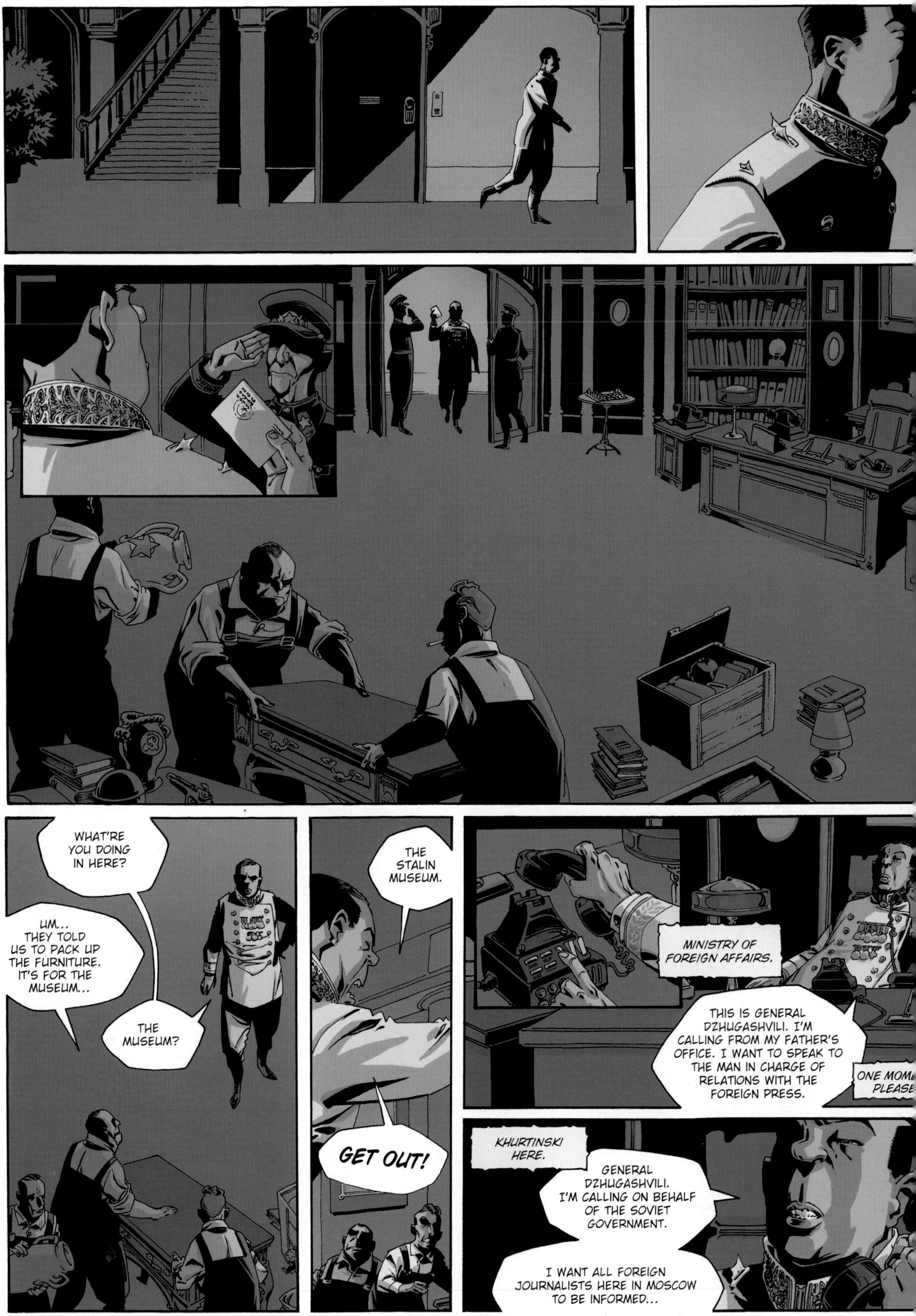
WHAT'RE YOU DOING IN HERE?
UM... THEY TOLD US TO PACK UP THE FURNITURE. IT'S FOR THE MUSEUM...
THE MUSEUM?
THE STALIN MUSEUM.
GET OUT!
MINISTRY OF FOREIGN AFFAIRS.
THIS IS GENERAL DZHUGASHVILI. I'M CALLING FROM MY FATHER'S OFFICE. I WANT TO SPEAK TO THE MAN IN CHARGE OF RELATIONS WITH THE FOREIGN PRESS.
ONE MOM PLEASE
KHURTINSKI HERE.
GENERAL DZHUGASHVILI. I'M CALLING ON BEHALF OF THE SOVIET GOVERNMENT.
I WANT ALL FOREIGN JOURNALISTS HERE IN MOSCOW TO BE INFORMED...

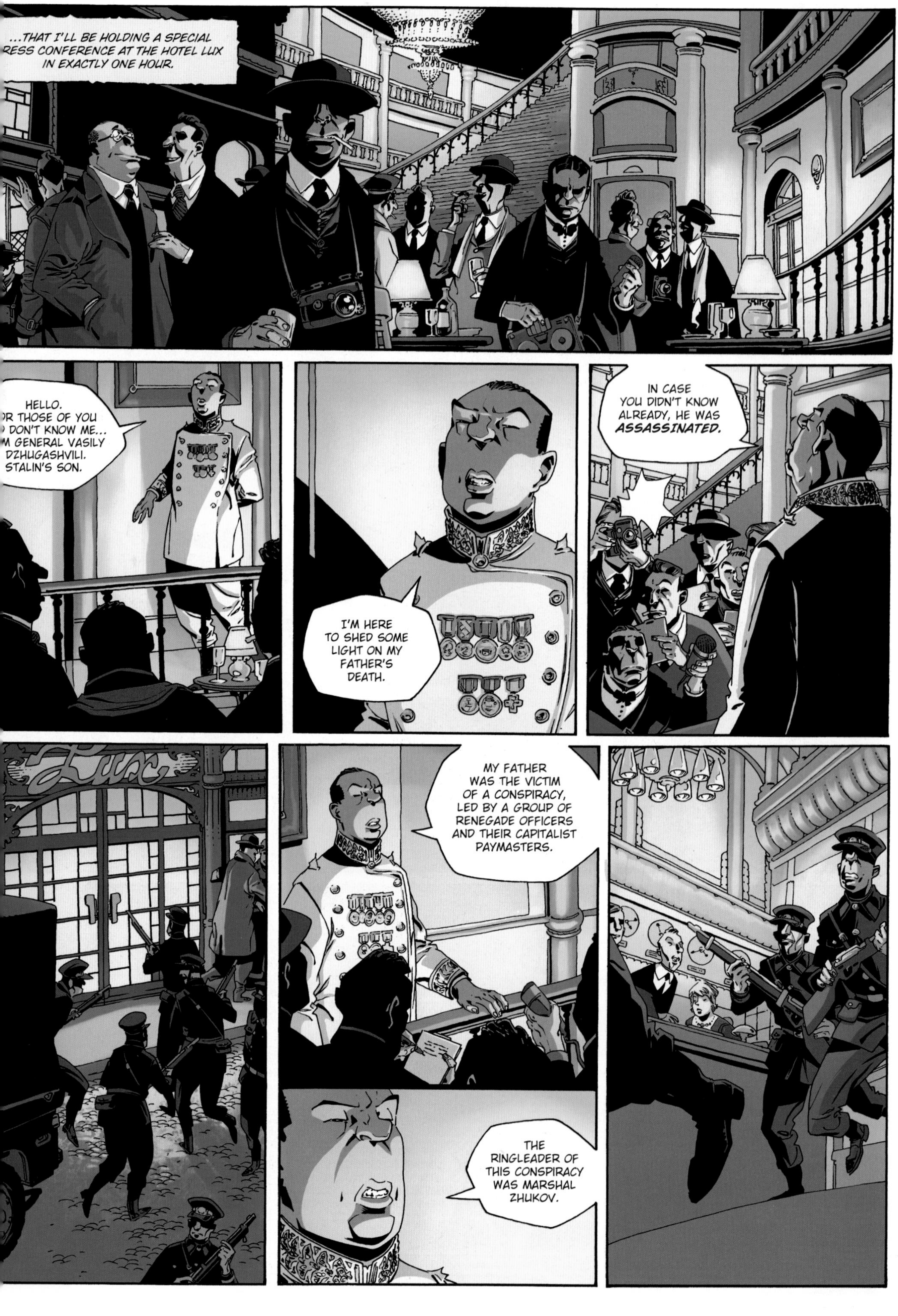
...THAT I'LL BE HOLDING A SPECIAL RESS CONFERENCE AT THE HOTEL LUX IN EXACTLY ONE HOUR.
HELLO. OR THOSE OF YOU D DON'T KNOW ME... M GENERAL VASILY DZHUGASHVILI. STALIN'S SON.
I'M HERE TO SHED SOME LIGHT ON MY FATHER'S DEATH.
IN CASE YOU DIDN'T KNOW ALREADY, HE WAS ASSASSINATED.
MY FATHER WAS THE VICTIM OF A CONSPIRACY, LED BY A GROUP OF RENEGADE OFFICERS AND THEIR CAPITALIST PAYMASTERS.
THE RINGLEADER OF THIS CONSPIRACY WAS MARSHAL ZHUKOV.

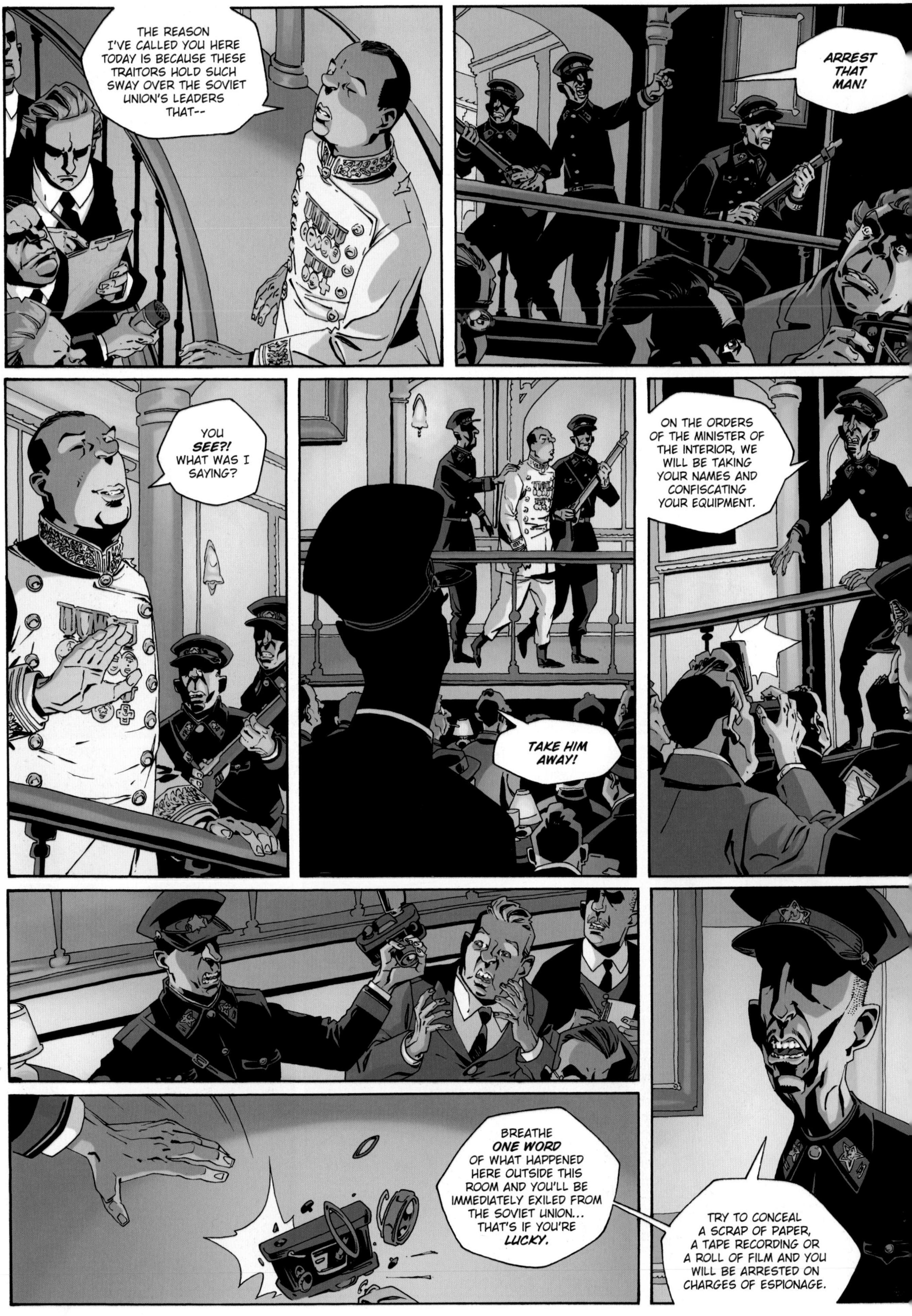
THE REASON I'VE CALLED YOU HERE TODAY IS BECAUSE THESE TRAITORS HOLD SUCH SWAY OVER THE SOVIET UNION'S LEADERS THAT--
ARREST THAT MAN!
YOU SEE?! WHAT WAS I SAYING?
TAKE HIM AWAY!
ON THE ORDERS OF THE MINISTER OF THE INTERIOR, WE WILL BE TAKING YOUR NAMES AND CONFISCATING YOUR EQUIPMENT.
BREATHE ONE WORD OF WHAT HAPPENED HERE OUTSIDE THIS ROOM AND YOU'LL BE IMMEDIATELY EXILED FROM THE SOVIET UNION... THAT'S IF YOU'RE LUCKY.
TRY TO CONCEAL A SCRAP OF PAPER, A TAPE RECORDING OR A ROLL OF FILM AND YOU WILL BE ARRESTED ON CHARGES OF ESPIONAGE.

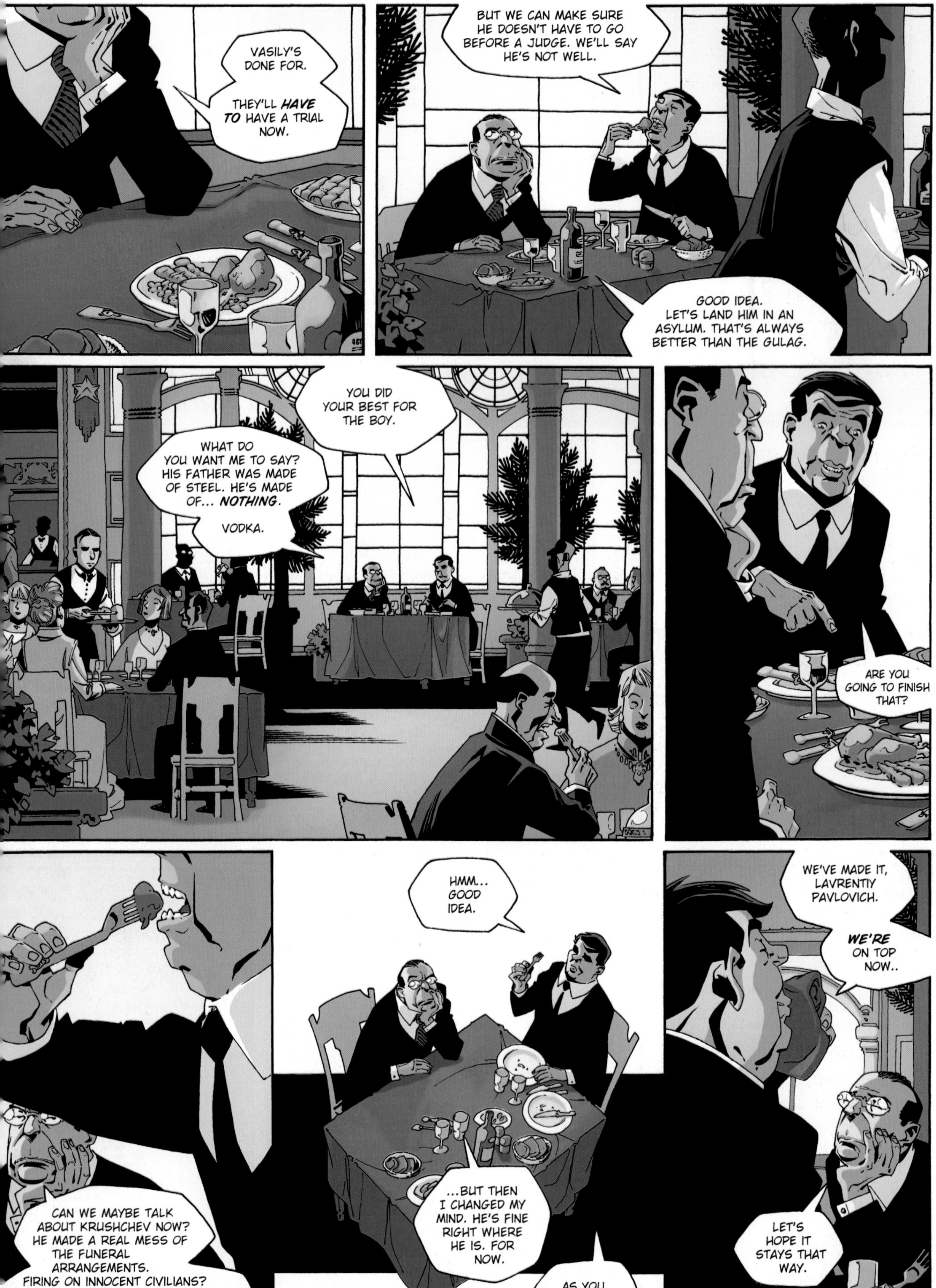
VASILY'S DONE FOR.
THEY'LL **HAVE TO** HAVE A TRIAL NOW.
BUT WE CAN MAKE SURE HE DOESN'T HAVE TO GO BEFORE A JUDGE. WE'LL SAY HE'S NOT WELL.
GOOD IDEA. LET'S LAND HIM IN AN ASYLUM. THAT'S ALWAYS BETTER THAN THE GULAG.
YOU DID YOUR BEST FOR THE BOY.
WHAT DO YOU WANT ME TO SAY? HIS FATHER WAS MADE OF STEEL. HE'S MADE OF... **NOTHING**.
VODKA.
ARE YOU GOING TO FINISH THAT?
CAN WE MAYBE TALK ABOUT KRUSHCHEV NOW? HE MADE A REAL MESS OF THE FUNERAL ARRANGEMENTS.
FIRING ON INNOCENT CIVILIANS? IT'S **SHOCKING!** I THOUGHT WE COULD HAVE HIM KICKED OFF THE COMMITTEE FOR INCOMPETENCE...
HMM... GOOD IDEA.
...BUT THEN I CHANGED MY MIND. HE'S FINE RIGHT WHERE HE IS. FOR NOW.
AS YOU WISH.
WE'VE MADE IT, LAVRENTIY PAVLOVICH.
WE'RE ON TOP NOW..
LET'S HOPE IT STAYS THAT WAY.

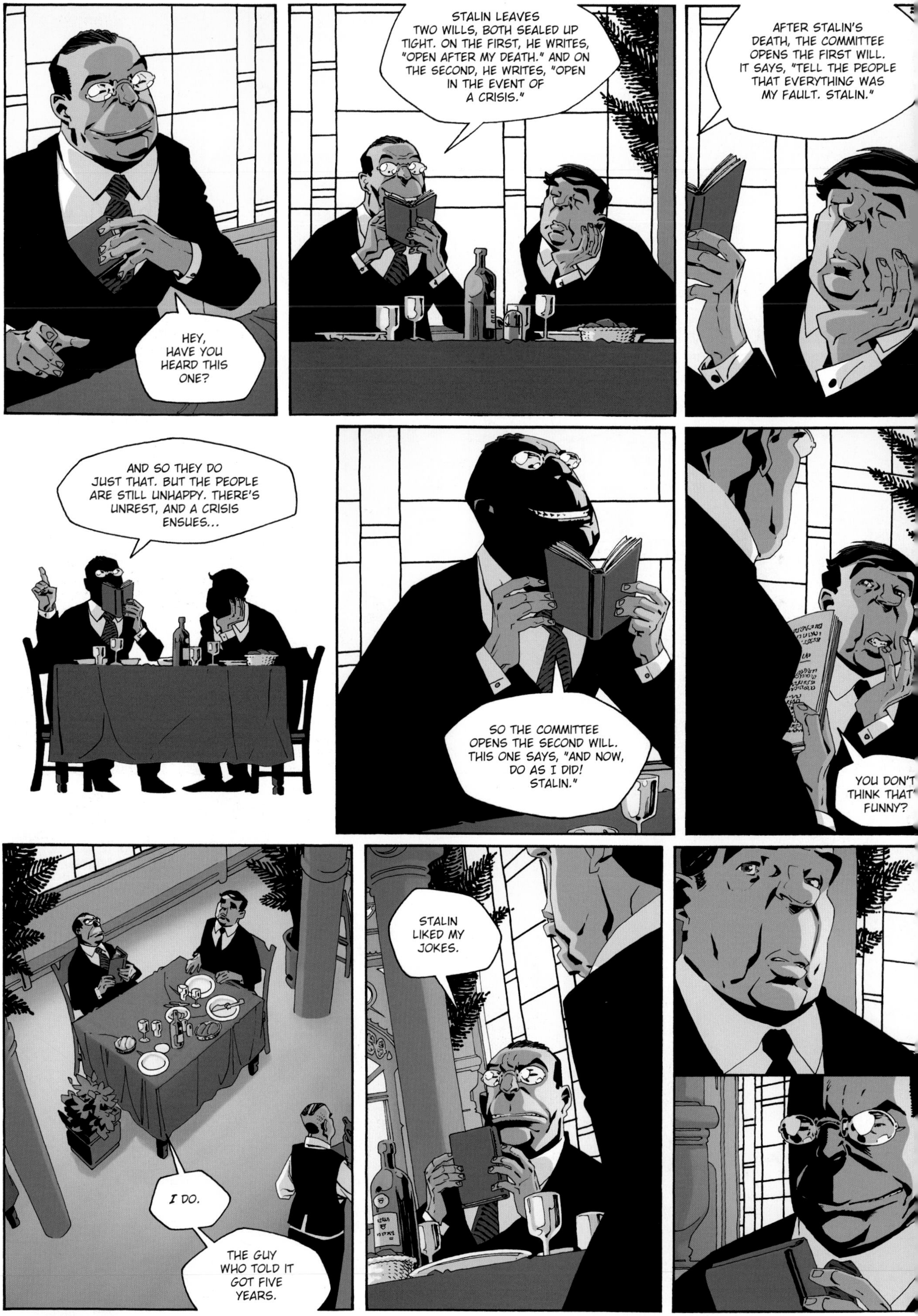
HEY, HAVE YOU HEARD THIS ONE?
STALIN LEAVES TWO WILLS, BOTH SEALED UP TIGHT. ON THE FIRST, HE WRITES, "OPEN AFTER MY DEATH." AND ON THE SECOND, HE WRITES, "OPEN IN THE EVENT OF A CRISIS."
AFTER STALIN'S DEATH, THE COMMITTEE OPENS THE FIRST WILL. IT SAYS, "TELL THE PEOPLE THAT EVERYTHING WAS MY FAULT. STALIN."
AND SO THEY DO JUST THAT. BUT THE PEOPLE ARE STILL UNHAPPY. THERE'S UNREST, AND A CRISIS ENSUES...
SO THE COMMITTEE OPENS THE SECOND WILL. THIS ONE SAYS, "AND NOW, DO AS I DID! STALIN."
YOU DON'T THINK THAT FUNNY?
I DO.
THE GUY WHO TOLD IT GOT FIVE YEARS.
STALIN LIKED MY JOKES.

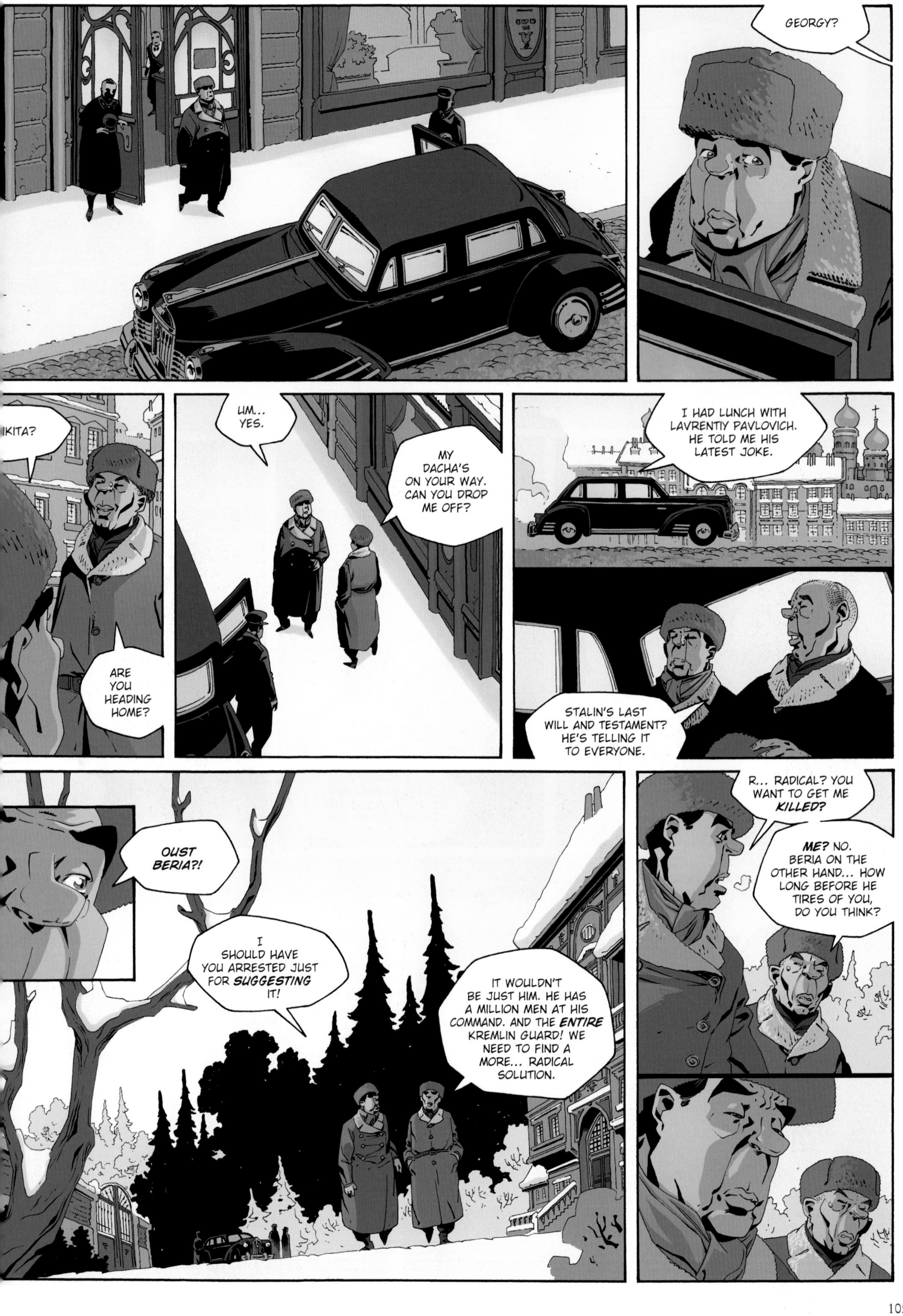
GEORGY?
...KITA?
ARE YOU HEADING HOME?
UM... YES.
MY DACHA'S ON YOUR WAY. CAN YOU DROP ME OFF?
I HAD LUNCH WITH LAVRENTIY PAVLOVICH. HE TOLD ME HIS LATEST JOKE.
STALIN'S LAST WILL AND TESTAMENT? HE'S TELLING IT TO EVERYONE.
OUST BERIA?!
I SHOULD HAVE YOU ARRESTED JUST FOR SUGGESTING IT!
IT WOULDN'T BE JUST HIM. HE HAS A MILLION MEN AT HIS COMMAND. AND THE ENTIRE KREMLIN GUARD! WE NEED TO FIND A MORE... RADICAL SOLUTION.
R... RADICAL? YOU WANT TO GET ME KILLED?
ME? NO. BERIA ON THE OTHER HAND... HOW LONG BEFORE HE TIRES OF YOU, DO YOU THINK?

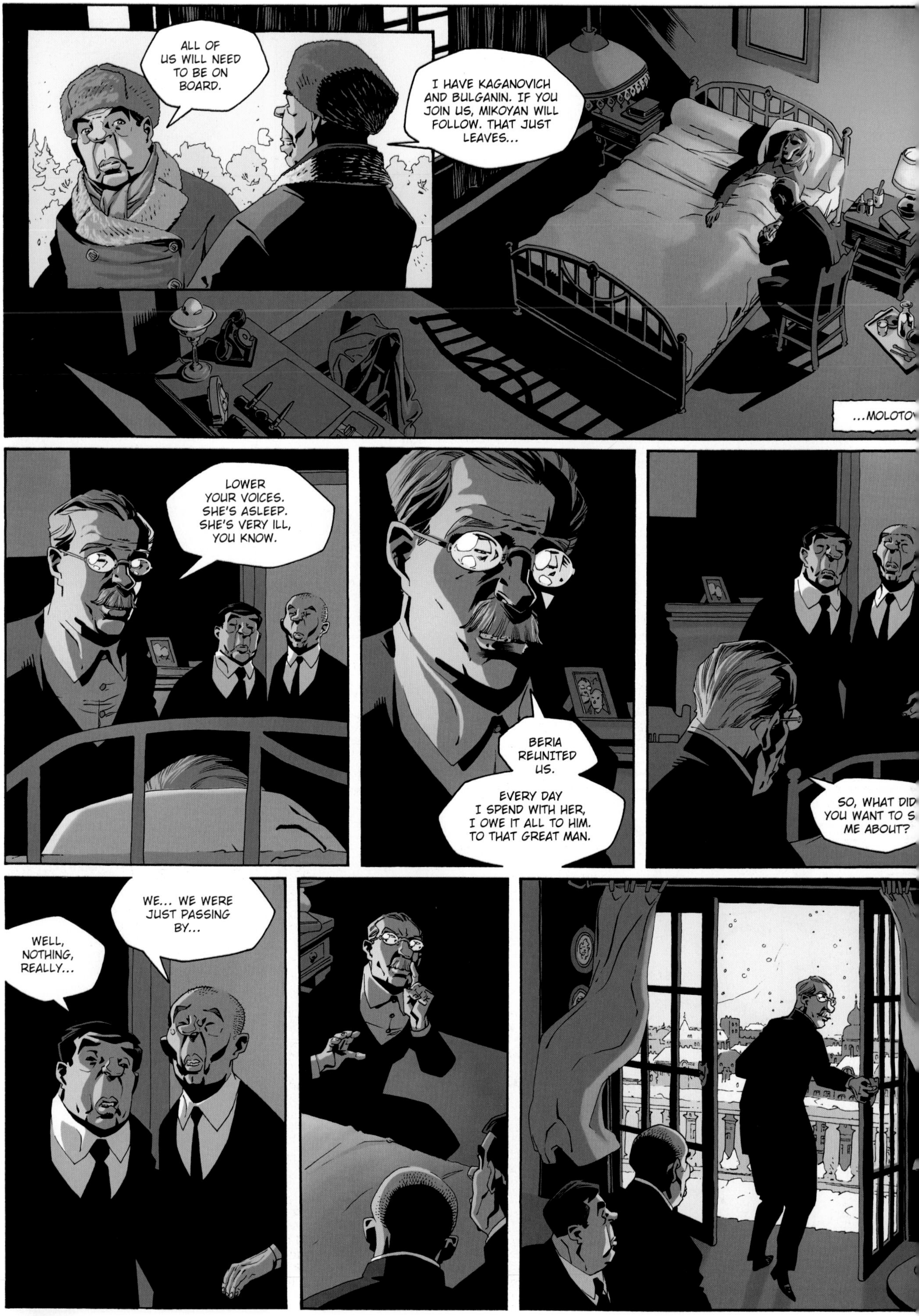
ALL OF US WILL NEED TO BE ON BOARD.
I HAVE KAGANOVICH AND BULGANIN. IF YOU JOIN US, MIKOYAN WILL FOLLOW. THAT JUST LEAVES...
...MOLOTO
LOWER YOUR VOICES. SHE'S ASLEEP. SHE'S VERY ILL, YOU KNOW.
BERIA REUNITED US.
EVERY DAY I SPEND WITH HER, I OWE IT ALL TO HIM. TO THAT GREAT MAN.
SO, WHAT DID YOU WANT TO S ME ABOUT?
WELL, NOTHING, REALLY...
WE... WE WERE JUST PASSING BY...

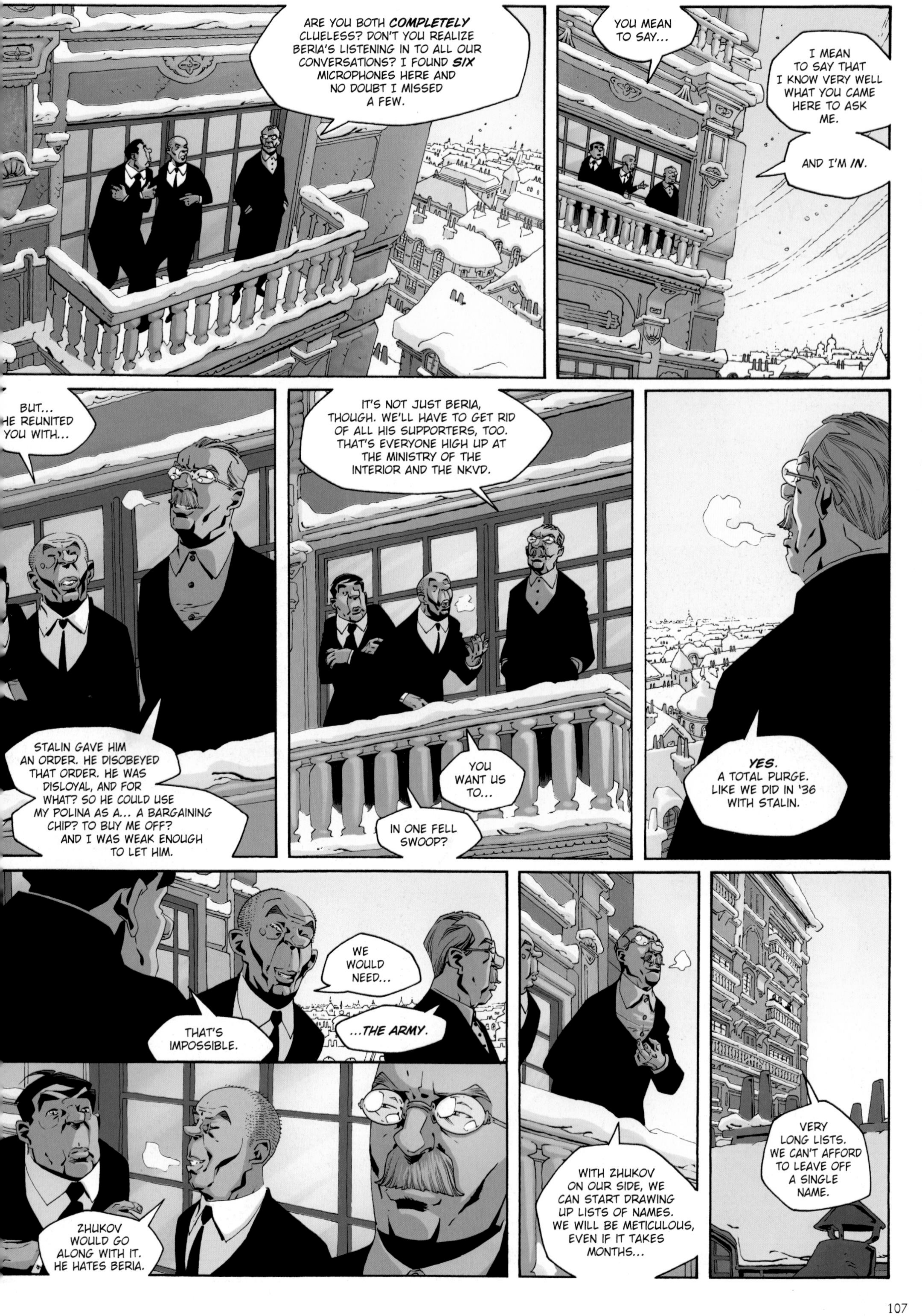
ARE YOU BOTH **COMPLETELY** CLUELESS? DON'T YOU REALIZE BERIA'S LISTENING IN TO ALL OUR CONVERSATIONS? I FOUND **SIX** MICROPHONES HERE AND NO DOUBT I MISSED A FEW.
YOU MEAN TO SAY...
I MEAN TO SAY THAT I KNOW VERY WELL WHAT YOU CAME HERE TO ASK ME.
AND I'M ***IN***.
BUT... HE REUNITED YOU WITH...
STALIN GAVE HIM AN ORDER. HE DISOBEYED THAT ORDER. HE WAS DISLOYAL, AND FOR WHAT? SO HE COULD USE MY POLINA AS A... A BARGAINING CHIP? TO BUY ME OFF? AND I WAS WEAK ENOUGH TO LET HIM.
IT'S NOT JUST BERIA, THOUGH. WE'LL HAVE TO GET RID OF ALL HIS SUPPORTERS, TOO. THAT'S EVERYONE HIGH UP AT THE MINISTRY OF THE INTERIOR AND THE NKVD.
YOU WANT US TO...
IN ONE FELL SWOOP?
YES. A TOTAL PURGE. LIKE WE DID IN '36 WITH STALIN.
WE WOULD NEED...
THAT'S IMPOSSIBLE.
...THE ARMY.
ZHUKOV WOULD GO ALONG WITH IT. HE HATES BERIA.
WITH ZHUKOV ON OUR SIDE, WE CAN START DRAWING UP LISTS OF NAMES. WE WILL BE METICULOUS, EVEN IF IT TAKES MONTHS...
VERY LONG LISTS. WE CAN'T AFFORD TO LEAVE OFF A SINGLE NAME.

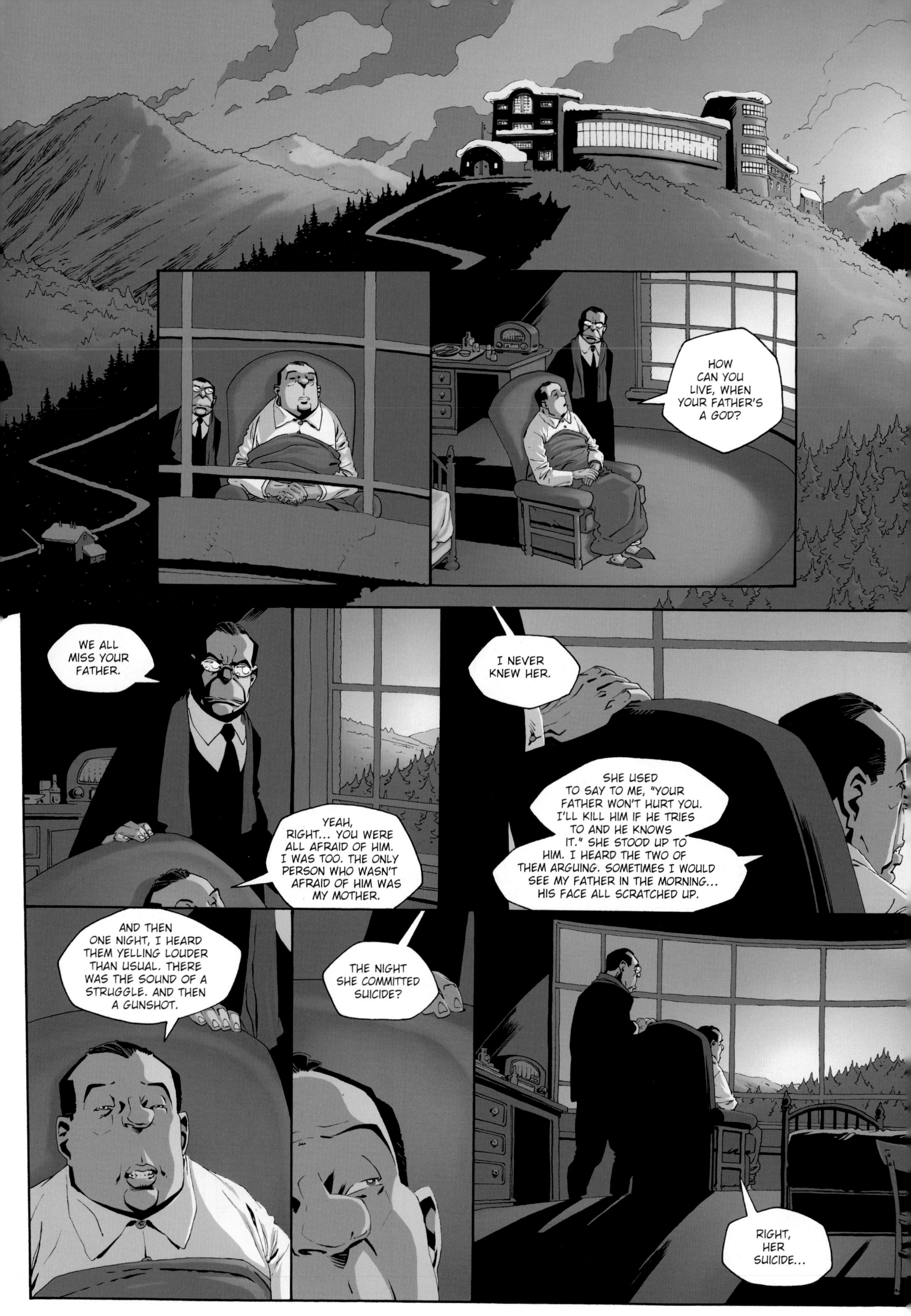
HOW CAN YOU LIVE, WHEN YOUR FATHER'S A GOD?
WE ALL MISS YOUR FATHER.
YEAH, RIGHT... YOU WERE ALL AFRAID OF HIM. I WAS TOO. THE ONLY PERSON WHO WASN'T AFRAID OF HIM WAS MY MOTHER.
I NEVER KNEW HER.
SHE USED TO SAY TO ME, "YOUR FATHER WON'T HURT YOU. I'LL KILL HIM IF HE TRIES TO AND HE KNOWS IT." SHE STOOD UP TO HIM. I HEARD THE TWO OF THEM ARGUING. SOMETIMES I WOULD SEE MY FATHER IN THE MORNING... HIS FACE ALL SCRATCHED UP.
AND THEN ONE NIGHT, I HEARD THEM YELLING LOUDER THAN USUAL. THERE WAS THE SOUND OF A STRUGGLE. AND THEN A GUNSHOT.
THE NIGHT SHE COMMITTED SUICIDE?
RIGHT, HER SUICIDE...

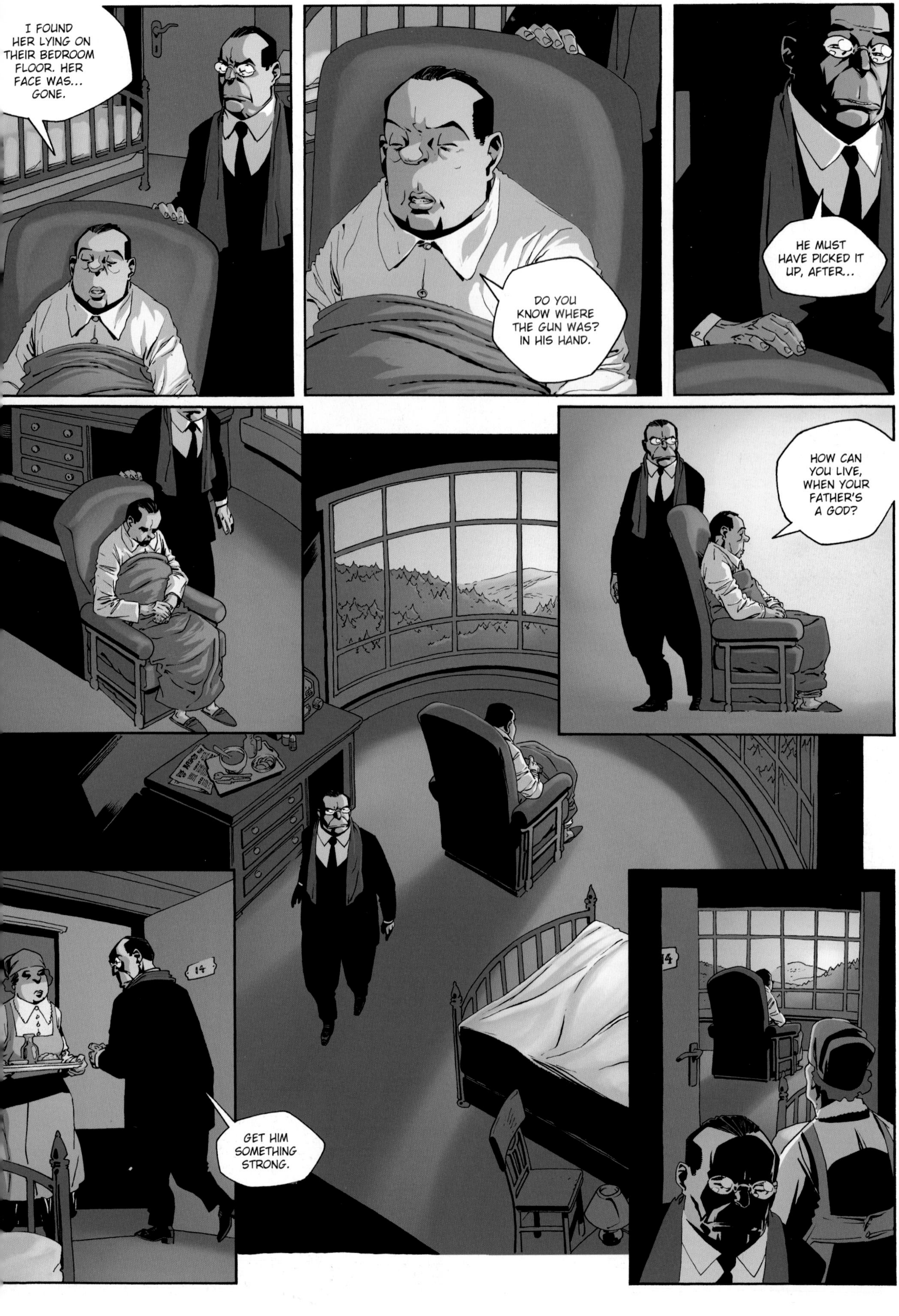
I FOUND HER LYING ON THEIR BEDROOM FLOOR. HER FACE WAS... GONE.
DO YOU KNOW WHERE THE GUN WAS? IN HIS HAND.
HE MUST HAVE PICKED IT UP, AFTER...
HOW CAN YOU LIVE, WHEN YOUR FATHER'S A GOD?
GET HIM SOMETHING STRONG.

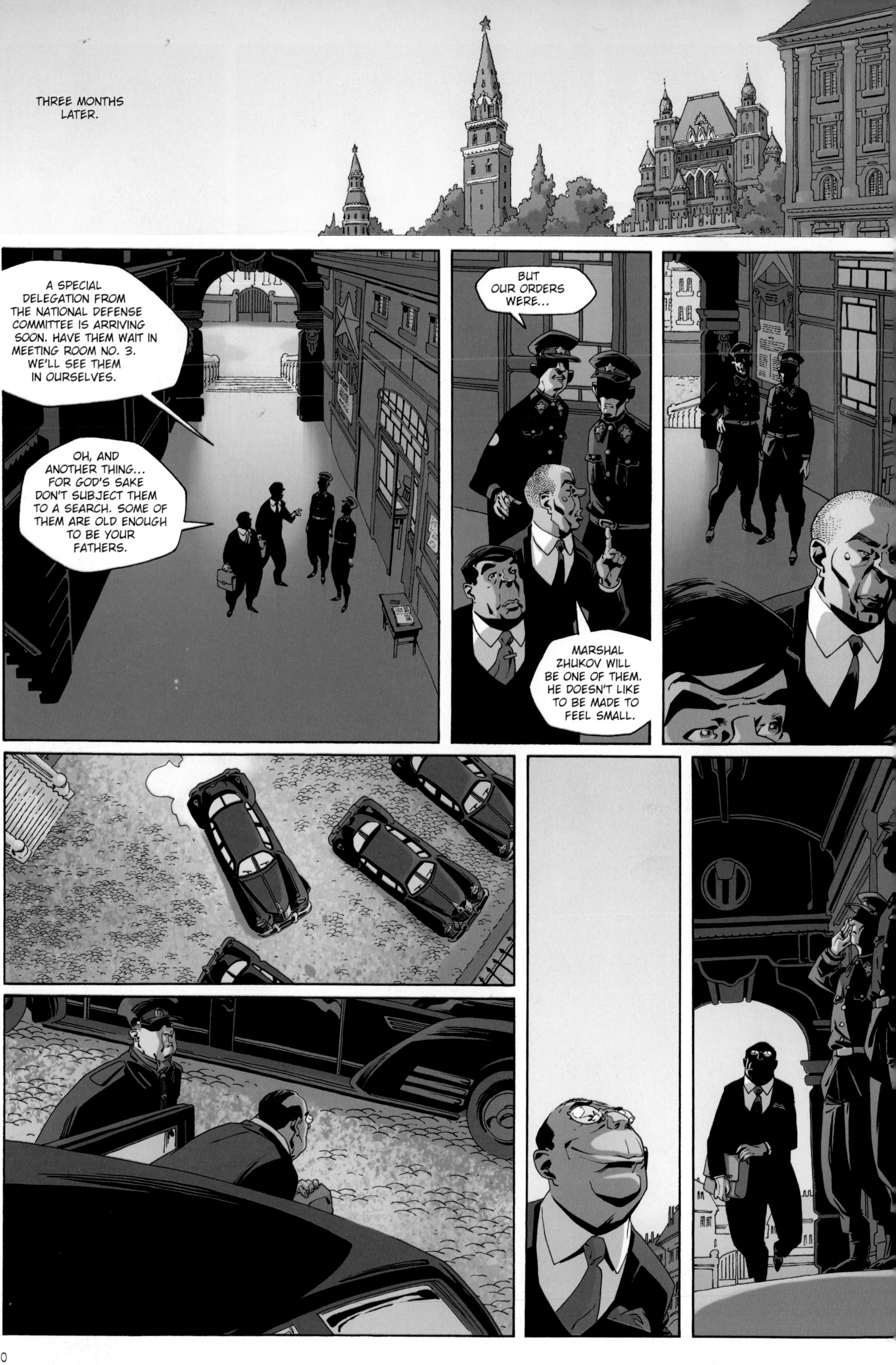
THREE MONTHS LATER.
A SPECIAL DELEGATION FROM THE NATIONAL DEFENSE COMMITTEE IS ARRIVING SOON. HAVE THEM WAIT IN MEETING ROOM NO. 3. WE'LL SEE THEM IN OURSELVES.
OH, AND ANOTHER THING... FOR GOD'S SAKE DON'T SUBJECT THEM TO A SEARCH. SOME OF THEM ARE OLD ENOUGH TO BE YOUR FATHERS.
BUT OUR ORDERS WERE...
MARSHAL ZHUKOV WILL BE ONE OF THEM. HE DOESN'T LIKE TO BE MADE TO FEEL SMALL.

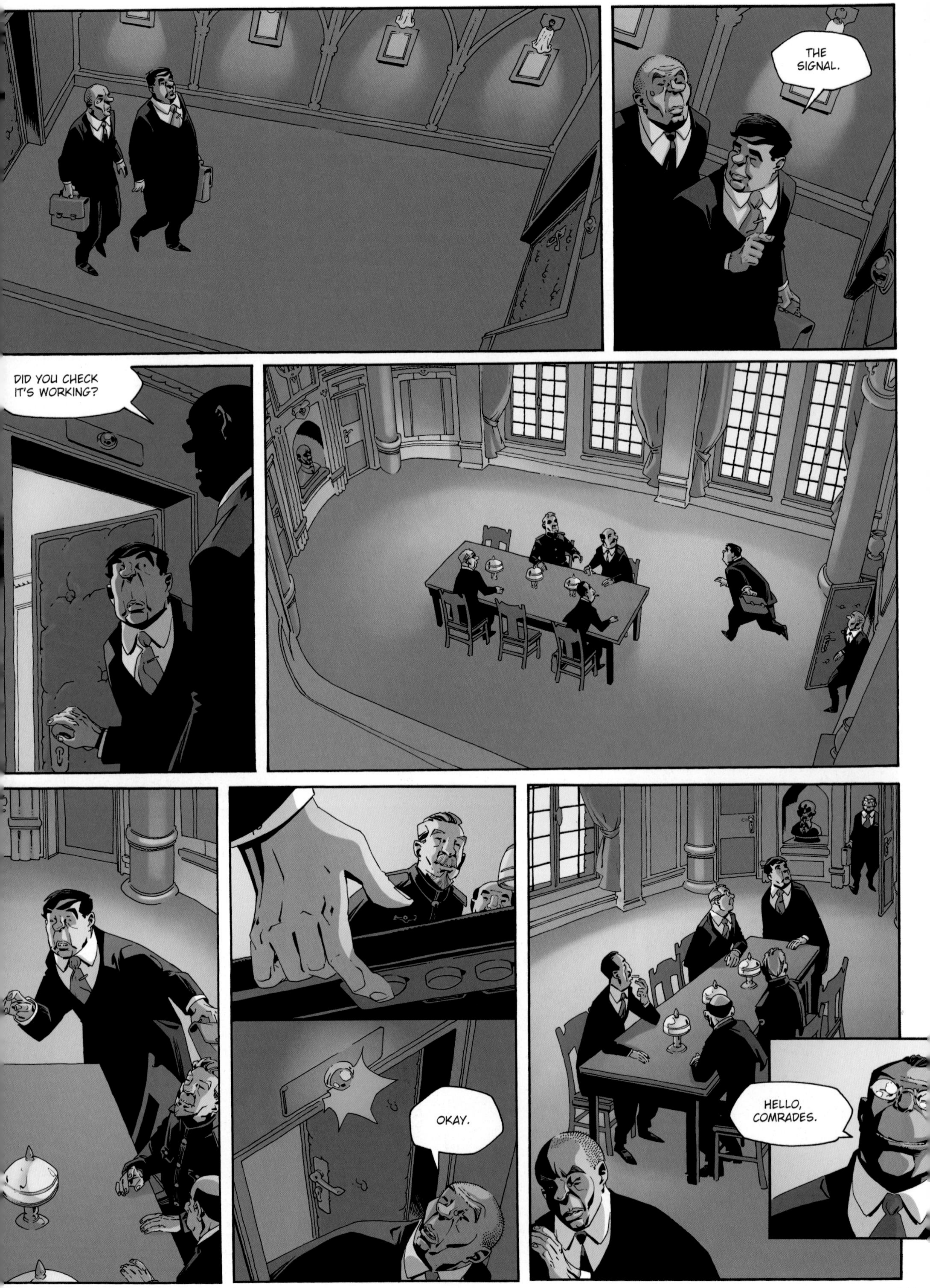
THE SIGNAL.
DID YOU CHECK IT'S WORKING?
OKAY.
HELLO, COMRADES.

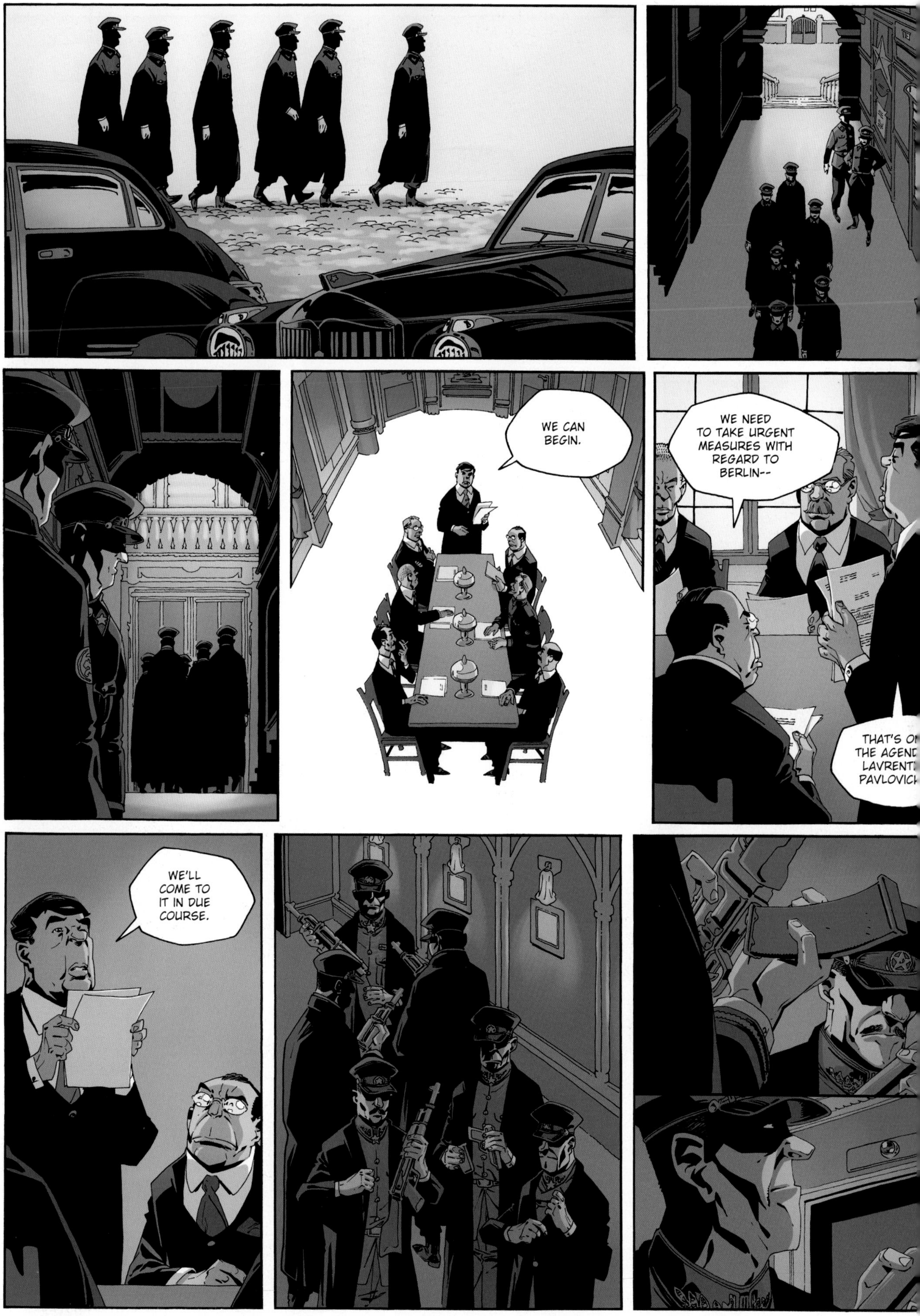
WE CAN BEGIN.
WE NEED TO TAKE URGENT MEASURES WITH REGARD TO BERLIN--
THAT'S O THE AGEND LAVRENT PAVLOVICH
WE'LL COME TO IT IN DUE COURSE.

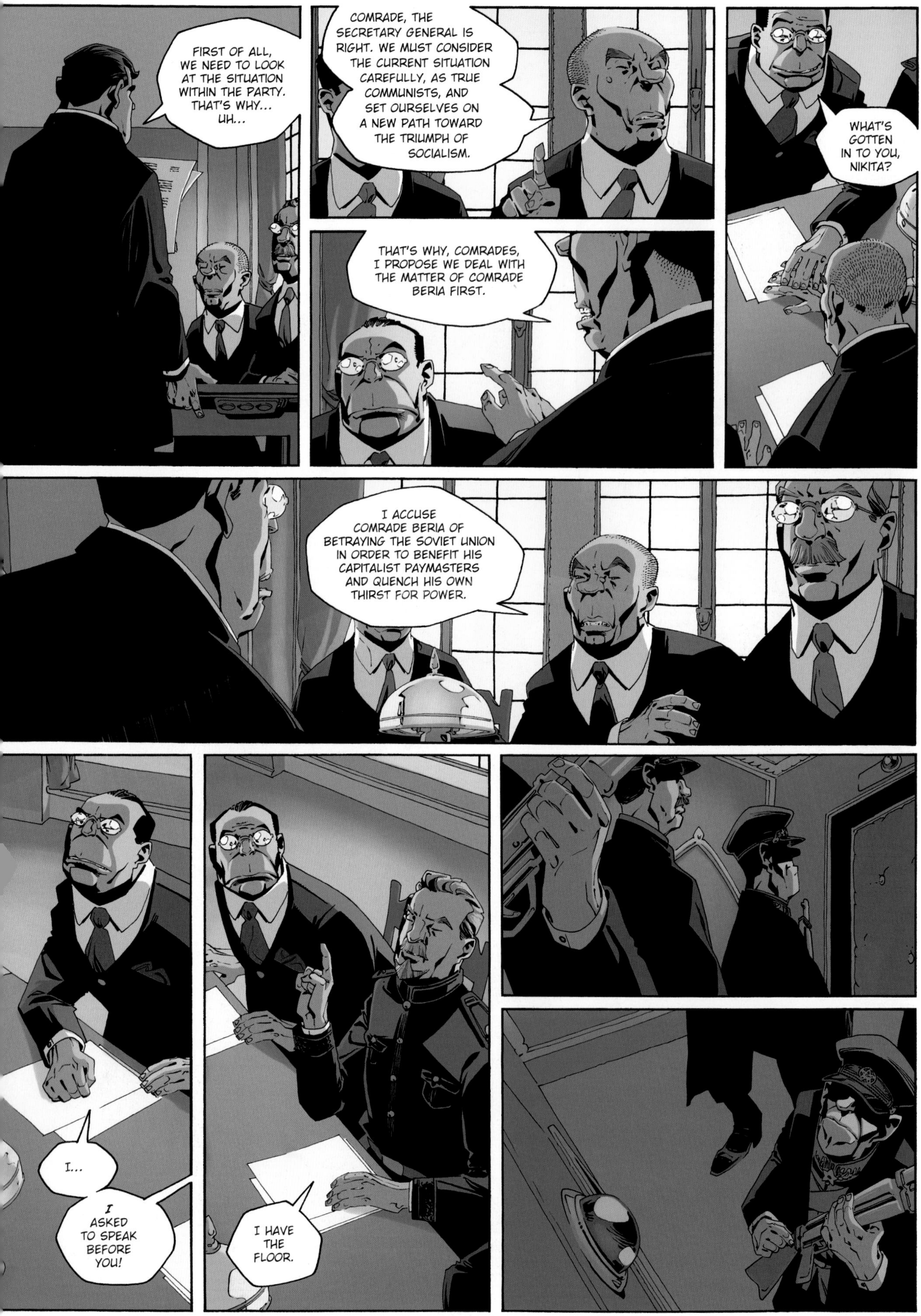
FIRST OF ALL, WE NEED TO LOOK AT THE SITUATION WITHIN THE PARTY. THAT'S WHY... UH...
COMRADE, THE SECRETARY GENERAL IS RIGHT. WE MUST CONSIDER THE CURRENT SITUATION CAREFULLY, AS TRUE COMMUNISTS, AND SET OURSELVES ON A NEW PATH TOWARD THE TRIUMPH OF SOCIALISM.
THAT'S WHY, COMRADES, I PROPOSE WE DEAL WITH THE MATTER OF COMRADE BERIA FIRST.
WHAT'S GOTTEN IN TO YOU, NIKITA?
I ACCUSE COMRADE BERIA OF BETRAYING THE SOVIET UNION IN ORDER TO BENEFIT HIS CAPITALIST PAYMASTERS AND QUENCH HIS OWN THIRST FOR POWER.
I...
I ASKED TO SPEAK BEFORE YOU!
I HAVE THE FLOOR.

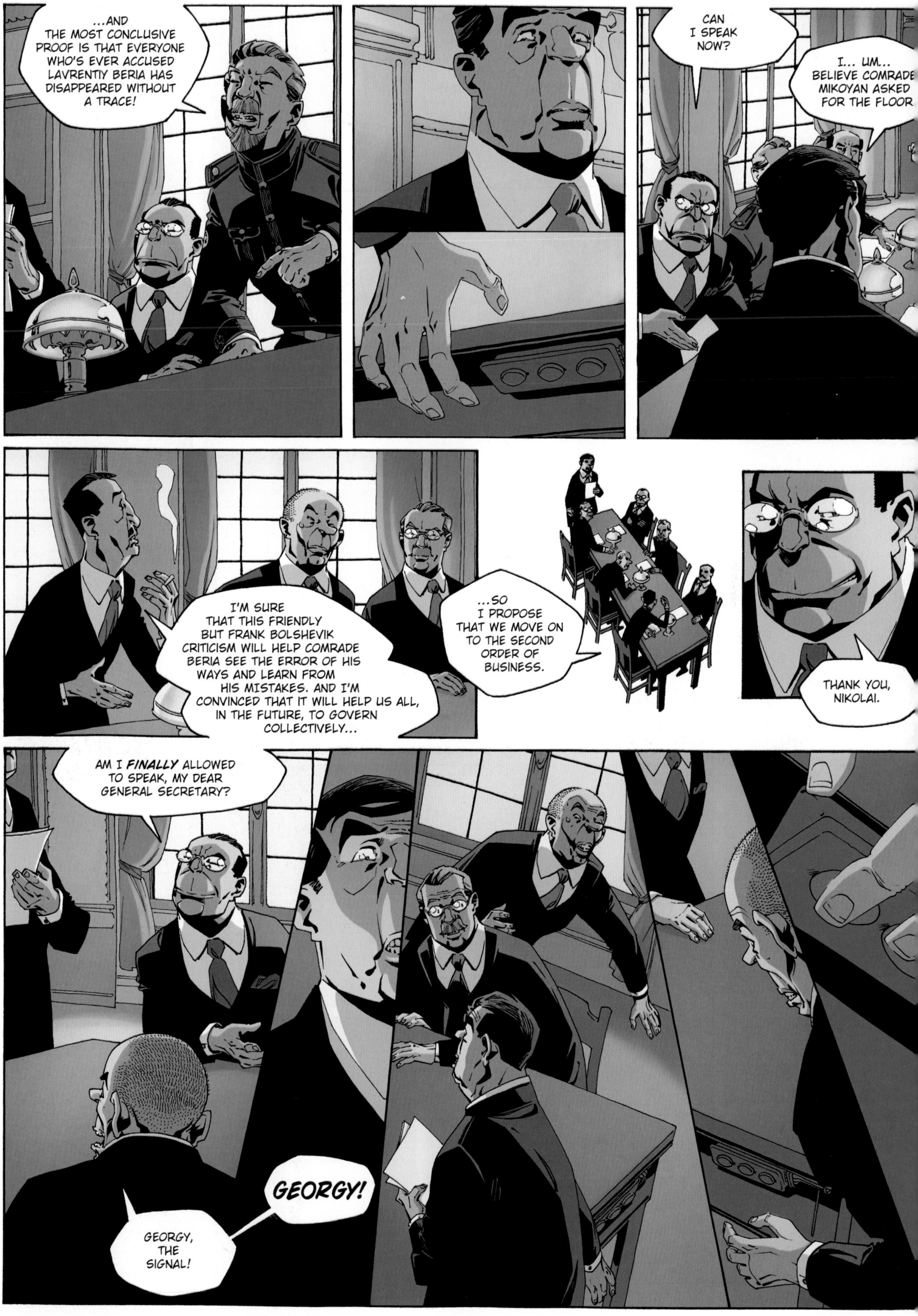
...AND THE MOST CONCLUSIVE PROOF IS THAT EVERYONE WHO'S EVER ACCUSED LAVRENTIY BERIA HAS DISAPPEARED WITHOUT A TRACE!
CAN I SPEAK NOW?
I... UM... BELIEVE COMRADE MIKOYAN ASKED FOR THE FLOOR
I'M SURE THAT THIS FRIENDLY BUT FRANK BOLSHEVIK CRITICISM WILL HELP COMRADE BERIA SEE THE ERROR OF HIS WAYS AND LEARN FROM HIS MISTAKES. AND I'M CONVINCED THAT IT WILL HELP US ALL, IN THE FUTURE, TO GOVERN COLLECTIVELY...
...SO I PROPOSE THAT WE MOVE ON TO THE SECOND ORDER OF BUSINESS.
THANK YOU, NIKOLAI.
AM I *FINALLY* ALLOWED TO SPEAK, MY DEAR GENERAL SECRETARY?
GEORGY, THE SIGNAL!
GEORGY!

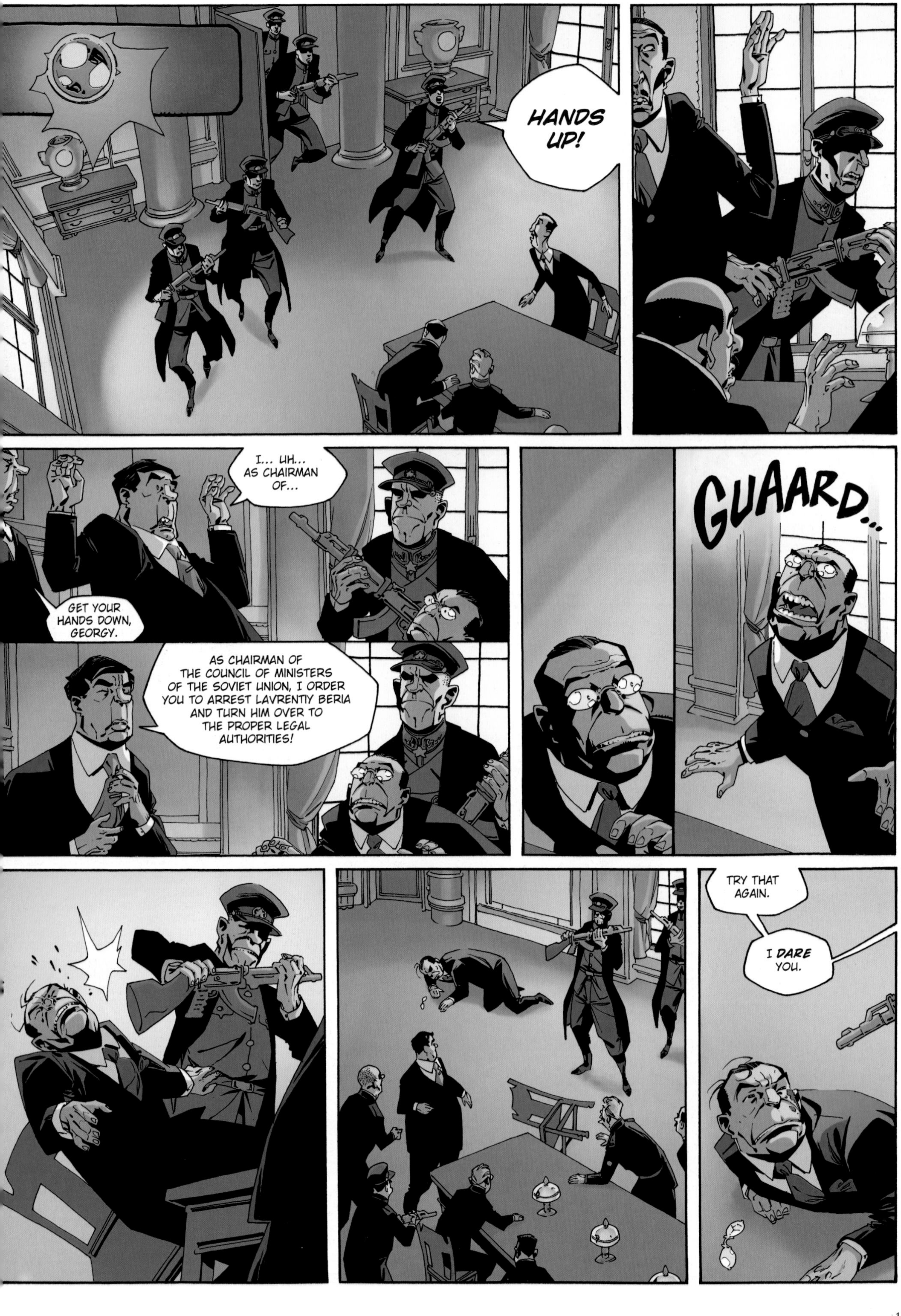
HANDS UP!
I... UH... AS CHAIRMAN OF...
GET YOUR HANDS DOWN, GEORGY.
AS CHAIRMAN OF THE COUNCIL OF MINISTERS OF THE SOVIET UNION, I ORDER YOU TO ARREST LAVRENTIY BERIA AND TURN HIM OVER TO THE PROPER LEGAL AUTHORITIES!
GUAARD...
TRY THAT AGAIN.
I DARE YOU.

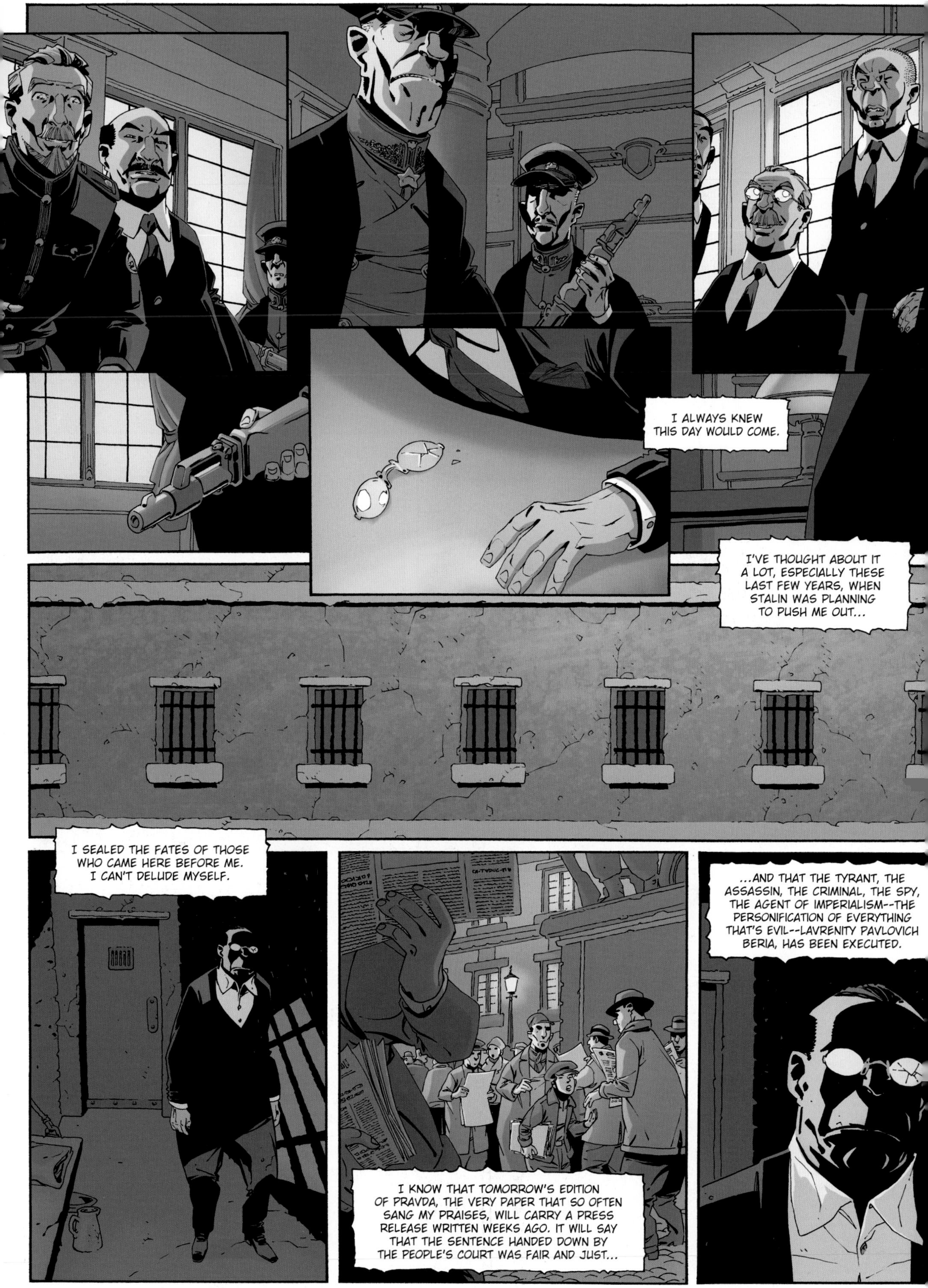
I ALWAYS KNEW THIS DAY WOULD COME.
I'VE THOUGHT ABOUT IT A LOT, ESPECIALLY THESE LAST FEW YEARS, WHEN STALIN WAS PLANNING TO PUSH ME OUT...
I SEALED THE FATES OF THOSE WHO CAME HERE BEFORE ME. I CAN'T DELUDE MYSELF.
I KNOW THAT TOMORROW'S EDITION OF PRAVDA, THE VERY PAPER THAT SO OFTEN SANG MY PRAISES, WILL CARRY A PRESS RELEASE WRITTEN WEEKS AGO. IT WILL SAY THAT THE SENTENCE HANDED DOWN BY THE PEOPLE'S COURT WAS FAIR AND JUST...
...AND THAT THE TYRANT, THE ASSASSIN, THE CRIMINAL, THE SPY, THE AGENT OF IMPERIALISM--THE PERSONIFICATION OF EVERYTHING THAT'S EVIL--LAVRENITY PAVLOVICH BERIA, HAS BEEN EXECUTED.

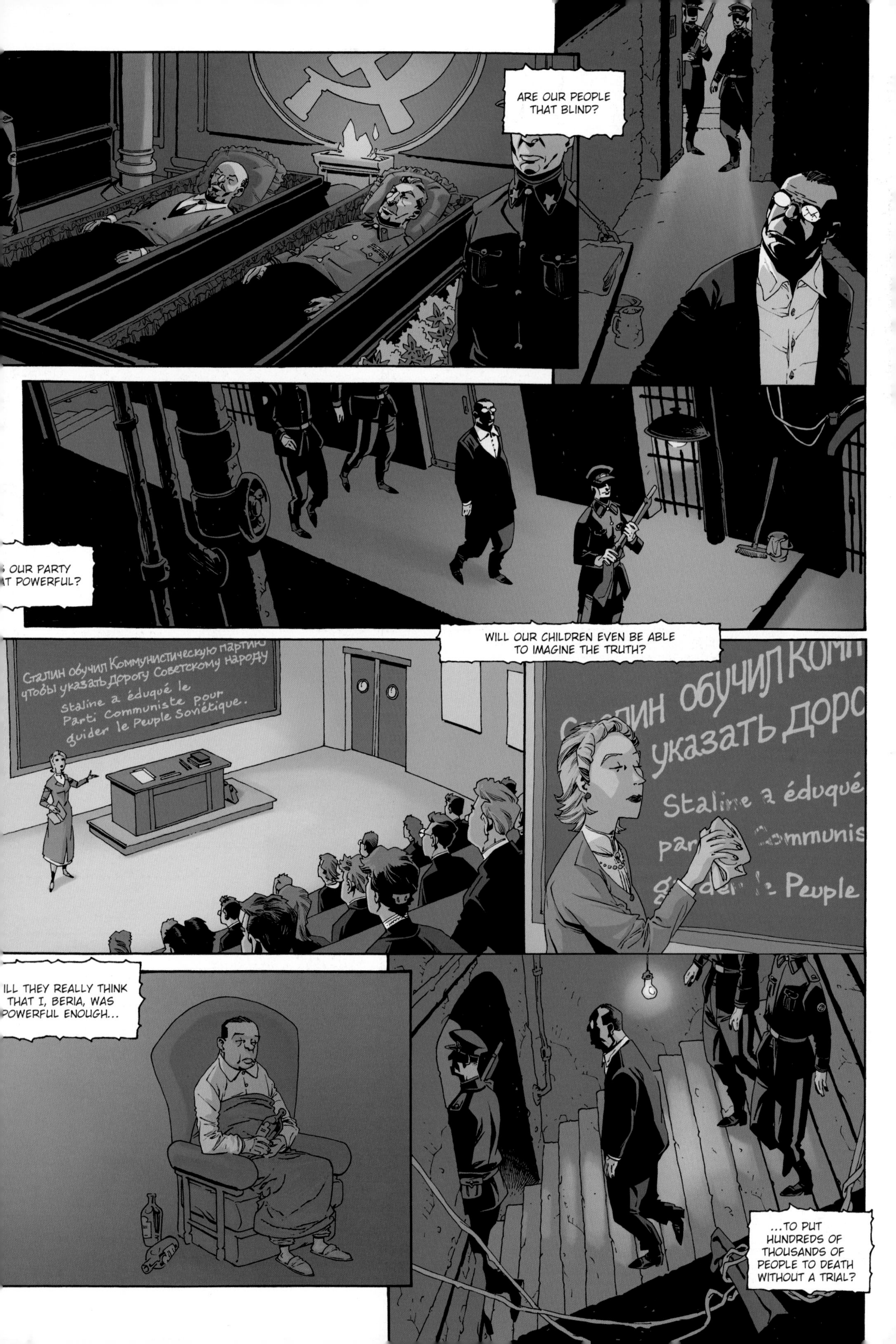
ARE OUR PEOPLE THAT BLIND?
S OUR PARTY T POWERFUL?
WILL OUR CHILDREN EVEN BE ABLE TO IMAGINE THE TRUTH?
Сталин обучил Коммунистическую партию чтобы указать Дорогу Советскому народу
Staline a éduqué le Parti Communiste pour guider le Peuple Soviétique.
ILL THEY REALLY THINK THAT I, BERIA, WAS POWERFUL ENOUGH...
...TO PUT HUNDREDS OF THOUSANDS OF PEOPLE TO DEATH WITHOUT A TRIAL?

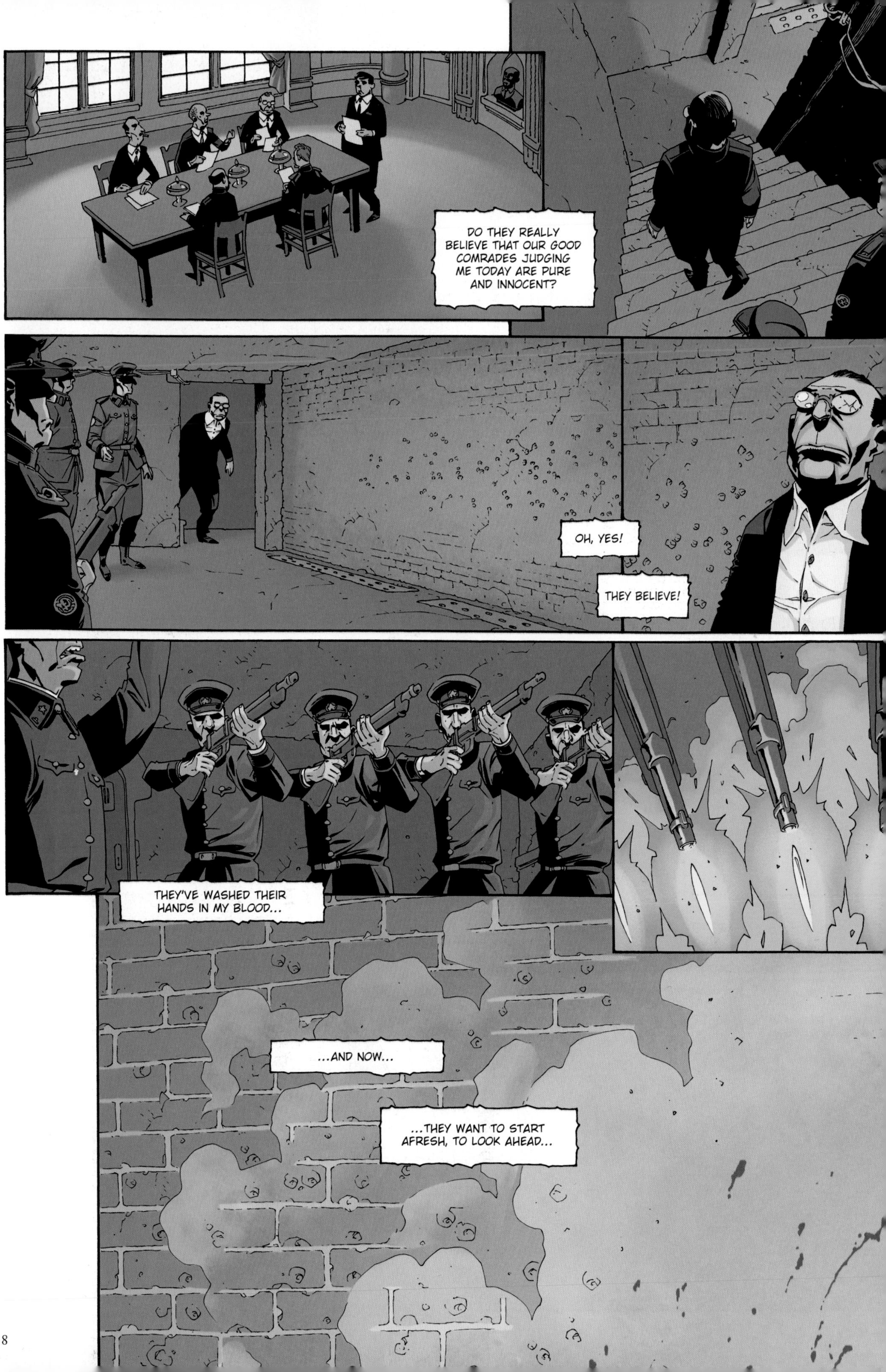
DO THEY REALLY BELIEVE THAT OUR GOOD COMRADES JUDGING ME TODAY ARE PURE AND INNOCENT?
OH, YES!
THEY BELIEVE!
THEY'VE WASHED THEIR HANDS IN MY BLOOD...
...AND NOW...
...THEY WANT TO START AFRESH, TO LOOK AHEAD...

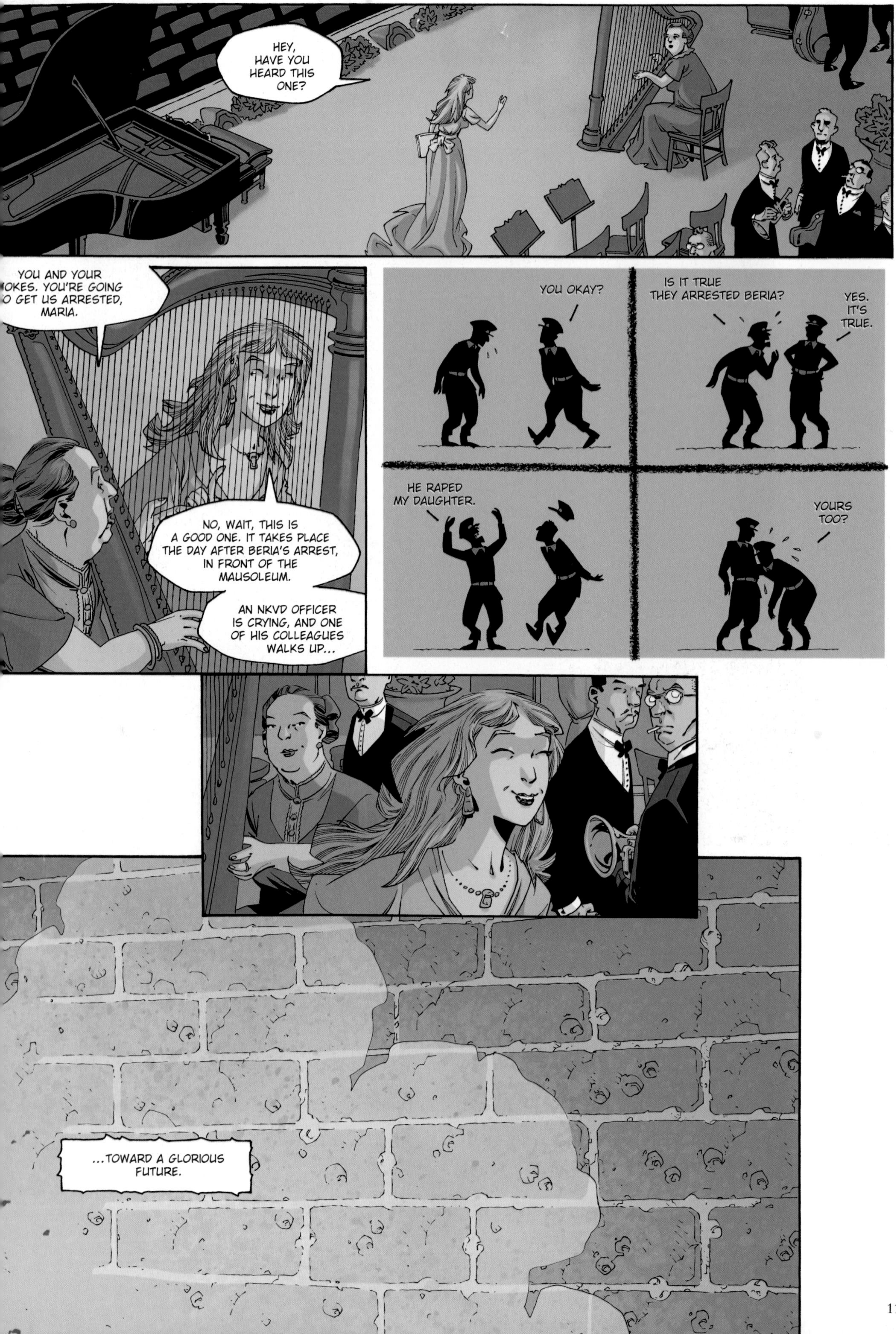
HEY, HAVE YOU HEARD THIS ONE?
YOU AND YOUR OKES. YOU'RE GOING O GET US ARRESTED, MARIA.
NO, WAIT, THIS IS A GOOD ONE. IT TAKES PLACE THE DAY AFTER BERIA'S ARREST, IN FRONT OF THE MAUSOLEUM.
AN NKVD OFFICER IS CRYING, AND ONE OF HIS COLLEAGUES WALKS UP...
YOU OKAY?
IS IT TRUE THEY ARRESTED BERIA?
YES. IT'S TRUE.
HE RAPED MY DAUGHTER.
YOURS TOO?
...TOWARD A GLORIOUS FUTURE.

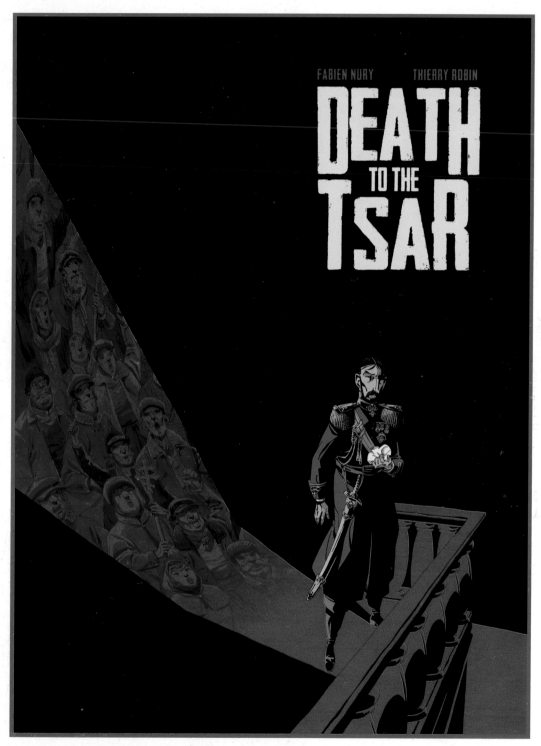

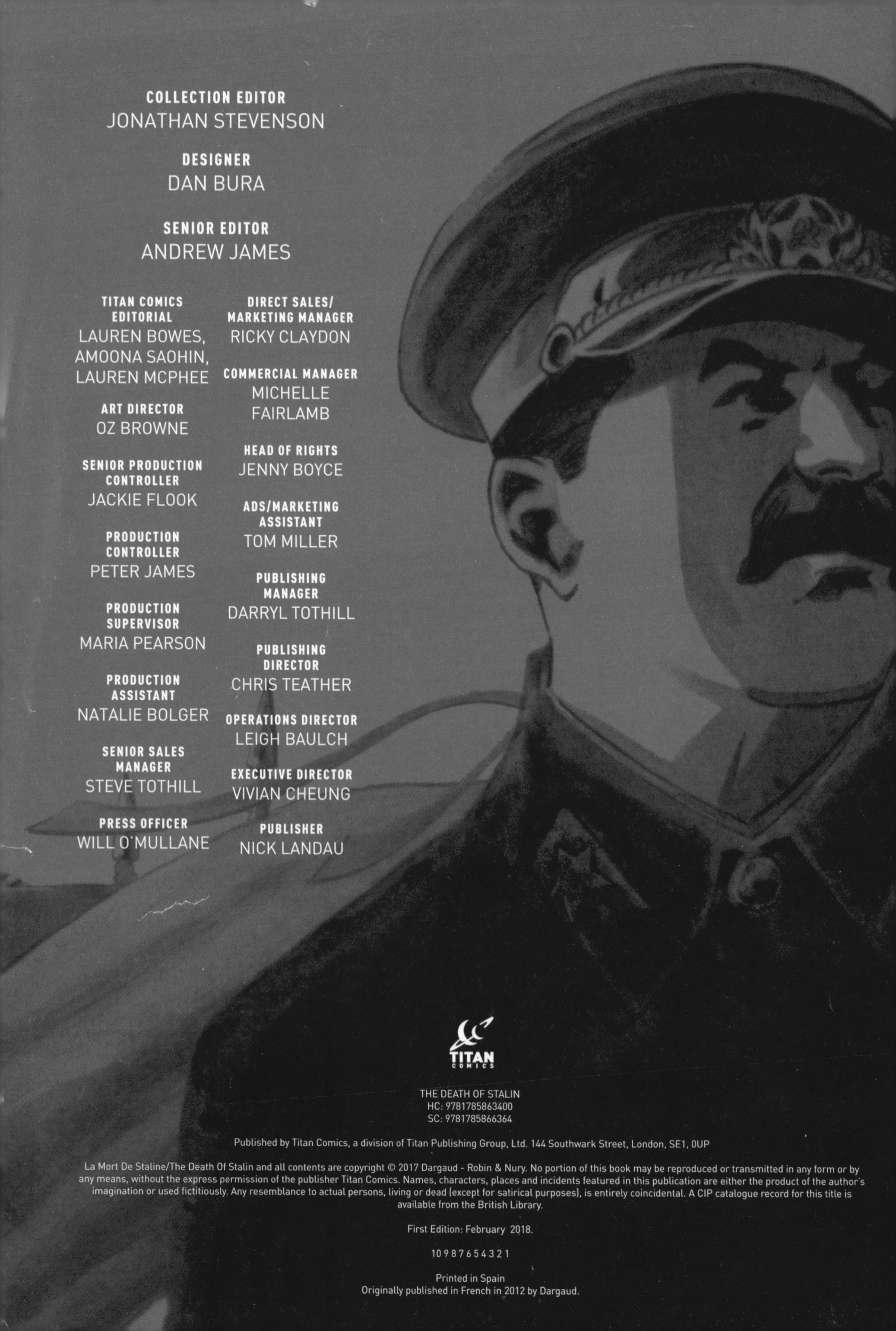

COLLECTION EDITOR
JONATHAN STEVENSON

DESIGNER
DAN BURA

SENIOR EDITOR
ANDREW JAMES

TITAN COMICS EDITORIAL
LAUREN BOWES, AMOONA SAOHIN, LAUREN MCPHEE

ART DIRECTOR
OZ BROWNE

SENIOR PRODUCTION CONTROLLER
JACKIE FLOOK

PRODUCTION CONTROLLER
PETER JAMES

PRODUCTION SUPERVISOR
MARIA PEARSON

PRODUCTION ASSISTANT
NATALIE BOLGER

SENIOR SALES MANAGER
STEVE TOTHILL

PRESS OFFICER
WILL O'MULLANE

DIRECT SALES/ MARKETING MANAGER
RICKY CLAYDON

COMMERCIAL MANAGER
MICHELLE FAIRLAMB

HEAD OF RIGHTS
JENNY BOYCE

ADS/MARKETING ASSISTANT
TOM MILLER

PUBLISHING MANAGER
DARRYL TOTHILL

PUBLISHING DIRECTOR
CHRIS TEATHER

OPERATIONS DIRECTOR
LEIGH BAULCH

EXECUTIVE DIRECTOR
VIVIAN CHEUNG

PUBLISHER
NICK LANDAU

THE DEATH OF STALIN
HC: 9781785863400
SC: 9781785866364

Published by Titan Comics, a division of Titan Publishing Group, Ltd. 144 Southwark Street, London, SE1, 0UP

 A CIP catalogue record for this title is available from the British Library.

First Edition: February 2018.

10 9 8 7 6 5 4 3 2 1

Printed in Spain
Originally published in French in 2012 by Dargaud.

THE DEATH OF STALIN